What the press has said . . .

"Pithy quotes and upbeat prose will chase away those negative thoughts."

—*Detroit Free Press*

"This may sound like yet another book on positive thinking, but it is in fact the first book that makes clear the limitations of positive thinking. It advocates, instead, full acceptance of the current reality before *focusing* on what is positive. This distinction, like so much else in the book, unlocks new possibilities and makes for compelling reading."

—*Ariana Stassinopoulos Huffington*

"*You Can't Afford the Luxury of a Negative Thought* is as complete a discourse on personal growth as one can find among the numerous self-help books available today."

—*Tim Janulewicz,*
St. Joseph News-Press/Gazette

"The book is much too big, much too full of great stuff to select any one thing to quote here. Suffice to say that if you were to flip through it at a bookstore, you'd surely want to take it home."

—*The Union Leader, Manchester, NH*

What our readers have said . . .

"Thanks for all the pleasant happy thoughts."
—*Mrs. B., Adelphi, MD*

"I'm just calling to tell you I'm reading your book and enjoying it tremendously. I found out about it in a cancer support group. My daughter just ordered two books from you because of me. I think it is one of the finest things of its type I've read in a long time."
—*Lorraine O., Livermore, CA*

"I'd like to order a case. I'll be waiting for the books to share them with my friends and I'm so happy that this book is out. God bless all of you."
—*Myrna B., Coronado, CA*

"I've already got two copies of the book and I'm sure I'll buy more later but I just wanted to leave a happy loving thought for you. Take care. Bye."
—*Anonymous*

"This is the 4th book I've ordered from you. I think it's a phenomenal book. It's kind of become my Bible. I just love the fact that it's so easy and humorous to read and so gentle. The book doesn't take itself seriously. So, thank you guys for writing it."
—*Roni S., Pleasantown, CA*

"I read your book. It was NEEDED. I will recommend your book to others."
—*Anita H., Red Bluff, CA*

"I love your book. Do you have others available?"
—*Betty B., Tampa, FL*

"Your book came highly recommended from a friend who has two copies and is always lending them out so she's thinking about buying a third for herself."
—*Patricia H., Livermore, CA*

"I appreciate it and tell all my friends. Thank you."
—*John Z., San Diego, CA*

"I'm just reading the book I got at the La Jolla Public Library and that's how I heard about it. It's an excellent book. Thanks so very much for writing it."
—*Pearl S., Lakeworth, FL*

"A friend, a therapist actually, gave this book to my chiropractor who gave it to me. That's how I heard about it. Thank you. You have a good day."
—*Thurman, Talmage, CA*

"Sincere thanks and God reward you."
—*Father John M., Little Rock, AR*

"Thank you. It is a wonderful book!"
—*Minnie F., Annandale, VA*

"The book is fantastic! My husband recently had cancer surgery and usually will *not* read anything but 'technical' (engineering) books. He is now reading your book and loves it. Thank you very much."
—*Donna D., Burney, CA*

"I saw your book in a bookstore in a shopping mall and I was blown away by how fantastic it was and is! I'm a 12-step person. Thank you for the book. Thank you for everything that's gone into it."
—*Jim R., Arleta, CA*

"We'd like to get this as soon as we can. It's a great book; we all love it here. We're just dying to get our hands...no we're living to get our hands on more because everybody here wants more. We're looking forward to getting our order soon."
—*Clybourn Chiropractic Health Center, Chicago, IL*

"I love the book. Thank you. God bless!"
—*Juliana L., Bayonne, NJ*

"By now, I'm sure you're aware of the world-changing events that are occurring in the Persian Gulf. The war here affects not only us soldiers in the region, but also our friends and families halfway around the world. There aren't too many amenities of home we can have—those are just dreamt-of, almost forgotten luxuries. But one of the most important things I brought with me is your book, *You Can't Afford the Luxury of a Negative Thought*. Over the period of time my unit has been here, your book has helped me keep my focus, raise my spirits, and just clarify my sense of purpose. Everyday, when I wake, I read a section of the book, and I feel I can handle any challenge that comes my way throughout the day. One section in your book, about "faithing" is so poignant that I'm reading *that* section every single time I get a chance.

"I just want to thank you gentlemen again for such a wonderful book, and I'd like to have a bookmark, and if at all possible, the audiocassette package that you speak of at the end of the book. The book is loved by my entire unit—it's frayed and worn, but it keeps its universal appeal..."
—*SPC Yael Pacis, NY*

"Hi. We heard about your book over Wisconsin public radio. We started to peruse the book and just think it's great."

Robert P., Columbus, OH

"It's a very, very nice book. I've enjoyed it immensely and thank you so very, very much."

Dorothy C., Baton Rouge, LA

"You just made my day, my whole afternoon. Thank you very much."

Polly H., Goleta, CA

"I really appreciate your exploration and research into this field. It's one that we all need. Thank you very much."

Bob M., Houston, TX

"Thanks for the many hours, pleasant hours of reading."

Linda H., Los Angeles, CA

"They're flying like hotcakes! We need another carton quick."

Clybourn Chiropractic Health Center, Chicago, IL

"Have just started reading your book and feel sure you have provided me with the tool to break out of my self-imposed imprisonment and shake my inferiority complex. I shall be ever be in your debt. Again my heartfelt thanks to you, and may your God richly bless you."

Grace W. (Age 80), West Palm Beach, FL

"This is the best book I've ever read. I read it at home. I put it in the car and read a page or two before going in to work. I read a few pages before going to bed. I've carried it around so much the pages are starting to fall out. I really do enjoy it."

—*Pally H., Gaffney, SC*

What famous (and marvelous) actresses have said . . .

"Thank you for your wonderful book. I've surrounded myself with every conceivable work on self knowledge, realization, universal consciousness and the rest from Jung to Alice M. Baily. You two have created a work of unique simplicity which offers a way of thinking and living in which motives are high but realistic and available. I love it."

—*Pauline Collins*
Tony Award Winner
Academy Award Nominee
Best Actress
Shirley Valentine

"This is a terrific book. I keep buying cases of it and giving copies to my friends. It is a joy to read and I recommend it highly."

—*Sally Kirkland*
Academy Award Nominee
Best Actress
Anna

A companion workbook for
*You Can't Afford the Luxury
of a Negative Thought*
is available.

It is entitled
**Focus on the Positive:
The You Can't Afford the Luxury
of a Negative Thought Workbook.**
$12.

Also available is a *new* recording of
*You Can't Afford the Luxury
of a Negative Thought.*
Read by David Warrilow.
It is complete and unabridged,
$22.99.

Both items ready for shipment November, 1991.
Please check your local bookstore, or call

1-800-LIFE-101

ACKNOWLEDGMENTS

As soon as the idea for this book was announced, people came from everywhere offering their skills, support and encouragement. A "serious" topic—life-threatening illness—seems to bring out the worst in people (fear, blame, panic), and it also brings out the best (generosity, compassion, love). These people—and all the others offering support—are the best.

Our thanks to John Morton for the original idea; Laurie Lerner for her extensive research in the John-Roger Archives; Paul LeBus for the brilliant design of the book, cover and all; Betsy Alexander, Sandy Barnert and Marsha Winborn for their invaluable editorial assistance; John Ward, John Forrister and Margalit Finger of *FingerPrint* for the more-than-generous gift of the typesetting; Ron Wodaski and Susan Wylie for their desktop publishing expertise; Theresa Hocking for the indexing; and Betty Bennett for the photos. A special thanks to Mark Katz, M.D., for his learned medical perspective.

You Can't Afford the Luxury of a Negative Thought

by
John-Roger
and
Peter McWilliams

Published by Prelude Press
Distributed by Bantam Books

Prelude Press
8165 Mannix Drive
Los Angeles, California
90046

Published simultaneously in the United States and Canada

Bantam Books are published by Bantam Books, a division of Bantam Doubleday Dell Publishing Group, Inc. Its trademark, consisting of the words "Bantam Books" and the portrayal of a rooster, is Registered in U.S. Patent and Trademark Office and in other countries. Marca Registrada. Bantam Books, 666 Fifth Avenue, New York, New York 10103.

PRINTED IN THE UNITED STATES OF AMERICA

Life! Can't live with it,
can't live without it.

CYNTHIA NELMA

This book is dedicated to
all those who seek the new,
but keep the best of the old.

Contents

'Tis the good reader
that makes the good book;
in every book he finds passages which
seem to be confidences or asides
hidden from all else
and unmistakably meant for his ear;
the profit of books is according to
the sensibility of the reader;
the profoundest thought or passion
sleeps as in a mine,
until it is discovered by an
equal mind and heart.

EMERSON

The way a book is read—
which is to say,
the qualities a reader
brings to a book—
can have as much to do
with its worth as anything
the author puts into it.

NORMAN COUSINS

You Can't Afford the Luxury of a Negative Thought

*The quotations
when engraved upon
the memory
give you good thoughts.
They also make you
anxious to read
the authors
and look for more.*

SIR WINSTON CHURCHILL

Introduction

This is not just a book for people with life-threatening illnesses. It's a book for anyone afflicted with one of the primary diseases of our time: negative thinking.

Negative thinking is always expensive—dragging us down mentally, emotionally and physically—hence we refer to any indulgence in it as a *luxury*. If, however, you have the symptoms of a life-threatening illness—be it AIDS, heart trouble, cancer, high blood pressure or any of the others—negative thinking is a *luxury* you can no longer afford.

We remember a bumper sticker from the 1960's—"Death Is Nature's Way of Telling You to Slow Down." Well, the signs of a life-threatening illness are nature's way of telling you to—as they say in California—lighten up.

Be easier on yourself. Think better of yourself.

Learn to forgive yourself and others for the many mistakes that flesh is heir to.

JOHN-ROGER:* After I worked with a woman for a few months on her habit of always looking at the dark side of things, she came to me and sighed in mock exasperation, "I'm getting way behind on my worrying!"

This is a book about getting behind on your worrying. Way, *way* behind. The further behind on your worrying you get, the further ahead you'll be.

---

*Throughout the book, one or another of us may pop up with a personal comment, aside or experience. At that point we will simply identify the speaker and let him at it. This saves us from the awkward attempt of trying to tell a story that obviously happened to one person with "we" or the even more torturous, "The senior author of this book finds that. . . ."

3

We are, perhaps,
uniquely among the
earth's creatures,
the worrying animal.
We worry away our lives,
fearing the future,
discontent with
the present,
unable to take in
the idea of dying,
unable to sit still.

LEWIS THOMAS

PETER: My favorite quote on worry: "Worrying is a form of atheism." Second favorite: "Worrying is the interest paid on a debt you may not owe."

This is not so much a book to be read as it is a book to be *used*. It doesn't have to be read cover to cover. We like to think you can flip it open at any time to any page and get something of value from it. This is especially true of the second—and largest—section of the book.

This book has two sections: *The Disease* and *The Cure*. The disease is not any specific illness, but what we believe to be the precursor of all life-threatening illnesses—negative thinking.

The cure is not a wonder drug or a vaccination or The Magic Bullet. The cure is very simple: (1) spend more time focusing on the positive things in your life *(Accentuate the Positive)*; (2) spend less time thinking negatively *(Eliminate the Negative)*; and (3) enjoy each moment *(Latch on to the Affirmative)*.

That's it. Simple. But far from easy.

It's the aim of this book to make the process simple and, if not easy, at least easier.

Above all, enjoy the journey.

Please don't use anything in this book *against* yourself. Don't interpret anything we say in *The Disease* as blame. When we use the word *responsibility,* for example, we simply mean you have the *ability* to *respond*. (And you *are* responding or you wouldn't be reading this book.)

And please don't take any of the suggestions in *The Cure* as "musts," "shoulds" or "have-tos." Think of them as joyful activity, creative play—not as additional burdens in an already burdensome life.

*To love oneself
is the beginning
of a lifelong romance.*

OSCAR WILDE

This book (or any of the ideas in it) is not designed to replace proper medical care. Please use this book *in conjunction with* whatever course of treatment your doctor or health-care provider prescribes. If you have a life-threatening illness, you are going to have to take some life-supporting actions, and naturally these include proper medical attention.

You are far more powerful than you ever dreamed. As you discover and learn how to use your power, use it only for your upliftment and the upliftment of others.

You are a marvelous, wonderful, worthwhile person—just because you are. That's the point of view we'll be taking. Please join us for a while—an hour, a week, a lifetime—at that viewing point.

PART I

THE DISEASE

*Thinking is an
experimental dealing
with small quantities
of energy,
just as a general
moves miniature figures
over a map
before setting his troops
in action.*

SIGMUND FREUD

The Power of Thoughts
(Part One)

A simple thought. A few micromilliwatts of energy flowing through our brain. A seemingly innocuous, almost ephemeral thing. And yet, a thought—or, more accurately, a carefully orchestrated series of thoughts—has a significant impact on our mind, our body and our emotions.

Thoughts have responses in the body. Think of a lemon. Imagine cutting it in half. Imagine removing the seeds with the point of a knife. Smell the lemon. Now, imagine squeezing the juice from the lemon into your mouth. Then imagine digging your teeth into the center of the lemon. Chew the pulp. Feel those little things (whatever those little things are called) breaking and popping inside your mouth. Most people's salivary glands respond to the very thought of a lemon.

For some people, the mere thought of the sound of fingernails on a chalkboard is physically uncomfortable. Try this—imagine an emery board or a fingernail file or a double-sided piece of sandpaper. Imagine putting it in your mouth. Bite down on it. Now move your teeth from side to side. Goosebumps?

Thoughts influence our emotions. Think of something you love. What do you feel? Now think of something you hate. What do you feel? Now, something you love again. We don't have to change our emotions consciously—just change our thoughts, and our emotions quickly follow.

Now imagine your favorite place in nature. Where is it? A beach? A meadow? A mountain top? Take your time. Imagine lying on your back, your eyes closed. Feel the sun on your face. Smell the air.

Every good thought you think is contributing its share to the ultimate result of your life.

GRENVILLE KLEISER

Hear the sounds of creation. Become a part of it. Feel more relaxed?

Most people who take the time to try these little experiments know what we're talking about.

Those who thought, "This stuff is silly. I'm not going to try anything as stupid as this!" are left with the emotional and physiological consequences of *their* thoughts—perhaps a sense of tightness, irritability, impatience or maybe outright hostility. These people (bless their independent hearts!) proved the point we're making as well as those who followed along with the "suggested" thoughts did. The point being: thoughts have power over our mind, our body and our emotions.

Positive thoughts (joy, happiness, fulfillment, achievement, worthiness) have positive results (enthusiasm, calm, well-being, ease, energy, love). Negative thoughts (judgment, unworthiness, mistrust, resentment, fear) produce negative results (tension, anxiety, alienation, anger, fatigue).

To understand why something as miniscule as a thought can have such a dramatic effect on our mind, body and emotions, it helps to understand the automatic reaction human beings have whenever they perceive danger: the Fight or Flight Response.

*And we are here
as on a darkling plain
Swept with confused
alarms of struggle
and flight,
Where ignorant armies
clash by night.*

MATTHEW ARNOLD

The Fight or Flight Response

Human beings have been around for a long, long time. One of the main reasons the human animal has survived as long and as successfully as it has is its highly developed, integrated and instantaneous response to perceived danger, known as the Fight or Flight Response.

The Fight or Flight Response works like this:

Let's consider our not-too-distant ancestor, Zugg. Zugg is far more advanced than a simple caveman—he has learned to manipulate tools, to till the fields and to build shelters. Zugg is out hunting one day (or tilling his field, as you prefer) when he hears a twig snap in the underbrush.

Zugg, because he has a fairly well-developed mind, remembers that one time when he heard a twig snap, a wild animal came out of the underbrush and ate his sister, Zuggrina. He immediately associates twig snapping with ravenous wild animals. Without even having to think about it, he prepares.

He focuses all his attention on the geographical area of the snap. His brain concentrates on the input of his senses. His mind whirls through possible defense strategies and paths of retreat. His emotions flare, a heady combination of fear and anger. Adrenaline, sugar and other stimulants surge into his system. Blood is diverted from relatively unimportant functions of the body—such as digesting food, fighting infections, healing wounds and other "inner" processes—and rushes to the skeletal muscles, especially the arms and legs. The eyes narrow, the muscles tense.

I'll moider de bum.

TONY TWO-TON GALENTO

He is ready.

Ready for what? He has only two choices—to do battle or to run, to combat or to escape, "to take a stand and fight or take off out of here," as Joni Mitchell put it.

Hence, the Fight or Flight Response. It's an automatic, physiological response to danger, either real or perceived.

The Fight or Flight Response has been an essential tool for the survival of our species. Back in Zugg's time, the more laid-back humans were, for the most part, eaten. These gentler folk might hear a twig snap and say, "Hark, a twig snapping. Isn't that a lovely sound?" and the next thing they knew they were dinner. This group did not, uh, persevere.

But Zugg and his kind? Victorious. They got through the animal wars, and then, having seemingly nothing better to do, spent the last 5,000 years fighting one another in human wars. The ones with the most intensely honed Fight or Flight Responses lived to fight another day, and, more importantly from a genetic point of view, lived to reproduce another night.

The Zuggrinas played an important role in all this, too. The offspring of the women who could defend their young the fiercest and/or grab their young and run the fastest survived. The most protected children were the ones with the genetically strongest Fight or Flight Response.

In the past few hundred years—in the Western world, at least—the need for the Fight or Flight Response has, for all practical purposes, disappeared.

When was the last time you had to physically fight or flee to save your life?

*Give them great meals of
beef and iron and steel,
they will eat like wolves
and fight like devils.*

SHAKESPEARE

We're talking about *you*, not people you read about in the newspapers or saw on TV.* And how many times have you had to fight or flee *for your life?* Most people—even those living in New York City—can count the times on the fingers of one hand.

The Fight or Flight Response has become, ironically, *counter* to survival in these newfangled civilized times. The veneer of civilization is thin—a few hundred years papered over millions of years of biological evolution. The "beast" within is still strong. The Fight or Flight Response is alive and well.

And it's killing us.

When we are cut off in traffic, are spoken unkindly to, fear that our job may be in danger, get a rent increase, hear about Nostradamus' revised predictions for an earthquake (even if you don't live in California, don't you plan to move there someday?), are told the restaurant lost our reservation, or have a flat tire, the Fight or Flight Response kicks in with full force as though our lives depended on slugging it out or running away *in that very moment*.

Worse, the Fight or Flight Response is activated whenever we *think* about being cut off in traffic, *think* that our job may be in danger, *think* about getting a rent increase, *think* about Nostradamus'

*One of the easiest ways to negate new information is to apply it to someone else—preferably someone you don't know and, even more preferably, to a fictional character. "What about James Bond (or Rambo or Road Warrior or Road Runner)? He's got to fight for his life *all the time*." Yes, but you're not James Bond (or, etc.). In fact, *nobody* is. Please apply everything in this book to *your* life, not the fictional lives of television, movies and novels, or the almost-fictional lives of "real people" reported in The Press (both print and electronic). Also, please avoid the temptation to apply this information to "the average person." There is no such person, and even if there were, he or she is not you. You are a unique individual. Use this book to take an honest, perceptive look at yourself—the good, the bad, the ugly and the beautiful—and learn to accept and love it all.

Not to the swift, the race:
Not to the strong, the fight:

HENRY VAN DYKE

The race is not always
to the swift,
nor the battle to the strong,
but that's the way to bet.

DAYMON RUNYON

earthquake predictions, *think* about moving to California, *think* about the restaurant losing the reservation, or *think* about having a flat tire.

Even if none of these "disasters" (only one of which is genuinely life-threatening) comes to pass, just *thinking* they *might* happen is enough to trigger the Fight or Flight Response.

Let's take a look at how negative thoughts, activating the Fight or Flight Response, affect the mind, the body and the emotions.

*The mind
is its own place,
and in itself can make
heaven of Hell,
a hell of Heaven.*

MILTON

Negative Thoughts and the Mind

When the Fight or Flight Response is triggered, the mind immediately focuses on the area of perceived danger. It is intent on finding further evidence on what's wrong. It's *looking* for danger, evil, disturbance, wild beasts.

It's a good bet that our friend Zugg didn't spend too much time appreciating the color of the sky or the fragrance of the flowers as he squinted in the direction of the twig snap. No. He was looking for trouble. His mind *automatically filtered out* anything that didn't pertain to the perceived danger. If the evidence wasn't bad, it was no good.

The mind is a marvelous filtering mechanism. It shelters us from large amounts of information. If it didn't, we would probably go mad. We simply cannot pay conscious attention to every single detail being collected by our five senses.

Without moving it, be aware of your tongue. Were you aware of it before we asked? Probably not. The sensation was there, but your mind filtered it out—you didn't need that information. Look carefully at the paper on this page. What's the texture like? Had you noticed that before? Unless you are in the printing or paper trade, probably not. Are there any smells in the room? How about noises? Ticking clock? Air conditioner? Feel the sensation of your body against whatever you're sitting (or lying) on. Have you forgotten about your tongue again?

When the Fight or Flight Response is activated, we begin to look for everything wrong with a situation, person, place or thing. And we find it, too! There's always *something* wrong. We're living in a

*Wisdom entereth not into
a malicious mind.*

RABELAIS

material world. Material things are, almost by definition, imperfect.

So there's our mind, automatically filtering out the positive, automatically focusing on the negative. Sounds like the perfect recipe for misery, doesn't it?

But it gets worse.

Zugg's mind, you will recall, also reviewed past moments of his life in which snapping twigs played a part. There was, of course, that terrible time with Zuggrina. Poor Zuggrina. Then there was that time with OggaBooga. Poor OggaBooga.

Zugg is now looking not just for twig-snap memories, but for memories of *all* wild beasts devouring *anything*. He even thinks back to times he *thought* about wild beasts devouring anything, including his foot. He is searching his memory for real and imaginary images of mutilation, and there are plenty to be found.

We often do the same thing. If someone cuts us off in traffic, our mind goes reeling back to all the rude and inconsiderate people we've ever seen driving cars, then to all the rude and inconsiderate people we've ever seen anywhere (and, of course, how terrible they are).

If someone is five minutes late for an appointment, we often spend four minutes and fifty-nine seconds of that five minutes remembering every other time the person was late, all the other people who were ever late, and every other situation—either real or imagined—of being disappointed or unloved.

The mind—an incredibly perceptive and accurate tool—is looking both within and without for negativity. It finds it. That thought triggers a more active level of the Fight or Flight Response, which

The mind,
in proportion
as it is cut off
from free communication
with nature,
with revelation,
with God,
with itself,
loses its life,
just as the body droops
when debarred from
the air and the cheering
light from heaven.

WILLIAM CHANNING

triggers an even more enthusiastic negative mental search, which discovers even more hideous evidence, which kicks off a stronger Fight or Flight Response, which . . .

Get the idea? It's known as a temper tantrum or losing one's cool or an anxiety attack or getting steamed—or life as we know it in this century.

*Most of the time
we think we're sick,
it's all in the mind.*

THOMAS WOLFE

Negative Thoughts and the Body

The Fight or Flight Response puts a body through its paces. All the resources of the body are mobilized for immediate, physical, demanding action—fight or flee.

All the other bodily functions are put on hold—digestion, assimilation, blood cell production, body maintenance, circulation (except to certain vital skeletal muscles), healing, and immunological responses.

In addition to this, the body is pumping chemicals—naturally produced drugs, if you will—into the system. The muscles need energy and they need it *fast*.

Zugg was lucky in this respect. Quite often he would actually *use* these chemicals by running them off or climbing them off or fighting them off. In our civilized world, we usually don't. The most we do is bang our fists or throw something (which only hurts our hands and breaks things).

Occasionally we yell, but that's not physical enough. Our body has armed itself to *fight or flee for its life,* and usually we just sit and seethe.

The repeated and unnecessary (and, as we pointed out before, it's almost always unnecessary) triggering of the Fight or Flight Response puts enormous physiological stress on the body.

It opens us to diseases (the immune system being told, "Hold off on attacking those germs—we have wild beasts to fight!"), digestive troubles (ulcers and cancers at the far side of it) poor assimilation (preventing necessary proteins, vitamins and

*I don't do anything
that's bad for me.
I don't like to be made
nervous or angry.
Any time you get upset
it tears down your
nervous system.*

MAE WEST

minerals from entering the system), slower recovery from illnesses (conquering a disease is far less important than conquering a wild beast), reduced production of blood cells and other necessary cells, sore muscles, fatigue and a general sense of ick, blah, and ugh.

Sound bad? It gets worse.

The emergency chemicals, unused, eventually begin breaking down into other, more toxic substances. Our body must then mobilize—yet again—to get rid of the poisons.

The muscles stay tense for a long time after the Response is triggered, especially around the stomach, chest, lower back, neck and shoulders. (Most people have chronic tension in at least one of these areas.) We feel jittery, nervous, uptight.

The mind always tries to find reasons for things. If the body's feeling uptight, it wonders, "What is there to feel uptight about?" Seldom do we conclude (correctly), "Oh, this is just the normal aftereffects of the Fight or Flight Response. Nothing to be concerned about." Usually we start scanning the environment (inner and outer) for something out of place. And, as we mentioned before, there will *always* be something out of place.

The mind's a remarkable mechanism. Given a task, it will fulfill it with astounding speed and accuracy. When asked, "What's wrong?" it will compile and cross-reference a list of grievances with blinding swiftness and precision. Everything everyone (including ourselves) should have done but didn't and shouldn't have done but did is reviewed, highlighted, indexed and prioritized. All this sparked by a sensation in the body.

Naturally, this mental review of negative events prompts a new round of Fight or Flight Responses,

*Wherever there is a heart
and an intellect,
the diseases of
the physical frame
are tinged with the
peculiarities of these.*

NATHANIEL HAWTHORNE

which promotes more tension in the body, which promotes more mental investigation into What's Wrong?

Do you see how this downward mind/body spiral can continue almost indefinitely? When it's gone on for a while, it's generally known as depression. But because depression, we hear, is a form of mental illness and mental illness is considered bad by our culture, we feel depressed about feeling depressed, and a whole new cycle of the Fight or Flight Response is triggered.

Considering all this, it's not surprising that some people make a decision deep inside themselves that life is just not worth living.

To hate and to fear
is to be psychologically ill.
It is, in fact,
the consuming illness
of our time.

H. A. OVERSTREET

Negative Thoughts and the Emotions

The primary emotions generated by the Fight or Flight Response are anger (the emotional energy to fight) and fear (the emotional energy to flee).

Contained within these two are most of the feelings we generally associate with the word *negative*.

Consider these lists:

ANGER	FEAR
hostility	terror
resentment	anxiety
guilt (anger at one-self)	timidity
	shyness (a general fear of others)
rage	
seething	withdrawal
depression	reticence
hurt (you're usually upset with someone else, or yourself, or both)	apprehension
	grieving (fear that you'll never love or be loved again)

Any others you'd care to add from your own repertoire could probably be considered a variation of anger or fear—or a combination of the two.

Zugg, while deciding what to do, probably experienced a good deal of both. Anger ("Win one for Zuggrina!") and fear ("What happened to Zuggrina ain't gonna happen to me!").

*Anger is one of
the sinews of the soul;
he that wants it hath
a maimed mind.*

THOMAS FULLER
1642

The problem with either emotion—in addition to the obvious unpleasantness—is that both tend to mar logical, rational, life-supporting decisions.

In his passionate anger for sibling revenge, Zugg might wade into the tall grass, spear in hand, and discover a whole gathering of wild beasts. Maybe the beasties didn't even know Zugg was around. Maybe they were just breaking twigs to roast weenies, but when Zugg appeared they decided on a quick change of menu.

How often have you waded into a confrontation, only to find that, as the saying goes, you had stirred up a hornet's nest?

> PETER: While on vacation, I received a traffic ticket from a particularly obnoxious police officer. A ticket *plus* insults! Too much was enough. I stormed over to the local police station and reported the offending public servant to his superior. While listening to my story, the police captain was tapping into his computer. I thought he was taking some sort of formal report. Oh, boy. The nasty policeman was really in trouble now. What the captain was doing, however, was looking up my driving record. He discovered an unpaid traffic ticket of mine from a vacation I had taken seven years before. I was placed under arrest. The anger quickly turned to fear. My anger cost me $110 and several hours in the cooler. Now I know why they call it the cooler.

On the other hand, Zugg could have, at the first sound of a snap, run away. (Remember the movie *Monty Python and the Holy Grail?* Whenever King Arthur's men were in even the slightest danger,

*All violent feelings
produce in us a falseness
in all our impressions
of external things,
which I would generally
characterize as
the "Pathetic Fallacy."*

JOHN RUSKIN

their battle cry, as they fled in all different directions, was, "Run away! Run away!") This meant that every time a rabbit snapped a twig or two gophers were going for it in the underbrush, Zugg would abandon his plowing and head for the high country. He would eventually abandon his field, vowing never to return to such a wild and savage place again.

How many fields have you abandoned in your life? The field of a challenging new career? The field of a more fulfilling place to live? The field of relationships? (That's "relationships" as in "true love, a many-splendored thing.") The field of your dreams?

Because people are afraid of fear, they give up acre after acre of their own life. Some find the snapping of twigs so uncomfortable that they abandon the territory of life altogether.

*Habit with him was all
the test of truth,
"It must be right:
I've done it from my youth."*

GEORGE CRABBE

The Addictive Quality of Negative Thinking

For many, negative thinking becomes a habit—a bad habit—which, over time, degenerates into an addiction. It's a disease, like alcoholism, compulsive overeating or drug abuse.

A lot of people suffer from this disease because negative thinking is addictive to each of The Big Three—the mind, the body, and the emotions. If one doesn't get you, the others are waiting in the wings.

The mind becomes addicted to being "right." In this far-less-than-perfect world, one of the easiest ways to be right is to predict failure, especially for ourselves. The mind likes being right. When asked, "Would you rather be right or be happy?" some people—who really take the time to consider the ramifications of being "wrong"—have trouble deciding.

The body becomes addicted to the rush of chemicals poured into the blood stream by the Fight or Flight Response. The thrill and stimulation of a serious session of negative thinking is something of a high. Some people "get off" on the rush of adrenaline.

The emotions become addicted to the sheer intensity of it all. They may not be pleasant feelings, but they're a long way from boredom. As the emotions become acclimated to a certain level of stimulation, they start demanding more and more intensity. It's not unlike the slash-and-gash movies—too much is no longer enough. Remember when the shower scene from *Psycho* was considered the ultimate in blood and gore? Now it's *Friday the 13th, Part Seven.* (Seven?!)

To fall into a habit
is to begin to cease to be.

MIGUEL DE UNAMUNO

Negative thinking must be treated like any addiction, with commitment to life, patience, discipline, a will to get better, forgiveness, self love, and the knowledge that recovery is not just possible but, following certain guidelines, inevitable.

Most people live,
whether physically,
intellectually or morally,
in a very restricted circle of
their potential being.
They make use of a very
small portion of
their possible consciousness,
and of their soul's
resources in general,
much like a man who,
out of his whole
bodily organism,
should get into a habit of
using and moving only
his little finger.
Great emergencies and crises
show us how much greater
our vital resources are than
we had supposed.

WILLIAM JAMES

The Power of Thoughts (Part Two)

What we've discussed thus far is pretty much accepted, mainline medical fact. The most "controversial" subject we've presented is the idea that negative thinking is an addictive disease. The doctors who have taken a close look see that the pattern of negative thinking, in its extreme, fits all the criteria of addiction in the medical sense. But some have not yet taken a close look.

With that possible exception, if you take this book to your local physician, he or she will probably read it, nod knowingly, and agree that it is fairly accurate. (Thirty years ago, of course, most of the medical establishment wouldn't admit that thoughts had any causal effect on organic illness. If you mentioned such a thing, they'd think you were nuts. We all live and learn.)

Now we're going to explore some thoughts about thoughts they don't teach you at The Harvard Medical School.

You can take the next few pages with as many grains of salt as you like. The accepted medical theory—that thoughts are a contributing factor of symptomatic illness, and that improving one's thoughts can help improve one's health—is all we need to meet the premise of this book.

The rest is, well, interesting, fun, provocative, stupid, enlightening—use your own adjectives to describe it. Even if it's just the rantings of two California boys, it doesn't negate the fact that, in anyone's book—medical or metaphysical—if a life-threatening illness threatens, you can't afford the luxury of a negative thought.

*There is nothing I love
as much as a good fight.*

FRANKLIN D. ROOSEVELT
January 22, 1911

The Creative Power of Thoughts

Thoughts are powerful. All the spectacular and terrible creations of humanity began as thoughts—an idea, if you will. From the idea came the plan and from the plan came the action and from the action came the object. Whatever you're sitting on or reclining upon began as a thought. The room you're in—and almost everything in it—began as a thought.

All the wars and fighting the world has known began with thoughts. (Usually, "You have it, I want it," "You're doing this, I want you to do that," or "I just don't like you.")

All the good, fine, noble and creative acts of humanity were conceived as a spark in a single human consciousness. The Eiffel Tower, the Mona Lisa, the Magna Carta, the Declaration of Independence, movies, books, television began in the human mind. (Granted, some of it should have stayed there. As someone once said, "In every journalist is a novel, and that's where it should remain.")

Even the creation of a human being begins as a thought. As the old saying goes, "I knew you before you were a twinkle in your father's eye."

Victor Hugo described it this way—"An invasion of armies can be resisted, but not an idea whose time has come." Often misquoted as "There is nothing so powerful as an idea whose time has come," it has been used so often it's almost become a cliché. (There is nothing less powerful than a cliché whose time has passed.)

Enlighten
the people generally,
and tyranny
and oppressions
of body and mind
will vanish like evil spirits
at the dawn of day.

THOMAS JEFFERSON

Although we probably don't think about it often, it's easy to see that everything created by humans—both good and bad—began as a thought. (The categorization of "good" and "bad," of course, is just another thought.) The only difference between a thought and a physical reality is a certain amount of time and physical activity.

The amount of time and physical activity varies from project to project. Sometimes it's seconds, sometimes it's years, and sometimes the thought must be passed from generation to generation. Some of the great cathedrals took a century and three generations of stone cutters to complete. On the other hand, there was the Hundred Years' War.

Leonardo da Vinci invented the helicopter four hundred years before one ever flew. Two hundred years ago, Thomas Jefferson envisioned a nation free from religious persecution, of people ". . . with certain unalienable rights, that among these are life, liberty and the pursuit of happiness. . . ." We're still working on that one.

To illustrate: Imagine the corner of this page turned over. Let it be an idea in your mind. Now reach up and fold it over. A thought was passed from our minds to your mind, and you turned that thought into a physical reality. (If you're not the first person to read this book, you might have wondered, "Why is the corner of this page turned over?" Now you know.)

Some people are particularly good at turning ideas into realities. Edison was one. Imagine: the phonograph, movies, an improved telephone and the electric light all from one man. Henry Ford wanted to make a cheap, reliable automobile and invented the assembly line in order to do it.

*Great men
are they who see
that spiritual is stronger
than any material force,
that thoughts
rule the world.*

EMERSON

Without thoughts, things that involve any sort of human action just don't happen. Where we are is the result of a lifetime of thinking, both positive and negative. If you wonder what your thinking's been like, take a look at where you are in life. Behold the answer.

If you're pleased with some parts of your life, then your thinking in those areas has no doubt been what you would call generally "positive." If you're not pleased with other parts of your life, then your thoughts about those areas probably have not been as positive as they could have been. The good news is that thoughts can be changed, and with that change come changes in manifestation.

Thoughts, if persisted in, can produce states of consciousness that, if persisted in, can produce physical manifestation.

If you persist in your thoughts of wealth, for example, this produces a consciousness of wealth—an overall state of being that is open, accepting, abundant and flowing—and this consciousness of wealth tends to produce the physical manifestations of wealth: houses, cars, cash, and a special edition of *Lifestyles of the Rich and Famous.*

"But," someone once protested, "I don't have any money and I worry about it *all the time.*" This person was proving the point, but in reverse. Worry is a form of fear, in this case a fear of poverty. This person, in holding an ongoing series of thoughts about poverty, created a consciousness of poverty, which created a lack of everything but bills, which caused more worry, which creates more poverty.

Positive thoughts yield positive results—loving, caring and sharing; health, wealth and happiness; prosperity, abundance and riches.

*All that is comes
from the mind;
it is based on the mind,
it is fashioned
by the mind.*

THE PALI CANON
500-250 B.C.

Negative thoughts bring negative results—dislike, indifference and withholding; dis-ease, poverty and misery; fear, lack and alienation.

Our thoughts, in other words, create our physical reality—not instantly, necessarily, as in "Poof! There it is"—but eventually. Where we put our vision—our inner and outer vision—is the direction we tend to go. That's our desire. The *way* we get there—well, there are many methods.

*Follow your desire
as long as you live;
do not lessen the time
of following desire,
for the wasting of time
is an abomination
to the spirit.*

PTAHHOTPE
2350 B.C.

Intention and Desire vs. Method and Behavior

If we were in New York and wanted to go to Toledo (God knoweth why—writers have to stretch reality sometimes in order to come up with examples), what are some of the ways we could get there?

Plane? Car? Train? Bus? Bike? Walk? Hitchhike? Pogo stick? Crawl? Roll? Skip? Hop? Somersault? You, no doubt, have some other ways we haven't mentioned. (Somersault. What a strange-looking word, huh?)

In this example, Toledo would be the *intention* or *desire*. The many ways of traveling there are the *methods* or *behaviors*.

Each intention or desire we have in life can be fulfilled by any number of methods or behaviors. The idea is to hold your intetion or desire clearly in mind, and then be open to whatever methods or behaviors appear—even unexpected ones.

For example, in traveling from New York to Toledo, what general direction should we take? West, right? That would be the generally accepted method—directionally speaking. Some might even argue that it is the *only* direction that would get us to Toledo. But what if you went east, and kept going east? Would you eventually find yourself in Toledo? Sure.

As Niels Bohr said, "The opposite of a correct statement is a false statement. But the opposite of a profound truth may well be another profound truth." Some people say the way to get more money is to hoard it. Others say the way to get more

*It is common sense to
take a method and try it.
If it fails,
admit it frankly
and try another.
But above all,
try something.*

FRANKLIN D. ROOSEVELT

money is to give it away. Some say health is gained through more rest. Others say it's obtained through more activity. Be open to all methods and behaviors, even *seemingly* contradictory ones.

Back to Toledo. Which direction is the faster route from New York to Toledo, east or west? It can only be west, right? Not necessarily. If we went west doing somersaults and you went east on the Concorde, who do you suppose would get to Toledo faster? (Hint: We are not listed in *Guinness' Book of World Records* as The Somersault Twins.)

Again, keep open to various methods and behaviors, and remember: life often offers more surprising answers than we do.

Back again to Toledo. All silly examples aside, if we really wanted to get from New York to Toledo, which is the right way to go? A westerly course, of course. As you can tell, we're being trickier than usual in this section. We're challenging some popular assumptions people have about methods and how to choose them. Is west really a "right" direction and east a "wrong" one? Of course not.

As methods go, "right" and "wrong" are just opinions. The only valid criterion of a method or a behavior is that it be *workable*. In the New York-Toledo journey, both east and west are workable methods and, therefore, acceptable. North and south are not workable; therefore, not acceptable. North and south are not wrong; they just aren't appropriate for a journey from New York to Toledo.

Methods and behaviors can sometimes indicate desires and intentions. If you were driving west from New York, for example, we could reasonably assume that your immediate desire was not to visit New England. The operative words are *sometimes* and *indicate,* because it's not until you land in

*Bring me my bow
of burning gold,
Bring me my arrows
of desire,
Bring me my spear—
O clouds, unfold!
Bring me my chariot
of fire!*

WILLIAM BLAKE

Toledo and say, "Yes! This is it!" that we'll know your desire was truly Toledo.

≈

Let's say someone has a desire to hide. He (let's make him a he) discovered at an early age that to be spontaneous and outgoing and sensitive and expressive got him into trouble with some of his authority figures. ("Be quiet! Can't you see we're watching television?" "Settle down." "Be a good little boy and sit still." Etc.) He decided to hide these parts of himself.

If his desire was to hide his sensitivity and enthusiasm, what methods could he use? Being withdrawn, not going out, shyness, not participating. He might start creating some physical methods: a stammer, putting on weight, or even developing an illness, such as asthma or a heart problem—perfectly reasonable reasons not to participate. He might generate a need for glasses—which can be wonderful things to hide behind. In later years, he may let his hair cover part of his face and maybe grow a beard.

And what if life at certain points became too intolerable? What if he decided, time and again, "I can't take this anymore. I don't want to live"? If he formed a desire to die, what are some of the methods or behaviors he might use to fulfill that desire?

Gunshot, car accident, poison, tuberculosis, leukemia, cancer, drowning, carbon monoxide, knife wound, slit wrist, heart attack, stroke, diphtheria, decapitation, a relationship with Blue Beard, bubonic plague, earthquake, flood, volcano, anorexia, falling, syphilis, wild beasts, cholera, guillotine, hanging, shark, piranha, electric chair, gas chamber,

Of all escape mechanisms,
death is the most efficient.

H. L. MENCKEN

lethal injection, polio, flu, meningitis, hepatitis, or the relative newcomer, AIDS.

If someone has a desire or intention to die, a life-threatening illness is just one of the many methods to fulfill that desire. It might just be that somewhere inside, the person has or has had a desire to die.

Maybe.

It's worth a look. Desires are often unconscious. But, once discovered, desires can be changed.

*The strangest
and most fantastic fact
about negative emotions
is that people actually
worship them.*

P. D. OUSPENSKY

Where Does Negative Thinking Come From?

Or,

Why Are We Doing This to Ourselves?

Why do we use the power of our mind to create a negative reality? If our mind can generate health, wealth and happiness as easily as illness, poverty and despair, why aren't we healthy, wealthy and happy all the time?

If a genie appeared and offered you a choice—health, wealth and happiness or illness, poverty and despair—which would you choose? If positivity is the obvious choice, why do we sometimes choose the negative? There must be something else, something deeper within us generating the impulse to think negatively.

Although you may have another word to describe the phenomenon, we call this wellspring of negative thinking *unworthiness*. It's more than just a feeling or a passing thought. It's a ground of being, a deep-seated belief that "I'm just not good enough." Other phrases for it include insecurity, undeservingness or low self-esteem.

Unworthiness undermines all our positive ideas and validates all our negative thoughts.

When we think something good about ourselves, unworthiness pops up and says, "No, you're not." When we desire something positive for ourselves,

You have no idea
what a poor opinion
I have of myself—
and how little I deserve it.

W. S. GILBERT

unworthiness says, "You don't deserve it." When something good happens to us, unworthiness says, often with our own lips, "This is too good to be true!"

When we think something bad about ourselves, unworthiness agrees, "Yes, that's true, and furthermore. . . ." When we tell ourselves we can't have or do something we want, unworthiness says, "Now you're being realistic." When something bad happens to us, unworthiness is the first to point out, "See, I was right all along. I told you so."

You can think of unworthiness as a vulture that sits on your shoulder, squawking in your ear a seemingly endless stream of: "You can't do it," "You're not good enough," "Don't even try," "Who do you think you are?" "You'll never make it," "Settle down," "You don't deserve it," "Somebody better than you should have it," *ad infinitum, ad nauseam.*

Some people cover their unworthiness with an air of self-confidence and an outward bravado bordering on arrogance. Their cover-up includes a self-indulgence and self-absorption that are almost selfish. These people, it appears on the surface, could use a healthy dose of unworthiness.

But, in reality, they are merely involved in a desperate attempt to hide—from themselves as much as from anyone else—the fact that they just don't feel worth it. They think the unworthiness is *true,* not just another illusion, and they respond by concealing it rather than laughing at it. (Did you ever try to conceal a vulture? It can be pretty funny—to everyone but the person concealing.)

If unworthiness is so fundamental, does this mean we're born with it? We believe humans were born to have joy and to have it more abundantly; that the birthright of everyone is loving, caring,

The childhood shows
the man,
As morning shows
the day.

JOHN MILTON

sharing and abundance. All the negative stuff has just been layered on top of our essential core of goodness.

So where does unworthiness come from? A look at how children are raised might offer a clue.

Imagine a child—at two, three or four—playing alone in a room. An adult, usually a parent, is nearby. What for? To come in and praise the child every five minutes? No. For "supervision." (Did your parents have super-vision? Ours did.) The adult is there to be on hand "in case there's any trouble."

The child is playing and having a wonderful time. Two hours go by. The child is "behaving" wonderfully. The interaction with the adult has been minimal.

Suddenly, the child knocks a lamp off a table. It crashes to the floor. What happens next? *Lots* of interaction with the adult, almost all of it negative. Yelling, screaming ("This was my favorite lamp," "How many times have I told you?" "Bad, bad, bad"), and probably, for good measure, some form of physical punishment (spanking, deprivation of a toy, etc.). Almost the only interaction in two-hours from the adult community was, "You are bad. Shame on you."

As an infant, we get unconditional, almost never-ending praise. Goo-goo ga-ga. Once we grow a little and begin exploring our world, our primary form of interaction with adults—the symbols of power, love, authority and life itself—is usually corrective. *Don't* do this. *Don't* do that. (This phase in growth is known as "The Terrible Twos" by the people who write the how-to-raise-children books—real positive, huh?)

If we draw a picture, we get praise. If we draw the same picture again, we get less praise. If we

Few parents nowadays
pay any regard
to what their children
say to them.
The old-fashioned respect
for the young
is fast dying out.

OSCAR WILDE

draw the same picture five times in a row, we are told to try something new.

If we pour jam on the cat, we are scolded. If we pour jam on the cat a second time, we are scolded more severely. If we pour jam on the cat five times, we may begin wishing that, like the cat, we had nine lives.

The more we do something good, the less praise we get for it. The more we do something bad, the more punishment we receive. Some children learn to do negative things just to get attention, because even negative attention is better than no attention at all. Being ignored, to a child, can seem like abandonment.

A part of us inside begins to add up all the times we're called "wonderful" and all the times we're called "bad." The bad seems to outnumber the wonderful by a significant margin.

We may begin to believe we *are* bad. That unless we do something new and remarkable and tremendous, we're not going to be thought of as good. That we must strive, work hard and never disobey if we hope to get even a little appreciation in this world. That our goodness must be *earned* because we are, after all, essentially bad.

Bad, unlovable, not good enough, undeserving, unworthy.

We may grow to believe this about ourselves, and from this fertile ground springs our negative thoughts. Sure, we have a lot of positive thoughts, but the negative ones tend to be more believed. A positive thought, checked against this belief of unworthiness, is labeled "False." A negative thought feels right at home. The unworthiness proclaims it true, accurate, *right*.

*The highest possible stage
in moral culture
is when we recognize
that we ought to
control our thoughts.*

CHARLES DARWIN

Negative Thinking and Life-Threatening Illness

There are as many examples of how negative thinking helps bring about life-threatening illnesses as there are people who have them. We each have our own personal list of disasters, those things that push us "over the edge," that make us decide life isn't worth living anymore.

For some it's one or two tragedies, the depth and intensity of which created a desire to die. For others, it's just the daily dose of "slings and arrows," the situations to which we respond, "What's the use?" "Why bother?" "Who cares?" The accumulation of these over the years forms the desire to not have to bother anymore.

The following is an edited transcript of John-Roger working with a person with AIDS symptoms. Although this example applies only to the person J-R was working with, other people reading this might see a similar pattern in their own lives and their own life-threatening illnesses. Your specific examples may be different, but the general pattern may be similar.

> JOHN-ROGER: What's the probability of reversing this? Eighty to 90 percent. That 10-to-20-percent variable is where you won't do what you're required to do, because of a depression or an "I don't give a damn" attitude. That will be the part that will do you in, if you let it. You don't have to let it.
>
> Let me tell you psychologically how AIDS comes about, because that's where your cure can lie:

*Attachment is the great
fabricator of illusions;
reality can be attained
only by someone
who is detached.*

SIMONE WEIL

At some point you might think about someone, "They don't like me, but I really like them, and I would like them to like me." You go out of your way to get them to like you. And they do. Then you feel very good. Up to this point, there's no problem. You've just done things to get someone to like you. This is what we call dating or courtship—pretty average behavior.

Then they turn from you. And you still like them. At that moment, a little bit of you dies.

You give yourself over to, "Oh my God, what will I do with this love of mine? He's going out with other people. He doesn't love me anymore." You contract and pull in. It hurts your back, your neck. You want release from the pressures of the body and the pain of the emotions, so if you can numb them or dull them, you'll do that. Alcohol and drugs walk right in the door. Both of those will distract you from the symptoms of the body and the emotions.

The body and the emotions, however, are just trying to give you a message. They're telling you you're hurting because of your attachments to your desires.

The attachment is the killer, not the desire. You can desire something and, when you're through with it, detach yourself from it, and it doesn't hurt. It's the attachment that hurts. And if it's somebody you're attached to, and they leave, it's as though your arm is being stretched and stretched until you finally say, "I'd just as soon have it cut off."

*He was a poor
weak human being
like themselves,
a human soul,
weak and helpless
in suffering,
shivering in the toils
of the eternal struggle
of the human soul
with pain.*

LIAM O'FLAHERTY

Then when you cut it, it seems as though you cut part of your lifeline.

You immediately want to go and find somebody else to restore your life. Now you're giving yourself over to the cruising, the searching, the questing.

You find somebody, and they're OK for now, and you get involved with them—for a day, a night, two or three days, maybe a week, but probably not more than a month. And then it's over. In your mind you say, "They helped me get over that other one, so it's OK."

But in the unconscious, you have wished a death on yourself. You have given up your life to something outside yourself—a person or thing or idea.

You die many, many times during the day from that point on. You feel the need for cohabitation with somebody—not even necessarily sex, maybe just living with someone, companionship, friendship.

When you can't find that—or whatever it is you think would make your life worthwhile—this attachment to the desire demands on your life until the alcohol becomes a habit, the drugs become addictive, finding somebody to have sex with becomes irrational.

Attachments are very strong. They can act like an obsession or a possession. You say, "Even when I'm doing nothing, the thing comes at me. The only way I can get rid of it

*If we could read
the secret history
of our enemies,
we should find in each
man's life sorrow and
suffering enough to
disarm all hostility.*

LONGFELLOW

is to go with it." And then it has more life because you give your life to it.

Giving over your life to it is not a sustaining action. It drains and depletes you. You might say, "I'm tired of the bar scene. I'm tired of the bath scene. I'm tired of the cruising scene." This is the rational mind inside you saying, "Don't do these things anymore. They're not really doing anything for you. You're getting repetition, repetition without fulfillment."

Then, if you let your body run down because of, say, alcohol or drugs or exhaustion, the virus can come in because your defense mechanism is dulled.

≈

We're not saying negative thinking *causes* AIDS, or any other life-threatening illness. The AIDS virus causes AIDS. Negative thinking, we suggest, promotes conditions in the mind, body and emotions that make it possible for the AIDS virus (or any infection) to take root.

Negative thinking helps provide the *opportunity*. The infection takes it from there. Once it takes root, how quickly the virus progresses and grows depends a lot on how much manure we give it from that great fertilizer generator, negative thinking.

Right now, probably the most common negative thought surrounding AIDS is fear. Anyone in the so-called "high-risk group" is a candidate for the epidemic of fear that's spread far faster than the AIDS virus itself. (Actually, the only people in the high-risk

*The fear of death
is more to be dreaded
than death itself.*

PUBLILIUS SYRUS
First century B.C.

group are those who practice high-risk activities.) If you've had a test indicating the presence of HIV antibodies in your system, you probably are even more susceptible to the dis-ease of fear.

The disease we're talking about here is rampant, irrational fear—not AIDS. The epidemic of fear (a subset of the epidemic of negative thinking) is one of the most contagious diseases around. Unlike any viral-based illness, you can catch fear over the telephone, while reading newspapers or magazines, and even while watching television.

For those afraid of catching AIDS—especially people who have the antibodies to the HIV virus in their system—every symptom of every disease has the terror of imminent death.

A cold? "Oh my God, pneumocystis!" A bruise? "Kaposi's sarcoma!" A sore in the mouth? "Thrush!" A little perspiration because the bedroom is too warm? "Night sweats!" It's hypochondriac heaven: fear enlarges every minor symptom into a fatal illness.

This fear pattern extends to most life-threatening illnesses. There is a certain "high-risk group" for every illness, and the people within that group often torture themselves with worry. For cancer, it's smokers. Thirty percent of all cancer deaths are smoking-related. Smokers may worry so much about cancer that they need another cigarette.

People with possible genetic predispositions to illness tend to worry. "My father died at sixty-five of a heart attack, my grandfather died at sixty-five of a heart attack, and I'm almost sixty."

Fear, fear, fear.

The tragic results of this epidemic of fear are many:

*There is perhaps
nothing so bad
and so dangerous in life
as fear.*

JAWAHARLAL NEHRU

1. From a purely medical point of view, all this negative thinking suppresses the immune system, raises the blood pressure and creates a general level of stress and fatigue in the body. In short, infections, cardiovascular irregularities, the degeneration of muscles and the random growth of unwanted cells get more opportunity.

2. From a thoughts-are-creative point of view, our worry about a particular disease tends to create that disease. There's an old saying: "What you fear may come upon you." It's old because there's a degree of truth in it. Medical students and psychology students will often take on the symptoms of the disease or disorder they are currently studying and, in some cases, produce the full-blown disease. The thought, "Oh my God, it's cancer!" every time you cough might be misinterpreted as an invitation or even a directive.

3. If you're sick, thinking it might be AIDS or lung cancer or Lyme disease, and it turns out to be just the flu, you say, "Thank God, it's the flu!" Such enthusiasm over the flu may create more flu.

4. The more that people believe they are going to die "within a few years, at best," the less they tend to start long-term projects—career goals, relationships, moving—which, in turn, tends to make life less fulfilling and enjoyable, therefore less livable. After a while, the question, "What have I got to live for?" might not have a satisfactory answer. And the desire to die is rekindled.

5. It's a miserable way to live. If we had a bomb strapped to our chest and were told it could go off at any time, that might be something, over time, we could learn to live with. (We all have a similar situation in that we know we're going to die, but we don't know when.) If, however, we were told the

Death in itself is nothing;
but we fear
To be we know not what,
we know not where.

JOHN DRYDEN

bomb would tick precisely 1,243 times before exploding, every time the bomb started ticking, we'd stop everything we were doing and start counting. Some days it might only tick ten times. Other days it might get up to 287. But while it ticked: panic. And, after a while, the fear that it *might* start ticking begins. So, even when it's not ticking, we're scared. As we said, it's a miserable way to live.

≈

Once negative thinking has given the life-threatening illness the opportunity to enter the body, is it then too late? Is the progression of a life-threatening illness irreversible? We don't think so. We're not being hopelessly optimistic about this, however; some things *are* irreversible.

Let's say, for example, that negative thinking had thrown you from the top of a thirty-story building. Once you were in the air, we would probably say it's too late for a change in thinking to greatly affect the physical outcome.

But for anything short of the law of gravity, there's a chance. (That's why it's called the law of gravity—levity has no effect upon it.)

The AIDS virus (HIV) is an interesting one. It seems to have the ability to go dormant for indefinite periods. While dormant, it does no harm. It just sleeps quietly.

The vital question is, What puts the virus to sleep and what keeps it sleeping? We like to think the gentle lapping of positive thoughts on the shoreline of the mind acts as a virtual Sominex (or Demerol or chloroform or nitrous oxide, as you prefer) to HIV.

MACBETH: *Canst thou
not minister
to a mind diseased,
Pluck from the memory
a rooted sorrow,
Raze out the written
troubles of the brain,
And with some sweet
oblivious antidote
Cleanse the stuffed bosom
of that perilous stuff
Which weighs
upon the heart?*

DOCTOR: *Therein
the patient
Must minister to himself.*

SHAKESPEARE

Cardiovascular illnesses are directly related to the general mental-emotional-physical state of ease in the body. The more often the body is at ease, the less the heart must work and the less pressure is exerted on the entire cardiovascular system. A primary goal of exercise, in fact, is letting the heart work less as it becomes stronger.

When the pressures caused by negative thinking are released and a natural state of ease returns, the cardiovascular system can heal itself and function as it was designed to.

Degenerative muscle diseases may be helped along their course of degeneration by "degenerative thinking." Generating generative (positive) thoughts may help slow the degeneration and, perhaps, even regenerate muscles.

Cancer is, by definition, cells that are growing out of control. This pattern can be swift, or it can be slow. It can take over a vital organ in a matter of weeks, or it can take decades. The cells can stop growing altogether for indefinite periods of time. When discussing "incurable" cancer (and more than 50 percent of all cancers are now considered curable), the medical establishment doesn't quite know why a cancer would slow, stop or, more mysteriously still, *get smaller.*

It's known as "remission." When it happens because of medical treatment, it is understood. "Your cancer is in remission." When it happens for "no good reason" (the patient's rediscovered desire to live and related changes in life-style not being a good enough "reason"), it's called "spontaneous remission." It's spontaneous, as are lightning or earthquakes. It just happens sometimes. We don't know why.

What physic,
what chirurgery,
what wealth, favor,
authority can relieve,
bear out, assuage, or expel
a troubled conscience?
A quiet mind cureth all.

ROBERT BURTON
1622

Tens of thousands of cancer patients, whose cancers have been in "spontaneous remission" for years, know why. They changed their thinking, and the thinking changed the course of the cancer.

The same is true of any infection or life-threatening illness you can name. Some of the "miracle cures" were not miracles to the people who experienced them. They discovered why they desired death, changed that to a desire for life, and got busy changing everything in their lives that was contributing to their physical demise.

Consider the remainder of this book a lullaby for the AIDS virus or any other infection, a road map on ways to ease your cardiovascular system, lessons in how to heal the hurts of the heart and thereby heal the physical heart, instruction in generating generative thinking to counteract degenerative illness, a guidebook on creating spontaneity in your commissions and your remissions, and a wake-up call to the worthiness, well-being and wellness within you.

PART II

THE CURE

There is no cure
for birth and death
save to enjoy the interval.

GEORGE SANTAYANA

The Cure

Yes, Virginia, there is a cure for the disease of negative thinking—dozens of cures, in fact. Any one of the techniques, suggestions or ideas in this section may do it for you. Any one may be the key that opens whole new worlds of aliveness, enthusiasm and health.

Yours may be a combination lock that requires five keys, or ten, or twenty, or you may need everything in this book—and a hundred more you discover on your own—to open the doors to your inner kingdom of joy, self-confidence and happiness. Whatever it takes is whatever it takes.

Whatever it takes, the results will be worth it.

We're going to begin by talking about death (eeek!) and the fear of death (eeek! eeek!). After that, luncheon is served. We're laying out a smorgasbord of positivity, gathered from our cumulative sixty-plus years of working with people—and ourselves.

We're not going to pretend that anything we present is new. You already know everything here. Some of it you know intuitively; some of it you were taught long ago. (Our parents and teachers taught us a lot more than unworthiness.)

But mostly, these suggestions will seem familiar because they're good old-fashioned common sense. We tend to be a pragmatic pair—if something works, we use it; if not, we try something else. What we pass along to you was learned through our own process of trial and error. It is from a firm—and substantial—foundation of mistakes that we offer these suggestions.

*Common sense
is not so common.*

VOLTAIRE

There's no particular order to this gathering of ideas. No "Do this first, then this, then this." You are the architect of your own cure. Naturally, like all good architects, you'll be consulting with other professionals—but the Master Plan is in your hands.

The pathway to your cure is easy—just follow your heart.

Before you officially "start" (we know you actually started when you picked up this book), we suggest you read the book all the way through, turning over the corners or marking in some way the pages that appeal to you. Things will no doubt appeal in one of two ways:

1. Some things will seem fun, interesting or entertaining. Do them. You're worthy of things that are fun, interesting and entertaining. (The road from negative thinking to positive being need not be a hard one—far from it!)

2. Some things you won't want to do, but something inside will tell you it's time to do them anyway. Giving up bad habits is seldom "fun," but the success of overcoming them increases your self-confidence, reclaims your power and enhances your self-worth. So, although they may not be exactly "fun," they are, nonetheless, worthwhile.

We've included a broad range of techniques here. Some of the things you may have done years ago and have no need for. Others you may not need until years from now. Some, we trust, will be like the baby bear's porridge: just right. Listen to your heart as you read, and the ones that are right for you will be duly noted.

After reading through to the end of the book, return and reread those pages you marked. Do they still appeal? If so, put them into action.

The music that can
deepest reach,
And cure all ill,
is cordial speech.

EMERSON

Another way of selecting those to "go for" from those to "wait for" is to ask a good friend—someone who knows you well and whose opinion you respect—to read this section and pick out the one he or she feels you need the most. Whether you put that one into motion is up to you, but the suggestions of a loving, supportive friend can often be illuminating. You can try this, too, with your therapist, doctor, or anyone else you respect. But always remember—the Master Plan is in your heart.

Once you begin the active phase of the process (the doing), you may find that you're being too easy on yourself or, conversely, that you've set too many things in motion. You'll soon know. If it's too few, add a few more. If it's too many, back off. In either case, don't feel that you've "failed" in any way. It's an organic process. Vines don't "fail" because they twist and twine themselves in many directions as they reach for the sun.

From time to time, reread the entire book again. You may find that a technique you used for a few days or weeks or months produced the desired result, and now you're ready for a new one. Again, trust your heart. What you're ready for at that time will make itself known.

Of course, that's just one way of using this section. There are lots of others. You could, for example,

♦ Open it to any page and follow the suggestion on that page.

♦ Tear out all the pages, put them in a hat, and pick one (or five, or ten).

♦ Paste all the pages on a bulletin board and throw darts to make your selection.

*Healing is
a matter of time,
but it is sometimes also
a matter of opportunity.*

HIPPOCRATES
460-400 B.C.

♦Start at the very beginning and work your way through to the end.

♦Walk up to a stranger on the street and ask him or her to pick one for you. Repeat the process until (A) there is a clear consensus, or (B) you run out of strangers.

There's lots of room for flexibility and fun in these suggestions.

The most important thing is—don't just *read* this book, *use* it. *Do* some things. *Try* them out. *Find out* if they work for you, if they produce uplifting results. If so, *do* some more. If not, *throw* it away. As Dorothy Parker once said (not about one of our books, thank heaven), "This is not a book to be cast aside lightly, but to be hurled with great force."

And now with great force (and gentle prodding) we hurl (and coax) you into *The Cure*. (And may the Great Force be with you.)

*One who longs for death
is miserable,
but more miserable
is he who fears it.*

JULIUS WILHELM ZINCGREF
1628

*If I could drop dead
right now, I'd be the
happiest man alive!*

SAMUEL GOLDWYN

Death 101 (Part One)

This is a crash course in death. Why death? I mean, shouldn't we be focusing on *positive stuff?* Yes, but first we have to explore the motivation *behind* doing all the positive stuff.

If the reason you're going to think more positively is a fear of death, whatever you do—no matter how positive—will be an affirmation and validation of that fear.

As long as fear is looming large, you will probably continue with the process of improvement. As soon as the fear no longer threatens, you may revert to old habit patterns. When, for example, the medical cure for your illness is discovered, there's no need to fear dying of it any longer; therefore, you may feel you can return to your former habits of negative thinking.

That will, of course, recreate the desire to die, and a method of death other than that particular one is likely to appear.

If you use the techniques given in this section of the book because you want to live a fuller, happier, more joyful, loving and productive life, then you have a foundation that will hold firm. If you undertake these methods as a frantic attempt to outmaneuver the Grim Reaper, the whole venture is, to paraphrase Henry Higgins, "doomed before you even take the vow."

Not that you must be perfectly calm in the face of your own mortality before any of these suggestions will work. Not at all. Fear can be a good motivator to *start* something. But fear must gradually be replaced with the desire for a positive result if long-term progress is to be expected.

Once you accept
your own death,
all of a sudden
you're free to live.
You no longer care about
your reputation.
You no longer care
except so far as your life
can be used tactically—
to promote a cause
you believe in.

SAUL ALINSKY

It also feels better—running *from* something you're afraid of is far less enjoyable than running *toward* something you desire.

Running from fear only strengthens fear—you are demonstrating that it has enormous power over you. Fear must be faced and gone through. The procedure of "getting over" fear is succinctly stated in the title of the book *Feel Your Fear and Do It Anyway*. (A book neither of us has read, so we can't recommend it, but it does have a great title.) Only then do we learn the truth of fear—that it is merely an illusion, not a real thing.

Before we continue with our short course on death, let's stroll over to the next classroom and overhear a few pointers on fear.

Fear is the main source
of superstition,
and one of the main sources
of cruelty.
To conquer fear
is the beginning of wisdom.

BERTRAND RUSSELL

Yea, though I walk
through the valley of
the shadow of death,
I will fear no evil:
for thou art with me;
thy rod and thy staff
they comfort me.

PSALM 23

Fear 101

There are some things it's good to have a healthy fear of—drinking poisons, leaping off tall buildings, sex with gorillas—situations in which our physical body is in imminent danger of annihilation, dismemberment, mutilation and extinction.

All other fears—the ones we face most often every day—are illusions. They should be given no more credence or authority over our actions than television commercials, election-year promises or the people who try to sell us flowers in airports.

Most people approach a fearful situation as though the fear were some sort of wall. Let's say it's walking up to someone we do not know and saying, "Hello."

As we think about approaching the stranger, the wall begins to form. As we consider the thoughts about what the person may say in response, the wall grows denser. (The other person's response is almost always imagined in the negative—"Would you leave me alone!" Seldom do we imagine the other person looking up at us and singing "Some Enchanted Evening.") If we begin to take a physical move in the general direction of the person, the wall becomes almost solid. It seems an impenetrable barrier. We turn away, humming a chorus or two of "If I Loved You."

But the wall of fear *is not real*.

Fear as a barrier is an illusion we have been trained to treat as though it were real. This served us well in our childhood years. Our parents may have taught us to be afraid of everything new. We were too young to know the difference between the legitimately dangerous and the merely exciting.

I'm not afraid to die.
I just don't want to be there
when it happens.
It is impossible
to experience
one's death objectively
and still carry a tune.

WOODY ALLEN

Life does not cease to be funny
when people die
any more than it ceases to be
serious when people laugh.

GEORGE BERNARD SHAW

When we grew old enough to know the difference, however, no one ever retrained us to take risks, explore new territories and treat fears as the illusions they are. Fear should be tucked away with all those other cozy childhood myths—Santa Claus, the Easter Bunny and the Tooth Fairy. (The Tooth Fairy was a particularly hard one to let go of.)

If fear is not a wall, what is it? It's a feeling, that's all. It will not (cannot) keep you from physically moving toward something unless you let it. It may act up and it may kick and scream and it may make your stomach feel like the butterfly cage at the zoo, but it cannot stop you. You stop you.

The fear of meeting someone, for example, is a particularly silly fear. Given that it's in a place where they're not going to slug you (Hell's Angels bars are not recommended), the worst that can happen is that they will reject you. You are left with rejection. If you don't try, however, you have rejected yourself, and are left with exactly the same thing as if you had tried—nothing.

If you do try, however, you may get what you want.

Even if you get rejected, you'll learn more from the experience than if you had never tried. You may learn, for example, that certain ways of approaching certain people in certain situations work better than others. We can learn as much (sometimes more) by what doesn't work as by what does. If we don't explore all the ways that *really* do and don't work, we are left with only our imagination and what seems to work in the movies.

To quote from a T-shirt (we have a broad range of literary sources): "Anything that's worth having is worth asking for. Some say yes and some say no."

You gain strength,
courage and confidence
by every experience
in which you really stop
to look fear in the face.
You are able
to say to yourself,
"I lived through this horror.
I can take the next thing
that comes along."
You must do the thing
you think you cannot do.

ELEANOR ROOSEVELT

People living deeply
have no fear of death.

ANAIS NIN

To overcome a fear, here's all you have to do. Realize that the fear is there, *and do it anyway*. Move—physically—in the direction of what you want. Expect the fear to get worse. It will seldom let you down in that regard. After you do several times the thing your fear is protesting about, the fear will be less. Eventually, it goes away.

As Virgil Thomson once said, "Try a thing you haven't tried before three times—once to get over the fear, once to find out how to do it, and a third time to find out whether you like it or not." And Virgil lived *(really* lived) to the ripe age of ninety-two.

Fear is something to be *moved through*, not something to be *turned from*. In fact, if you feel carefully, you'll discover that the only difference between fear (a supposedly negative emotion) and excitement (a reputedly positive emotion) is what we choose to call it. The *sensation* is exactly the same. We just add a little "Oh, no!" to fear and a little "Oh, boy!" to excitement, that's all.

Fear, then, can be seen for what it *truly* is—the energy to do your best in a new situation.

So, with this in mind, let's return to death.

("Oh, boy!" "Oh, no!")

For certain is death
* for the born*
And certain is birth
* for the dead;*
Therefore over the inevitable
Thou shouldst not grieve.

BHAGAVAD GITA
2:27

Death and taxes
and childbirth!
There's never any convenient
time for any of them.

SCARLETT O'HARA

Death 101 (Part Two)

If you think about it, the fear of death is one of the most useless fears we have. Death is one of the few things in life that all of us will, sooner or later, experience.

If we're going to be afraid of death, we might as well be afraid of breathing or gravity or *I Love Lucy* repeats or all the other inevitabilities of life.

Our point of view is simple: unless you fully accept the inevitability of death, it's hard to enjoy this interval called life. ("This strange interlude," as Eugene O'Neill called it.) In other words, unless you get over your fear of death, you'll never really appreciate life. Unless it's OK to die, you'll never really live.

> PETER: Someone I know was captured during a war and sentenced to death. He was put in a cell with a window facing the execution ground. Day after day, hour after hour, he watched his comrades marched before a wall and shot. He had no idea when his turn would come. It went on for six weeks. The war ended and he was released. Although he's one of the busiest people I know, he's also one of the calmest. He knows that, no matter what, the worst thing that can happen to him is that he'll die, and he's already faced that fear and come to terms with it.

So, keeping in mind the section on fear, what do we suggest? Dying so we get over the fear of death? If death weren't so semi-permanent, that might not be a bad idea. (Ever notice how calm and yet playful cats—with their nine lives—seem to be?)

Death is nothing to us,
since when we are,
death has not come,
and when death has come,
we are not.

EPICURUS
341-270 B.C.

O death,
where is thy sting?
O grave,
where is thy victory?

I CORINTHIANS
15:55

What we're suggesting is taking a good look at your fear of death. Let yourself experience the fear. Find out what the fear's all about. Explore the many beliefs humans have about what happens after death. Are any of these really so terrible?

Let's take a look at some of the most popular ones:

DEATH IS IT, THE END, FINITO. As soon as the blood no longer flows to the brain, we have no more experience, and our time here on Earth—which is wholly biological and nothing else—is over.

Well, if that's the case, we have nothing to worry about. Everything we experience is bioelectrical-chemical reactions, and when that stops, it stops. Our fear of death is no more significant than the glow in a light bulb worrying about what's going to happen to it when the power is switched off. When the light is out, the light is out. Period. The end. Nothing.

IT'S HEAVEN OR HELL (OR MAYBE PURGATORY). When we die, we are judged by God and placed in one of three places: heaven (good), hell (bad) or (in at least one popular belief) purgatory (certainly not as good as heaven, but not as bad as hell).

If this is your belief, then you might consider life-threatening illness as a loving message from God: "Prepare yourself for Paradise." You may prepare yourself so well, in fact, and become so close to God, that God might ask, "Do me a favor?" and you'll say, "Sure. What?" and God may say, "Stick around Earth for another eighty years or so and

Either death is a state of
nothingness and utter
unconsciousness, or,
as men say,
there is a change and
migration of the soul
from this world to another.
Now if death be
of such a nature,
I say that to die is to gain;
for eternity is then only
a single night.

PLATO

Nothing can happen
more beautiful than death.

WALT WHITMAN

continue sharing the joy of Spirit with everyone you meet."

WE KEEP COMING BACK UNTIL WE LEARN WHAT WE NEED TO KNOW. The Soul (who we really are) never dies; only the physical body dies. If the Soul has not learned all it needed to learn in one body, it picks up another (at birth) and continues with its education. What does it have to learn? About the many levels, aspects and variations of God's creation. This is generally known as "reincarnation" and is the most popular belief about life and death worldwide—although not as popular in this country. If you believe it, *Time* magazine may make fun of you and some evangelical preachers will consider you damned.

Well, if this is the way things are, we *really* have nothing to worry about. Death is like going from one room to another in a house, or taking off a suit and putting on a bathrobe (silk, with our personal motto "What? Me Worry?" embroidered on the pocket). Death is then a rest stop, a changing room, a summer vacation between semesters.

≈

Some say death is such a wonderful experience that the news must be kept from us or we'd all be killing ourselves just to get there. Of course, if we could fully perceive the joys of The Other Side, then we'd also know why we're here in the first place, so

To be, or not to be: that is the question:
Whether 'tis nobler in the mind to suffer
The slings and arrows of outrageous fortune,
Or to take arms against a sea of troubles,
And by opposing end them? To die: to sleep;
No more; and, by a sleep to say we end
The heartache and the thousand natural shocks
That flesh is heir to, 'tis a consummation
Devoutly to be wished. To die, to sleep;
To sleep: perchance to dream: ay, there's the rub;
For in that sleep of death what dreams may come,
When we have shuffled off this mortal coil,
Must give us pause. There's the respect
That makes calamity of so long life;
For who would bear the whips and scorns of time,
The oppressor's wrong, the proud man's contumely,
The pangs of disprized love, the law's delay,
The insolence of office, and the spurns
That patient merit of the unworthy takes,
When he himself might his quietus make
With a bare bodkin? who would fardels bear,
To grunt and sweat under a weary life,
But that the dread of something after death,
The undiscovered country from whose bourn
No traveler returns, puzzles the will,
And makes us rather bear those ills we have
Than fly to others that we know not of?

SHAKESPEARE

we wouldn't kill ourselves after all. We're all here for a reason. We all have a purpose.

We'll all find out when we die. Until then, the fear of death may hold us here while we get on with whatever we're here to get on with. It is the subject, as well as the poetry, that makes Hamlet's soliloquy the most famous lines from any play ever written. It gives form to the thoughts and fears most of us have about death.

Here we, as responsible writers, are on the edge. We can't make death sound *too* exciting, or it would seem as though we were advocating suicide. We are not. A little fear of death, then, seems a healthy fear. It's the morbid, mostly unconscious, automatic terror that most people feel whenever the subject is even hinted at that we find counterproductive.

Take the time to conquer your fear of death. You can still live to be a hundred, and the years between now and then will be happier, healthier and more exciting. And when it comes time to die, well, *bon voyage*.

I must leave all that!
Farewell, dear paintings that
I have loved so much and
which have cost me so much.

JULES CARDINAL MAZARIN
1661

If you don't go
to other men's funerals
they won't go to yours.

CLARENCE DAY

How to Die

The final entry in our crash course on dying is ten suggestions on how to die. You can file these away until you need them.

Ten Suggestions on How to Die

1. Get things in order. Things you don't want people to see? Destroy them. Things you want people to have? Give them away. ("Let the season of giving be yours and not that of your inheritors." Gibran, *The Prophet.*) Pay debts. Make notes of what you've done. Make it easy for whomever you chose to take care of things after.

2. Make a will. Of things that weren't given away, decide who gets what. Put it in writing. Make it legal. Choose an executor. Do you want to be cremated or buried? Decide what kind of funeral—if any—you want. Bette Davis said, "I don't want donations made to any charities in my name. I want lots and lots of flowers!" If that's how you feel about it, say so. In writing.

3. Say good-bye. Good-byes don't all have to take place on your deathbed. You can say good-by to people, and then see them every day for the next fifty years. Tell people what you would want them to know if you never saw them again. Give them the opportunity to do the same. Usually, it's simply, "I love you."

4. Don't spend time with people you don't want to spend time with. When people hear someone is dying, they all want to make a pilgrimage. Many of these people you haven't seen in years and, if you lived another hundred years, would probably

On no subject are our ideas
more warped and pitiable
than on death.
Let children
walk with nature,
let them see the beautiful
blendings and communions of
death and life, their joyous
inseparable unity,
as taught in
woods and meadows,
plains and mountains and
streams of our blessed star,
and they will learn that
death is stingless indeed,
and as beautiful as life,
and that the grave
has no victory,
for it never fights.
All is divine harmony.

JOHN MUIR

never see again. Say good-by on the phone. Tell them you're just not up to a visit. You don't owe anyone anything.

5. *Spend time alone.* Reflect on your life. Make peace with it. Come to terms with it. Forgive yourself for everything. Learn what you can from what's taken place, and let the rest go. Mourn the loss of your life. Come to a place of understanding and acceptance. You may be surprised how quickly you get there.

6. *Enjoy yourself.* Make a list of all the movies you want to see or see again. Rent them. Watch them. Read the books you never got around to. Listen to your favorite music.

7. *Relax.* Sleep. Do nothing. Lie around. Recline. Goof off.

8. *Pray.* Listen. People are closest to God at birth and at death. If you missed Him the first time around, catch Him on the return. Whatever inspirational or spiritual beliefs you hold dear, hold them very close. You are being held close, too.

9. *Enjoy each moment.* Appreciate what is. Be completely here and now. That is where eternity is found. You may have only a few here-and-now moments, but it's a few moments more than most people ever have.

10. *When it's time to go, go.* Let go. Say one last good-by and mean it. Say good-by so completely that you'll never want to come back, you'll never even look back. All the good you take with you. The rest is good-by and moving on.

≈

But I will be
A bridegroom in my death,
* and run into 't*
As to a lover's bed.
The stroke of death is as
* a lover's pinch,*
Which hurts, and is desired.

SHAKESPEARE

Saul and Jonathan
were lovely and pleasant
in their lives,
and in their death
they were not divided:
they were swifter than eagles,
they were stronger than lions.

II SAMUEL
1:23

Do the majority of these sound more like suggestions for living rather than dying? That's because they are. The best way to die is to live each moment fully. Then, when the time for death comes—be it next week or fifty years from now—it's just another event in an already eventful life.

≈

More on death (and, of course, life) can be found in our book *LIFE 101*. Please call 1-800-LIFE-101 for details.

Prayer indeed is good,
but while calling
on the gods
a man should himself
lend a hand.

HIPPOCRATES

Part II: THE CURE

ONE:

ACT-CEN-TU-ATE

THE

POSITIVE

We know *accentuate* is not spelled "act-centu-ate." We just wanted to stress the need for *act*-ion. Some say, "To do is to be." Others say, "To be is to do." We tend to agree with Francis Albert Sinatra, "Do, be, do, be, do." We'll even stoop to old jokes to emphasize the need for *action*.

We'll pull out songs from the forties, too—such as *Ac-Cent-Tchu-Ate the Positive*. That song was written by Johnny Mercer (lyrics) and Harold Arlen (music) during the darkest days of World War II. It became a theme song for an entire country actively involved in *doing something*. (Winning a war.) They did it, too.

And so can you.

O! who can hold a fire
in his hand
By thinking on the
frosty Caucasus?
Or cloy the hungry edge
of appetite
By bare imagination
of a feast?
Or wallow naked in
December snow
By thinking on fantastic
summer's heat?
O, no! the apprehension
of the good
Gives but the greater
feeling to the worse.

SHAKESPEARE

The Case Against "Positive Thinking" (Part One)

As you may have gathered from what you've read thus far, we are obviously against negative thinking. So, if we're against negative thinking, we must therefore—*ipso facto,* it follows as the night the day, obviously—be in favor of positive thinking.

No.

No?!

No.

Positive thinking, as taught and practiced by many people, is not as immediately dangerous as negative thinking, but it has its downside.

Thoughts are powerful, more powerful than most people give them credit for being. They are not, however, *all-powerful*. There is more to reality than just thoughts.

For example, try to turn a page in this book without doing anything physical. Don't touch it or move it; just hold the book still and try to turn a page with your thoughts. Or try to think a glass of water to your mouth, or pick up the phone and think-dial a number. You see what we mean? Thoughts are powerful, but not all-powerful. There's a lot of power in our physical body, too.

When some people first discover how powerful thoughts are, they begin worshiping the mind in the way some people worship God. They deny the truth of what's actually happening for a mental image they find more pleasant. This creates a separation between the positive thinker and his or her reality. This separation can be the cause of disorientation, confusion and, eventually, illness.

I am not a pessimist;
to perceive evil
where it exists is,
in my opinion,
a form of optimism.

ROBERTO ROSSELLINI

As an example, suppose you had a small cut on your forehead. The positive thinker might say, "Your head is fine. The cut is only an illusion. *Think* of your forehead as healed. *Imagine* your forehead perfect."

We would probably say, "Oh, you cut your forehead. Let's wipe the blood off and put on some antiseptic and bandage it." While we were physically taking care of what needed to be done, we might suggest you hold a positive image of it healing quickly. But most likely we'd ask, "What happened?" because there's a certain therapeutic quality in talking about the incident. Also, we'd be curious to know.

And, there may be a lesson in the accident—if nothing else, the way to avoid *that* happening again.

If we're not in favor of positive thinking, what are we in favor of? If we're against negative thinking, we must be in favor of *something* positive. We are.

We recommend *focusing on the positive*.

Why is it no one ever
sent me yet
One perfect limousine,
do you suppose?
Ah no, it's always
just my luck to get
One perfect rose.

DOROTHY PARKER

Focusing on the Positive

In any given moment, there is ample evidence to prove that life is a bed of thorns or a garden of roses. How we feel about life depends on where we place our attention, that is, what we focus upon.

Did you ever notice that every time you are given a rose, the stem is covered with thorns? (If you take the thorns off, the flower wilts more quickly. Florists know this and, therefore, leave the thorns on.) Do you say, "Why are you giving me this stick with thorns on it?" Of course not. You admire the beauty of the rose. Even if you prick yourself in your enthusiasm, it never seems to hurt—you are too involved in appreciating the rose and the person who gave it to you.

Right now, in this moment, without moving from where you are, you can find ample evidence to prove your life is a miserable, depressing, terrible burden, or you can find evidence to prove your life is an abundant, joyful, exciting adventure.

Let's start with the negative. Look at all the imperfections around you. No matter how good anything is, it could be better, couldn't it? Look for dirt, disorder and dust. See all the things that need cleaning, repairing and replacing? An endless array of clutter, chaos and catastrophe assaulting your senses. Dis-gusting.

Now, let go of the complaining consciousness and look at the situation with an attitude of gratitude and appreciation.

Look around the same area you just surveyed and find the good. You can start with whatever you're sitting or lying on. It's probably softer than a concrete floor. Look at all the other objects you use

*One should sympathize
with the joy, the beauty,
the color of life—
the less said about life's
sores the better.*

OSCAR WILDE

but take for granted—glasses (both seeing and drinking), tables, windows, the walls and ceiling sheltering you from the elements. Consider the wonder of the electric light. A hundred years ago, you would have to have been very rich or very lucky to have had even one. And you probably have more than one—and a TV and a radio and many of the other electronic marvels of the age.

What around you do you find aesthetically pleasing? A painting you haven't really looked at in years? The detail work on the clothes you're wearing? A flower? A vase? Wallpaper? Carpet? When was the last time you took a moment to appreciate *colors?*

Did you notice that you tended to feel better when you focused on the positive things in your surroundings? The process of focusing on the positive to produce more positive feelings works the same with things more intimate than your surroundings—your body, for example.

If you look for all the things wrong with the body, boy, are you going to find them. Pains here, bumps there, rough spots over here, too much fat down there—the list goes on and on (and, as we get older, goes on and on and on and on).

But take a look at all that's right with your body. Even if you have a pain in your left foot, you can be thankful there's not one in your right. How about all those processes we take for granted? Digestion, circulation, respiration, assimilation, thinking—yes, we think thoughts without having to even think about thinking them. And let's not forget the five senses. Some people take them so much for granted that they can't name all five without thinking, "Let's see, what's the fifth one?"

*Try thinking of love
or something.*

CHRISTOPHER FRY

It's as though there were two attorneys in your mind, one gathering evidence for "Life is Awful" and the other gathering evidence for "Life is Wonderful." You're the judge and can rule out any evidence you choose. Your decision is final. Which judicial ruling do you suppose would lead to more joy, happiness, peace and ease?

To focus on the positive is not to disregard certain warning signals of a "negative" nature that, if ignored, eventually lead to inconvenience at best and disaster at worst. (If we use these "negative" signals to avoid disaster, then they're not so negative after all. Some even call them guardian angels.)

Let's say you're driving down the freeway and the little light goes on, telling you you're running out of gas. We do not suggest ignoring that bit of "negativity" and focusing on how wonderful it is that none of the other warning lights are on. We suggest you get some gas.

Here, by the way, is where negative *thinking* can come in. The negative *reality* is that you're low on gas. Negative *thinking* begins the litany, "I wonder if I'm going to run out of gas before the next station. What will I do if that happens? I'm in the middle of nowhere. What if some highway robbers get me? If I do get to a gas station, will it be the kind I have credit cards for? I bet it will be more expensive than in town. I bet it will be self-service and the pump will be dirty and my hands will smell of gas. I knew I should have filled up in town. Why am I so lazy and so stupid?" Etc., etc., etc.

During this inner tirade (which, for most accomplished negative thinkers, takes place in about five seconds), the driver, in his or her anxiety, usually speeds up, which only wastes gas.

We are wide-eyed
in contemplating the
possibility that life
may exist elsewhere
in the universe,
but we wear blinders
when contemplating
the possibilities
of life on earth.

NORMAN COUSINS

What we suggest is this: take note of the negative information, decide what to do about it (whatever corrective action seems to be in order) and, while doing it, return to focusing upon the positive (in this case the music, the scenery, the passengers) while working on "eliminating" the negative.

With medical conditions, it's good to keep track of symptoms, but it does no good to dwell upon them. The positive thinker might deny the early symptoms of a disease, making a cure all the more difficult. The negative thinker might turn every mosquito bite into skin cancer.

Positive focusers take a middle road. They note symptoms accurately so they can be reported to their health-care provider. They make an appointment. Beyond that, there's no point in dwelling on the symptoms, so they turn their attention to things more positive.

In considering the idea that there is sufficient evidence in any given moment to prove that life is wonderful or that life is terrible, let's take a look at how this works even closer to home: in our mental process—our memories of the past and our anticipation of the future.

Here, too, we can muddle in the negative: "I was a jerk last night." "Tommy wouldn't play with me when I was six." "I have to go to the dentist next week, and I hate the dentist."

Or, we could do positive thinking: "I'm winning the Oscar this year," when we've never been in a movie. "I'm going hiking and camping next week," when we've just had major surgery. "I have so many wonderful friends," when the phone hasn't rung in two weeks.

*What a wonderful
life I've had!
I only wish
I'd realized it sooner.*

COLETTE

Or, we could try focusing on the good memories that actually happened and on realistic future plans we look forward to with pleasure: "That movie on TV last night was so good." "Helen's coming to visit tomorrow; that will be nice." "The book I ordered should be arriving any day."

Yes, it's a good goal to "live in the moment," but who does that all the time? As long as you're living in memories of the past and projections of the future, you might as well make them *happy* memories and *joyful* projections.

We will be giving some techniques later in which you can let your imagination run positively wild. There can be great value in this. What we're talking about here is day-to-day, ordinary thinking. In our view, negative thinkers need to get their mind out of the sewer and positive thinkers need to get their head out of the clouds. You can meet in the middle ground of your wisdom.

Have we made a clear distinction between *positive thinking* and *focusing on the positive?* It's a subtle but important difference. Positive thinking imagines any wonderful thing at all, no matter how unrelated it is to the actual events of one's life. Focusing on the positive starts with what's so, what's real, what's actually taking place, and moves forward from there in a joyful direction.

If you spend all your time in a positive future, when will you appreciate the present? The present is the future you dreamed of long ago. Enjoy it.

Optimism, said Candide,
is a mania for
maintaining that
all is well
when things
are going badly.

VOLTAIRE

The Case Against "Positive Thinking" (Part Two)

There is a story told of a Master who saw a dead dog decaying in the road. His disciples tried to keep the unsightly animal from him, but the Master looked down and said, "What pearly white teeth." Even amid the stench and decay, there was still something beautiful to behold.

The Master did not, as some positive thinkers might, say the dog was "only sleeping." The Master did not throw a stick and say, "Here, Rover, fetch!" The Master first perceived *what is* and then found something good about it.

Positive thinkers sometimes use positive thinking as a way to justify their inability to accept the moment. They have a long list of "shoulds," and, unless reality measures up to the imagined state of perfection (and it almost never does), they retreat into positive thoughts, affirming that, thanks to their thoughts, the future conditions of the world will be better for everyone.

In other words, some people use positive thinking as a holier-than-thou-sounding form of denial.

A major problem with positive thinking and illness—especially life-threatening illness—is, "What do you do about the illness?" If you are told to positively think yourself a healthy body and then you get sicker, you may add personal blame on top of the worsening illness. "If I had only thought *more* positively, I would be well by now. Where did I fail?"

This is especially true of positive thinkers who tell stories of miracle cures. "If only you think

*An optimist may see a
light where there is none,
but why must the
pessimist always run
to blow it out?*

MICHEL DE SAINT-PIERRE

positively, and believe, you, too, can have a miracle cure." Well, maybe, and maybe not, too.

It took a lot of negative thinking—decades in some cases—to bring on an illness. Why should a week or two of positive thinking get rid of it?

Now, we're all for miracles, and we've seen our share, but miracles can't be counted on. If they could, by definition, they wouldn't be miracles. We tend to follow the Pragmatic Creed: "Hope for the best, prepare for the worst, and shoot down the middle."

If you have a miraculous healing, wonderful! Take all the credit for it. If you have a slow, progressive recovery, great! If you have the usual series of ups and downs that life-threatening illnesses generally go through, find *something* to be grateful for every day, every hour, every minute. Each time you find something, it will make you smile in your heart. Own your life and its cures.

Positive thinking only puts a gap between where you are physically and where you think you "should" be. There are no "shoulds" to a life-threatening illness. You'll be happier, and probably heal faster, if you let go of as many shoulds as you can. (More on this later.)

Now we'd like to explore an area in which we take fundamental issue with positive thinkers— how to respond to loss. Positive thinkers might say, "There is no loss, only the opportunity for new experiences. Rejoice!" We say: loss hurts. It also infuriates. That's natural. That's human. To deny the pain and anger with an attitude of platitudes may do far more harm than good.

The sound of her
silk skirt has stopped.
On the marble pavement
dust grows.
Her empty room is
cold and still.
Fallen leaves are piled
against the doors.
Longing for
that lovely lady
How can I bring my
aching heart to rest?

HAN WU-TI
157-87 B.C.
On the death of his mistress

Learn to Mourn

This is a lifetime of good-byes. As the years go on, you'll be saying good-by to both people (through moving, change or death) and things (youth, that semi-tight body you once had, hair, prized possessions, etc.). Eventually you'll say good-by to it all with your own death.

Learning to mourn, to grieve, to say a good good-by, is an invaluable tool.

When a loss takes place, the mind, body and emotions go through a process of healing as natural and as miraculous as the healing of a physical injury. Know that feeling lost, sad, angry, hurt, fearful and tearful at good-byes is a natural part of that healing process.

Human beings recover from loss in three distinct but overlapping phases. The first is *shock/denial;* the second, *anger/depression;* the third, *understanding/acceptance.*

No matter what the loss—from a missed phone call to the death of a loved one—the body goes through the same three phases of recovery. The only difference is the *time* it takes to go through each stage and the *intensity* of the feelings at each point along the way.

The first stage is shock/denial. When we first hear of a loss, our initial reaction is usually "Oh, no!" We can't believe what we've heard. We go numb.

This ability to deny and go numb is a blessing. Catastrophic losses are too hard to take all at once. It has been suggested that the reason some people have slow, terminal illnesses as their method of

Warm summer sun,
shine kindly here;
Warm southern wind,
blow softly here;
Green sod above,
lie light, lie light—
Good-night, dear heart,
good-night, good-night.

MARK TWAIN
Epitaph for his daughter

dying is because it's going to take them a long time to say good-by, and they want to do it right.

The next stage, anger/depression, is the one most commonly associated with loss. We wail against the situations, people, things and unkind fates that "caused" the loss. (Anger.) We cry. We feel sad. We hurt. We don't want to go on. (Depression.)

One of the toughest areas to accept is the anger felt at the one who is dying (even if it's yourself). "Why are you leaving me?!" a voice inside wants to know. It's tough because, as a culture, we don't accept anyone as being responsible for his or her own death unless it's a clear-cut suicide. Even people who die of lung cancer after smoking two packs a day for thirty years are somehow deemed innocent at death.

We're not suggesting that anyone really is to blame—and blame is such a useless activity, anyway. But know that to feel angry at someone for dying, or angry at yourself over your own death, is perfectly normal. It's a natural stage of recovery that one must pass through. Pass through, that is —not remain in.

Finally we come to understanding/acceptance. We accept what is. What is, after all, is what is, and we can feel miserable about it or not. If we don't feel miserable, what is remains is. If we do feel miserable, what is remains is. We grow to understand that our misery isn't going to change what's happened; it's only making us miserable. And what's the point in that?

J-R: An excellent book on learning about emotional loss, survival, mourning and rejuvenation is one of Peter's earlier works, *How to Survive the Loss of a Love*.

*We are healed
of a suffering
only by experiencing it
to the full.*

MARCEL PROUST

PETER: I'm far too humble to mention it, but since J-R has, I'd like you to know the senior author is Melba Colgrove and it's available at most bookstores, or by calling 1-800-LIFE-101.

We put this information on grieving in the section "Actcentuate the Positive" because mourning is a positive human trait. It allows us the flexibility to adapt to change. It is not "negative" to feel pain and anger at loss. It's a natural, human response. The negativity enters when the process of healing—which is, in fact, a gift—is denied.

Accept the process. Accept the numbness, the pain, the anger, the sadness, the tears and, eventually, accept the acceptance.

Accepting the acceptance can be difficult. People may expect you to mourn longer than you find necessary, or, they may want your mourning to "hurry up." People often offer comfort due to their own discomfort. "There, there," they say, "everything's all right," when, in fact, everything is *not* all right.

Grieving must be done in its own time.

To deny the human reality that pain hurts only delays the process. Take the time to grieve, to mourn, to say a good good-by. At the point of genuine understanding and acceptance of your own death (not just a mentally constructed understanding and acceptance) lies the ability to understand and accept the entire process of life.

*I have set before you
life and death,
blessing and cursing:
therefore choose life,
that both thou and thy
seed may live.*

DEUTERONOMY
30:19

Choose You This Day

It's time for you to make a choice. The choice we're talking about is The Big Choice—to live or to die ("To be or not to be"). If you had to make the choice, once and for all, which would you choose?

The problem is, there's a Catch-22 in making that kind of choice.

If you know deep down inside that you no longer want to continue living—for whatever reasons—consciously knowing this can help you avoid a great deal of confusion, torment and anguish. If you've put yourself on a plane headed for Cleveland, there's no point complaining to yourself and others, "I don't want to go to Cleveland."

If you have chosen to die, the avoidance of negative thinking is still important. Negative thinking contaminates "the moment," and between now and your death, you might as well enjoy every moment.

The irony is that when people finally "give up" and do appreciate the moment, they often realize that life can be a wonderful place. They see it wasn't life itself, but their *reaction* to life that was causing the dis-ease.

Then they sometimes begin a negative-thinking pattern of "I don't want to die after all," which, once again, pollutes the moment, which makes life less livable, so why live anyway, so I might as well die, etc., etc.

Other people, when asked, "Do you want to live or die," say—at once and with great emotion—"I want to live!" These people may then spend so much time struggling against death that life becomes an agonizing battle, and some part of them again says, "Why bother?"

*Destiny is not
a matter of chance,
it is a matter of choice;
it is not a thing
to be waited for,
it is a thing
to be achieved.*

WILLIAM JENNINGS BRYAN

Can you see, then, the Catch-22 involved in a once-and-for-all decision to live or to die?

The decision to live or to die is not one that can be made once, and that's that. It is to be made in each individual moment. And that decision is demonstrated by *action*.

If you are taking part in non-life-supporting activities, wallowing in misery and indulging in negative thinking, then—no matter what you think you think—we'd say you were, in that moment, choosing to die.

If you are actively involved in life-enhancing activities and enjoying them with a positive focus and enthusiasm, we'd say, in that moment, you were choosing to live. (The word *enthusiasm* is a wonderful one. It comes from the Greek *en-theos,* which means "one *[en]* with God *[theos]*" or "inspired by God." We like to think of it as being "one with the energy of God.")

If you ask yourself in this moment, "Do I want to live or die?" we say, "Look to what you're doing, feeling and thinking for the answer."

Are you doing all you can for your health, happiness and positive focus? And are you doing it with an attitude of, "This *will* make me healthier, happier and more positive," or are you moaning, "If I don't do all this damn healthy stuff I'm gonna die and I don't want to die so I'll do it"?

Take a frequent look at your thoughts, feelings and activities. Set an alarm to go off at regular intervals—every hour, say. No matter what you're doing when the alarm goes off, stop and take an honest look at where you are and what you've been doing—mentally, emotionally and physically—since the alarm last sounded.

We should be careful
to get out of an experience
only the wisdom
that is in it—
and stop there;
lest we be like the cat
that sits down
on a hot stove lid.
She will never sit down
on a hot stove lid again
—and that is well;
but also she will never sit
down on a cold one
any more.

MARK TWAIN

If it's been life-supporting, joyful and positive—congratulate yourself. If it hasn't, you can "course-correct." (Commercial aircraft, flying over water, are off course 95 percent of the time. Nonetheless, they still get to where they're going. The onboard navigational system is continually making minute corrections in course.)

If your evaluation of the interval between alarms indicates some negativity—don't be surprised. Don't be upset. Just change it.

Being negative about being negative is one of the slickest traps negativity has going for it. It seems as though you're agreeing that negative thinking is bad—so bad, in fact, that's it's worth getting upset about whenever it happens. Then when you discover you've been feeling bad about feeling bad, you feel bad about that. And on and on—or should we say down and down?

Let it go. Forgive yourself. Make whatever corrections seem necessary. Move on. (We'll be giving specific techniques for all of these later.)

As Woody Guthrie said, "Take it easy, but take it."

Until one is committed,
there is hesitancy,
the chance to draw back,
always ineffectiveness.
Concerning all acts of initiative
(and creation) there is
one elementary truth,
the ignorance of which
kills countless ideas
and splendid plans:
That the moment one
definitely commits oneself,
then Providence moves too.
All sorts of things occur to
help one that would never
otherwise have occurred.
A whole stream of events
issues from the decision,
raising in one's favor all manner
of unforeseen incidents
and meetings and material assistance,
which no man could have dreamed
would have come his way.
I have learned a deep respect
for one of Goethe's couplet's:

"Whatever you can do,
or dream you can, begin it.
Boldness has genius,
power and magic in it."

W. H. MURRAY
THE SCOTTISH HIMALAYAN EXPEDITION

Commit to Life

No matter what you *think* your decision about living or dying is, commit yourself to life.

By committing to life, we don't mean committing to live another so many years. (How many years "should" we live anyway?) We mean, commit yourself to living each moment fully, productively, joyfully. Commit yourself to health, wealth and happiness—not as a distant dream, but as a here-and-now reality.

You may not know fully *how* to do that yet, but "hows" are just methods and behaviors. When the commitment is clear, a desire and intention arises from that commitment, and the methods and behaviors present themselves.

Rather than tell yourself, "I don't know how to fully live my life, so I can't commit myself," commit yourself and then set about discovering how to do it.

All this can be summed up in one of our favorite phrases: "The willingness to do creates the ability to do." Be willing to live your life fully. The ability, methods, behaviors and opportunities to do this will appear.

*Never put off till
tomorrow what you can
do the day after tomorrow.*

MARK TWAIN

Live Your Life Now

Don't put off living your life until you are "better." That's probably just the latest in a series of perfect reasons why you haven't fully lived up until this moment. ("I'll do it when I'm older." "I'll do it when I've learned more." "I'll do it when I have more money." "I'll do it when I find my soul mate." "I'll do it when I have the time." "I'll do it when. . . .")

Regarding all those things you've put off until "later," keep this in mind: you're in your "laters" now.

Start doing the things you've always wanted to do *now*. Start enjoying each moment (by finding something enjoyable in it) *now*.

We're not talking about executing every grand scheme your imagination has ever created. ("I've always wanted to be Ruler of the World.") We're talking about overcoming the tendency to say, "When my life is better, then I'll be able to start focusing on positive things."

Start now.

We often form a habit of procrastination. Yes, we put off unpleasant activities, but we also tend to put off the enjoyable ones, too. We dole out pleasure, contentment and happiness as though they were somehow rationed. The supply of these things is limitless (as, by the way, is the supply of misery, pain and suffering). We do the rationing ourselves.

If you look, you'll find all the perfect reasons why you shouldn't enjoy your life, why you should postpone enjoyment until certain things are different.

We say, the only thing that has to be different for you to enjoy your life is where you focus your

This is the true joy in life,
the being used for a
purpose recognized by
yourself as a mighty one;
the being thoroughly
worn out before you are
thrown on the scrap heap;
the being a force of
nature instead of a
feverish selfish little clod
of ailments and
grievances complaining
that the world will not
devote itself to
making you happy.

GEORGE BERNARD SHAW

attention. Look for all the positive things taking place in and around you *right now*. As you find them, naturally you'll feel more joyful.

In life we have either reasons or results. If we don't have what we want (results), we usually have a long list of reasonable reasons for why we don't have the results. We tend to rationalize (pronounced "rational lies"). All this is (A) a waste of energy and (B) a convincing argument that we can't have what we want, which becomes (C) another reason not to live.

We suggest that when you don't get what you want, rather than waste time and energy explaining why you don't have it, find another way to get it. If you can't find something positive about your environment, look again—with "fresh eyes." Try another point of view. Be creative. What good are you taking for granted? If you can't find anything, hold your breath. Within a few minutes, you'll *really* appreciate breathing.

*Death is not
the greatest loss in life.
The greatest loss
is what dies inside us
while we live.*

NORMAN COUSINS

Strengthen Your Desire to Live

The desire to live can be strengthened. You obviously have *some* desire to live, or you wouldn't be alive. (When people completely lose the desire to live, they fade very fast.)

Beyond that, you have gotten this far in a book that obviously affirms life. There is a self-selection process that takes place with personal-growth books: the people who aren't ready for them don't read them. Their desire *not* to grow is stronger than their desire to grow; therefore, the book is put down—literally and in other ways—and not picked up again. So, since you've gotten this far in the book, we'd say your desire to live is rather strong.

The desire to live can be made stronger by a simple, but often uncomfortable, technique.

The technique is this—go to a mirror, look into your eyes, and say out loud, over and over: "I want to live."

What generally happens is that the many thoughts, feelings and attitudes that created the desire *not* to live tend to surface. You may feel awkward, scared, unworthy, foolish, stupid, embarrassed, angry, tearful, enraged, or depressed. These are not easy feelings to feel, and the tendency is to avoid them—to stop the process.

We suggest you persevere. Behind all the fear, anger, unworthiness and frustration is the natural desire to live—the love you feel for yourself and for your life. When you connect with this love and affirm your desire to live, that desire becomes strengthened. Your will to live comes more alive.

You can do this process as often as you like, but start slowly. Set a timer and do it for, say, one

He who has a why to live can bear almost any how.

NIETZSCHE

minute. The next time, if one minute wasn't too bad, do it for two minutes. Then three. Then four.

Before you start, we suggest you ask a white light to surround, fill and protect you, knowing only that which is for your highest good can take place while you do this process. (More on using the light later.)

Although uncomfortable at times, saying "I want to live" will give you not only a strengthened desire to live, but also a diagram of your own negativity. Is it mostly angry or mostly fearful? How do you convince yourself you're not worth it? What feelings and thoughts make you want to run from life? This process will answer those questions in a short period of time.

The goal of the process is to strengthen your desire to live—not necessarily to live for a certain number of years, but to live life fully in each moment.

If you take good care of the moment, the years will take care of themselves.

In spite of illness,
in spite even of
the archenemy sorrow,
one can remain alive
long past the usual date
of disintegration if one
is unafraid of change,
insatiable in
intellectual curiosity,
interested in big things,
and happy in small ways.

EDITH WHARTON

The Willingness to Change

"The universe is change; our life is what our thoughts make it." Does that sound like some radical "New Age" thought to you? It wasn't even new when Marcus Aurelius Antoninus (121-180 A.D.) said it.

Conquering negative thinking may require some major changes, not just mental ones, but emotional and physical ones as well—what is generally known as your life-style. You may have to change your job, where you live, the city in which you live, friends, clothes, habits, all sorts of things. As the Koran (13:11) states, "God changes not what is in a people, until they change what is in themselves."

If you want to get better, be willing to change, be open to change. Welcome and invite changes of a positive nature into your life. Remember, "There is nothing so permanent in life as change." (More metaphysical psychobabble? Heraclitus said, "Nothing endures but change," around 500 B.C.)

If you're in a rut, if you've grown accustomed to tolerating intolerable situations, change may not be comfortable and change may not be easy. It takes courage to take an honest look at one's life, discover what's no longer working, and then change it. Mark Twain reminds us, "Courage is mastery of fear—not absence of fear."

If you're faced with a life-threatening illness, you, frankly, have little choice. (We are assuming you have made the decision to live.)

Whatever you have right now in your life is the result of what you thought, felt and did up until this time. If you want things to be different, to be better, you will have to change what you think, feel and do.

Courage is the price
that life exacts
for granting peace.
The soul that knows it
not, knows no release
From little things;
Knows not the livid
loneliness of fear,
Nor mountain heights
where bitter joy can hear
The sound of wings.

AMELIA EARHART

It's as simple as that. Simple, but not necessarily easy. Not necessarily easy, but necessary. As Anais Nin noted in her diary, "Life shrinks or expands in proportion to one's courage."

Take a good, honest look at everything in your life. Decide which things, situations and people you tend to think most negatively about. Get rid of them. Yes, *that* one. The one about which you thought, "If I could only get rid of _____, but I don't dare."

That one. Dare.

Throw it out, send them packing, walk away.

In other words, change.

Love thy neighbor
as thyself,
but choose
your neighborhood.

LOUISE BEAL

You Don't *Have* to Do Anything

Whatever you do, do it because you choose to do it, not from any misguided sense of duty, obligation or imperative.

Sometimes people need to be pushed to the brink before they realize that this life belongs to *them,* not to the demands and desires of others. If you have a life-threatening illness, you're on that brink. If you learn that this is *your* life, you can more easily take a few steps toward de-brinking yourself.

Try saying this out loud: "I don't *have* to do anything." Say it a few times. Feel the sense of release, of freedom, of unburdening?

You can add to it: "And what I choose to do, I can do."

Together they make a nice (and, perhaps, necessary) affirmation: "I don't have to do anything, and what I choose to do, I can do."

Repeat it—out loud or in your mind—often.

*I only have
"yes" men around me.
Who needs "no" men?*

MAE WEST

Avoid People and Situations That Upset You

Those things, people, situations and experiences you don't like—avoid them. Stay away. Walk away. Do something else.

Some might call this cowardly. We call it smart. The world is brimming with things, people and experiences. We will never experience all of them if we live to be 10,000. So why not associate with the ones that naturally please you?

Yes, in some situations you will really want C, and in order to have C you must pass through A and B. In those cases, keep your eye on C. Keep reminding yourself *why* you're messing with A and B. Tell yourself that soon you'll be at C, and that C will be worth it.

Some examples of things to avoid: parties you don't want to go to, people you don't want to see, TV specials you don't want to watch (but think you should), movies everybody else has seen that hold no appeal for you, and so on.

This idea goes contrary to the "Confront It All" attitude of some self-help books. These books claim you grow through confrontation.

Yes, this is true. Tribulation and confrontation are great teachers. There is, however, quite enough tribulation presented to you *naturally*. You don't have to *seek* it. It will seek you, and some of it will be unavoidable. *That's* the time to practice acceptance, patience and forbearance.

If you can avoid the unpleasantness in the first place, by all means do so.

*Its name
is Public Opinion.
It is held in reverence.
It settles everything.
Some think it is
the voice of God.
Loyalty to petrified
opinion never yet
broke a chain
or freed a human soul.*

MARK TWAIN

Don't Worship the God of Other People's Opinion

Some people (let's face it: *most* people) do things they don't want to do (or don't do things they want to do) because they're afraid of what others might think or say about them.

We call this "worshiping the god of other people's opinion." The opinion of another becomes more important than our own wants, needs and desires. As Charles Dudley Warner put it, "Public opinion is stronger than the legislature, and nearly as strong as the Ten Commandments." We sacrifice much to the Great God of Opinion—happiness, self-worth, freedom. And that opinion is often inaccurate. "Truth is one forever absolute," wrote Wendell Phillips, "but opinion is truth filtered through the moods, the blood, the disposition of the spectator."

If your faith in yourself is strong, the opinion of others (which, often, they got from the opinion of others, who got it from the opinion of still others) is not as influential. As Thoreau said, "Public opinion is a weak tyrant compared with our own private opinion. What a man thinks of himself, that is what determines, or rather, indicates, his fate."

And whenever one quotes Thoreau, one must also quote Emerson: "It is easy in the world to live after the world's opinion; it is easy in solitude to live after our own; but the great man is he who in the midst of the crowd keeps with perfect sweetness the independence of solitude."

Or, as George John Whyte-Melville stated more simply, "In the choice of a horse and a wife, a man must please himself, ignoring the opinion and advice of friends."

You may talk
of the tyranny of
Nero and Tiberius;
but the real tyranny
is the tyranny of your
next-door neighbor.
Public opinion is a
permeating influence,
and it exacts
obedience to itself;
it requires us to think
other men's thoughts,
to speak
other men's words,
to follow
other men's habits.

WALTER BAGEHOT

Of course, if you live in the freedom of your own thoughts and desires, you must also give the same freedom to others. Learn to accept the behavior of others that doesn't fit the pattern of your opinions. (Such as the opinion that other people shouldn't have opinions about you.)

Whenever you find yourself disapproving of another, examine your opinions. Explore your list of "shoulds" and "shouldn'ts." See your opinion as merely opinion, not truth, and therefore .not worth getting upset about.

Others' opinions of you and your opinions of others are the cause of a great deal of unnecessary negative thinking. (All negative thinking is unnecessary, but the guilt, fear and resentment generated by opinions are particularly unnecessary.)

Learn, in fact, to relish the differences between people. Imagine how dull the world would be if we all thought, spoke and acted the same. (Spend a summer in Maine sometime and see what we mean. On second thought, just take our word for it.)

"It were not best that we should all think alike," Mark Twain tells us. "It is difference of opinion that makes horse races."

Applaud freedom wherever it may appear. Learn to praise the idiosyncrasies, the eccentricities, the quirks and the singularities of others.

It will help you to praise your own.

*The return from your
work must be the
satisfaction which that
work brings you and the
world's need of that work.
With this, life is heaven,
or as near heaven
as you can get.
Without this—
with work which you
despise, which bores you,
and which the world
does not need—
this life is hell.*

WILLIAM EDWARD BURGHARDT
DU BOIS

Do You Like Your Job?

Mr. Du Bois knew whereof he spoke: this message was given to his newly born great-grandson on the occasion of Mr. Du Bois' ninetieth birthday. He loved his work (he was, among other things, a founder of the NAACP) and didn't give up the ghost (or his work) until he was ninety-five.

Most people tend to think of the division between work and play the way Mark Twain saw it: "Work consists of whatever a body is obliged to do. Play consists of whatever a body is not obliged to do."

Some people, however, have discovered, as Shakespeare pointed out, "If all the year were playing holidays/To sport would be as tedious as to work." Or, as Jerome Klapka Jerome put it, "It is impossible to enjoy idling thoroughly unless one has plenty of work to do."

If you go to a job you despise, filled with things you hate to do, populated with people you don't like, find another job. "If you cannot work with love but only with distaste," Kahlil Gibran tells us, "it is better that you should leave your work."

Work takes up entirely too many of our waking hours for it to be a drudgery. "Every really able man, in whatever direction he work," wrote Emerson, "if you talk sincerely with him, considers his work, however much admired, as far short of what it should be." (Whenever one quotes Thoreau, one must also quote Emerson, but not necessarily the other way around.)

Get a job you enjoy. Before finding that job, you may have to find your career first—your calling, your avocation. "Blessed is he who has found his

*I don't like work
—no man does—
but I like
what is in work—
the chance to
find yourself.
Your own reality
—for yourself,
not for others—
what no other man
can ever know.*

JOSEPH CONRAD

work," said Carlyle. "Let him ask no other blessedness."

"In order that people may be happy in their work," John Ruskin tells us, "these three things are needed: They must be fit for it. They must not do too much of it. And they must have a sense of success in it."

The idea of "work" implies there is something you do that you would not do without the reward. For most people, the reward is money. If you associate the primary reward of work with money, we suggest you change the reward. Try loving, maybe. Or service—knowing you are providing people with something they really need.

Sometimes you don't have to change your work. All you have to change is your *attitude* about work. Many good things have been said about work and working over the years: "Back of the job—the dreamer who's making the dream come true!" (Berton Braley) "Work keeps us from three great evils: boredom, vice, and need." (Voltaire) "Work is the scythe of time." (Napoleon)

If you want to make your dreams come true, it will require work—doing something you're not necessarily thrilled about doing for the sake of a desired goal. One who should know, Thomas Alva Edison, told us, "There is no substitute for hard work."

Some people get religious about work. The motto of the Benedictine order is *"Orare est laborare, laborare est orare."* ("To pray is to work, to work is to pray.") Some, such as Carlyle, wax poetic: "All work is as seed sown; it grows and spreads, and sows itself anew." While others, such as our old friend Marcus Aurelius Antoninus, are downright gruff: "In the morning, when you are sluggish about

*I will work
in my own way,
according to the light
that is in me.*

LYDIA MARIA CHILD

getting up, let this thought be present: 'I am rising to a man's work.' "

We doubt if that thought would get either one of us out of bed, but this one, from Gibran, might: "Work is love made visible."

If we think of work as a way of manifesting our love, then whatever job we do can be fulfilling.

If you're working at McDonald's, instead of thinking, "Oh, God, not another busload of tourists having a Big Mac Attack!" you can think, "I'm helping provide food so that these people can more fully enjoy their journey." Either way, you'll be wrapping the same number of burgers and boxing the same number of fries. With one attitude, however, you'll feel miserable; with the other, you'll feel loving.

So, if you hate your job, either change your job or change your attitude about the job. One or the other. Don't indulge in negative thinking about it.

You may say, "I can't afford to be without this job." If you're hopelessly mired in disliking the job, you can't afford to keep it.

If you have a life-threatening illness, regaining your health is Job #1. Until Job #1 is done, everything else is just filler.

*The spirit of self-help is
the root of all genuine
growth in the individual;
and, exhibited
in the lives of many,
it constitutes the true
source of national vigor
and strength.
Help from without
is often enfeebling
in its effects,
but help from within
invariably invigorates.*

SAMUEL SMILES
1859

What You Do, You Become Stronger In

A strong mental attitude is built in the same way physical strength is gained—by repetition. Manipulating weights builds physical strength. Manipulating thoughts builds mental strength.

You may have a habit of negative thinking, built up over years of repeating negative thoughts. This repetition has made the habit strong.

Focusing on the positive may not be as strong yet; it may, in fact, be somewhat weak. The way to make it strong is to exercise it. Use it often. Unlike physical exercise, if you do too much, you will seldom wake up sore the next morning.

Decide what you want to become stronger in, and become strong by doing it.

*I am different
from Washington;
I have a higher, grander
standard of principle.
Washington could not lie.
I <u>can</u> lie, but I won't.*

MARK TWAIN

Commitments

If you want to be happy in life, keep all of your commitments and don't expect other people to keep any of theirs.

When we make a commitment, we "give our word." Giving something as valuable and as powerful as our word should not be taken lightly. When we don't fulfill our word, a part of us begins to mistrust ourselves. Over time, the effects of broken commitments build up. One begins to have a serious case of self-doubt and feelings of being ill at ease.

This self-doubt feeds the unworthiness, causing tiredness, confusion, lack of clarity and a general sense of "I can't do it."

Parallel to this disintegration in our relationship with ourselves is the deterioration of our relationships with others. If you make a series of commitments and don't keep them, people—at best—don't trust you. At worst, it's a great deal of *Sturm und Drang*—hurt feelings, anger, betrayal, abandonment, etc.

Keeping this in mind, it's easy to see that if you've been, shall we say, *freewheeling* in your commitments—either with yourself or with others—you have plowed, irrigated and well-fertilized the soil in which negative thinking thrives.

To reverse this—and prevent future fertilization—we have a few suggestions:

1. Don't make commitments you're not sure you can keep. If you're not sure, say you're not sure. If a definite maybe is not good enough, it's better to tell the other person no.

*There's one way to find
out if a man is honest—
ask him.
If he says, "Yes," you
know he's a crook.*

GROUCHO MARX

2. Only make commitments that are important to you. If a commitment is important enough, you'll keep it. If it's not important enough, don't make it.

3. Learn to say no. Don't make commitments that are important to someone else but not important to you just because you're afraid of "hurting their feelings." In doing this, you will either (A) break the commitment later, causing more hurt feelings, or (B) keep the agreement, hurting your own feelings. It's better to say, "No, thank you" up front.

4. Communicate. As soon as you know you're not going to be able to keep a commitment, let the other person know. Even if you *think* you won't be able to keep it, let the other person know. And don't just say, "Sorry, can't make it." Renegotiate. Changing a commitment is asking for a favor. Do it nicely.

5. Write down your commitments with others. Keep a calendar and note your appointments. This (A) helps you remember them and (B) avoids scheduling conflicts.

6. Write down commitments with yourself. Write this on the first page of your calendar: "All commitments with myself will be put in writing. Everything else is just a good idea." This keeps you from thinking the "good idea" to go jogging tomorrow at 6 a.m. is actually a commitment. If it is a commitment, write "Jogging, 6 a.m." in your calendar. And do it.

7. Declare things finished. If you have a half-dozen half-read books lying around open, gathering dust, declare your reading of them finished. Put book marks in them and put them away. Tell yourself, "I'm done with this for now." You can always go back and pick them up again, but for now, release yourself from any implied commitment you have

*We can secure
other people's approval,
if we do right
and try hard;
but our own is worth
a hundred of it.*

MARK TWAIN

with yourself and have not finished. The same works with commitments with others. When you know you're not going to be taking part in something people expect you to be taking part in, let them know that, until further notice, you won't be there. It's amazing how much energy declaring things finished can free up within you.

8. *Forgive yourself.* Forgive yourself for any broken agreements in the past. Forgive yourself for judging yourself for having broken those agreements. While you're at it, forgive yourself for breaking any agreements you may make in the future. (More on the technique of forgiveness later.)

It may help you keep your agreements—and not make agreements you don't plan to keep—if you understand the four primary reasons people break agreements. They are:

1. *Approval.* We say we'll do something we really don't want to do because we're afraid someone might disapprove of us. The trouble is, we lose our own self-approval in the process—a poor trade-off.

2. *Comfort.* It's more comfortable not to keep the commitment. This is actually a false sense of comfort. If, for example, you want to lose weight and it *seems* more comfortable to go off your diet and eat some cake, the resulting post-cake discomfort is likely to be greater than not eating the cake in the first place.

3. *Rebellion.* Breaking agreements for rebels is a knee-jerk reaction to feeling hemmed in, limited or tied down in any way. Rebels especially feel rebellion toward (A) authority figures and (B) ultimatums. Unfortunately, rebelling against the "doctor's orders" (an authority figure issuing ultimatums!) can be fatal.

Love truth,
but pardon error.

VOLTAIRE

4. Unconsciousness. Unconsciousness is a very important reason why people break agreements. There are other important things to say about this, but we forgot them. Maybe we'll remember later. Uh, yeah.

Keeping agreements (and not making agreements you don't plan to keep) is a good way to learn about your need for other people's approval and how to replace it with self-approval, how to expand your "comfort zone" so you'll have more freedom, and how to move from automatic, unthinking rebellion into conscious, voluntary cooperation. And how to stay awake, too!

The second part of our little "secret of happiness" is simple—whenever anyone breaks an agreement with you, let it go. In your mind, let the other person out of the agreement at once. Imagine that they called with the best reason and apology in the world.

Let it go.

Expecting human beings to keep their agreements is (A) not realistic and (B) an invitation to aggravation.

When someone breaks an agreement—especially someone important to you—it may bring back earlier images and feelings of being let down, betrayed and abandoned. Use the opportunity to heal these memories from the past, not to add further injury to yourself in the present. (More on the healing of memories later.)

Tom appeared on the
sidewalk with a bucket of
whitewash and a
long-handled brush.
He surveyed the fence,
and all gladness left him
and a deep melancholy
settled down
upon his spirit.
Thirty yards of board
fence nine feet high.
Life to him
seemed hollow,
and existence
but a burden.

MARK TWAIN

The Thought-Feeling-Action Pyramid

In order to make progress in the physical world, three things are necessary—a thought, a feeling and an action (directed activity). They form a pyramid:

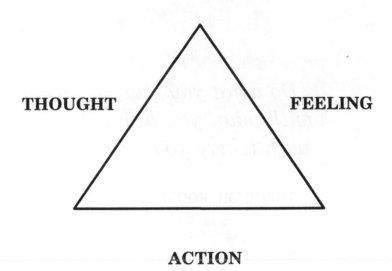

THOUGHT   FEELING

ACTION

If we have a thought and a feeling to match it, but no action, we're just spinning our wheels. If the thoughts and feelings are negative, this usually becomes worry, depression and "stewing in our own juices." If the thoughts and feelings are positive, it's often just unproductive "positive thinking." (Doing meditation, contemplation, visualization or spiritual exercises does not fall in the "unproductive" category.

Do what you can,
with what you have,
with where you are.

THEODORE ROOSEVELT

More on those later.) A *physical action* is necessary to make something real.

If we have a thought and an action but no feeling, the action will probably not continue for long. Our feelings are our greatest motivators. The mind can spark the feelings, but the feelings move the body. For sustained physical action, we need to *feel* something about what we're doing.

If we have a feeling and an action, but no directed thoughts, we're like a powerboat without a rudder. There's no direction of a logical, rational nature. This happens a lot with addictive behaviors— overeating, drug abuse, alcoholism, compulsive sex. The emotions say, "I want it." And the body says, "You got it," before the mind can even engage. Later, the mind may say, "You know you shouldn't have done that." I knew, but I "forgot." Temporary insanity.

If any one of the three sides of the pyramid is missing, the structure collapses. We cannot do productive, enduring, life-enhancing work. Life becomes frustrating. We cannot accomplish what we want to accomplish.

Knowing this, we offer the following advice: if you don't have all three—a thought, a feeling and an action—available at the same time, let the other ones go. If you don't have a matching thought, feeling and action, release yourself from whichever ones you have.

For example, if you have the thought, "I'd like to go swimming," and the emotions say, "Swimming! Oh boy, swimming!" but there's no available water, let the thought and the feeling go. You "let it go" by focusing on something else, something more physically available.

If you're by a lake, in a bathing suit, and your mind says, "Swimming would be good for us," and

God, give us grace to
accept with serenity
the things
that cannot be changed,
courage to change
the things
which should be changed,
and the wisdom to
distinguish the one
from the other.

REINHOLD NIEBUHR
1943

the body says, "I'm ready," but the feelings say, "I am not at this moment emotionally equipped to deal with the cold water," let go of the thought and the physical preparedness.

If the emotions want to go swimming and the body is ready to go swimming but the mind says, "I think this water is polluted and may not be safe," let go of the feeling and the physical readiness.

You "let go" by refocusing on something the mind, the emotions and the body are willing to do—and can do—*together. Now.*

When we hold on to one or two sides of the pyramid, but don't have the matching second and/or third, we're inviting frustration, futility, ineffectiveness, inadequacy, illness, desperation, despair, despondency, depression, glumness, gloom and guilt to come play havoc with our mind, our body and our emotions.

If we're thinking about the importance of losing weight, but our emotions and body are eating chocolate cake, to achieve a balance either the emotions and the body will have to give up the cake (and the feeling and physical craving for the cake) or the mind will have to give up its concept about weight loss. If things stay as they are—the mind's "should" vs. the emotions' feelings and the body's action—it's a perfect setup for guilt. (More on guilt—and chocolate cake—later.)

Did you ever feel you were going in three directions at once? Maybe you were. Maybe your mind wanted one thing (let's clean the garage), the emotions wanted another (let's go dancing) and the body wanted still another (let's take a nap). The same person cannot do all three things at the same time. Two of the three will have to go—or maybe all three

Harmony is pure love,
for love is
complete agreement.

LOPE DE VEGA

will go, and the mind-body-emotions triumvirate will agree to do something else.

It's as though the mind, body and emotions have little "minds" of their own. Sometimes you have to ask the Inner Henry Kissinger to step in and negotiate for you. "First we'll take a nap, then we'll clean the garage, then we'll go dancing, OK?"

Sometimes you have to simply lay down the law (lovingly) and tell the body, "No nap," the emotions, "No dancing," or the mind, "The garage is clean enough."

However you work it, don't let yourself be caught in nonproductive thinking, feeling or doing. The result is ineffectiveness, and ineffectiveness feeds a lack of self-worth ("I knew I couldn't do it"), which leads to more negative thinking, which leads to a triggered Fight or Flight Response, which leads to . . . well, you read that part of the book.

*The greatest pleasure I
know is to do a good
action by stealth,
and to have it found out
by accident.*

CHARLES LAMB

If You Want to Feel Good About Yourself, Do Good Things

We are, as Madonna was kind enough to point out, living in a material world. One of the easiest ways to feel good about ourselves is to do good things. The operative word is *do*.

What's "good"? We'll let you decide. Whatever you think is good—as long as it doesn't hurt yourself and doesn't hurt others—is fine with us.

It could be doing good things for yourself— mentally (learning something new, focusing on the positive, reading a good book—well, you're already doing that), physically (exercise, massage, meditation) or emotionally (practicing forgiveness, spending time with a loved one, seeing a good movie).

Or it could be doing something good for someone you know, or for someone you don't know, or for a service group, or for nature, or for the whales, or for world peace, or for the planet as a whole.

Again, the key here is *action, doing, movement, involvement*. As Madonna's spiritual teacher, Olivia Newton-John, once said, "Let's get physical." Sending someone nice thoughts is, well, nice, but sending them a note saying how nice you think they are is even nicer.

I always say,
keep a diary and
someday it'll keep you.

MAE WEST

Write Down the Good

Whenever something good happens, write it down. Buy a special notebook—perhaps one of those cloth-covered, fancy, hard-cover ones—and use it to list all the good in your life.

Include the good things that happen to you and the good things you do for yourself and for others. Spend at least ten minutes a day—or longer—remembering and writing the good.

The entries don't have to be long. They don't have to make sense to anyone but you. "Watched beautiful sunrise," "Talked to Grandma," "Saw great TV show," "Pain in left arm is less," "Got letter from John."

Begin your notebook with the entry, "Bought myself the most wonderful book," followed by, "Am writing the most wonderful book"—because you will be.

We tend to forget the good and remember the bad. We seem to be programmed that way. Writing down the good helps reprogram us. We retrain ourselves to focus on the positive and then to work with that positivity in a physical, material way (writing).

Use the book whenever you're feeling down or low. Read through it. Remember the good. It will lift your spirits.

*There are some days
when I think
I'm going to die
from an overdose
of satisfaction.*

SALVADOR DALI

Doing Things with Joy
Will Create More Joy

If you want more joy in your life, do whatever you're doing with more joy.

How? Just *do it*. How do you behave when you're joyful? Behave that way. What do you think when you're joyful? Think that way. How do you feel when you're joyful? Feel that way.

The joy begins a cycle of joy, which produces more joy, which produces even more joy.

You don't have to do anything special or different—driving the car or making the bed or reading a book will do. Just do whatever you're doing with joy.

The same is true of loving, happiness, compassion—all the good attitudes (or should we call them be-atitudes?) of life. Doing things with loving produces more loving. Doing things with happiness produces more happiness. Doing things with compassion produces more compassion.

It's a wonderful, upward spiral that starts whenever you decide to start it. How about now?

*I cannot give you
the formula for success,
but I can give you the
formula for failure—
which is:
Try to please everybody.*

HERBERT BAYARD SWOPE

You Can Have Anything You Want—You Just Can't Have Everything You Want

No matter how powerful we as humans are, we do have a few fairly significant limitations:

1. We can put our physical body in only one place at one time.

2. We have only twenty-four hours each day, 365 days each year. (Except every fourth year, when we get one more day.)

3. We have only so many years on this planet. (Somewhere between zero and one hundred fifty, tops.)

Given all this, it's obvious that we can't—contrary to the claims of some positive thinkers, self-help books and TV commercials—"Have it all." There's just too much it "all" and not enough time.

You can, however—contrary to the claims of negative thinkers, third-grade teachers and those who *always* listen to reason—have *anything* you want. The only limitations on that "anything" are, "Can it be gotten by anyone?" and "Is it available?" If the answer to those two questions is yes, it's there for you as well.

Don't get lost in "possible" or "impossible." If you have no money and say, "I want ten million dollars," some might think it's impossible. But it's not. Lots of people have started out with no money and made ten million dollars.

Just concern yourself with "workable" and "not-workable." Not-workable might be, "I want to be the first man on the moon." That's not workable. It's

One must not lose desires.
They are mighty
stimulants to creativeness,
to love and to long life.

ALEXANDER BOGOMOLETZ

already been done. But to be the first *woman* on the moon—that's workable. It hasn't been done yet.

To get what you want takes ten simple steps. Simple, but if your desire is gargantuan (not impossible, mind you, just gargantuan), not necessarily easy. These ten steps also work for less-than-gargantuan desires, in which case the fulfillment of the desire will be easier.

If you keep in mind that you can't have *everything* you want, here's how to get *anything* you want:

1. Focus all your attention on what you want. Be interested in it. Be "obsessed" by it.

2. Visualize and imagine yourself doing or having whatever it is you desire.

3. Be enthusiastic about getting and having it.

4. Know exactly what you want. Write down a detailed description. Draw pictures. Make models.

5. Desire it above all else. Above everything else. Above all.

6. Have faith with involvement. *Know* you can have it, that it's already yours. Be involved with whatever you need to do to get it.

7. Do the work required. How do you know how much work is required? When you have it, that was enough. Until you've got it, it's not enough.

8. Give up all things opposing your goal.

9. Pretend you already have it.

10. Be thankful for what you already have.

There. That's it. How to get anything you want.

If you have a life-threatening illness, this can be the blueprint for your recovery. As long as *one other person* has survived the illness you currently

We lived for days
on nothing
but food and water.

W. C. FIELDS

have, you can be number two. And if no one has survived the illness, you can be number one.

Frankly, however, the stickler in there—"the fine print," if you will—is number five: *Desire it above all else.* Some people, in their process of having a life-threatening illness, wonder if there is something beyond this physical world. They start to desire—above all else—an answer to the question, "What happens after death?"

If they believe in God, they often—above all else—want to know God, to feel God's presence more abundantly, to prepare, as they say, "to meet their maker."

Even W. C. Fields, shortly before his death, was discovered by a friend propped up in bed reading a Bible. "Bill!" his friend said. "You don't believe in God. What are you doing reading the Bible?"

"Looking for loopholes," Fields replied. We might like to think he found his loophole.

The struggle is not just between the habit of negative thinking and the positive focus required to heal your body; the struggle is also between staying here—in this body, on this planet—or going on to someplace many, many people have described as far greater than here.

As the King in *The King and I* said, "Is a puzzlement."

As the bumper sticker reads: "Everybody wants to go to Heaven, but nobody wants to die."

Or, as we say, "You can have anything you want; you just can't have everything you want."

(Lots more on getting what you want is contained in our book *DO IT! Let's Get Off Our Buts.* At your local bookstore, or call 1-800-LIFE-101.)

To every thing there is a season,
and a time to every purpose
under the heaven.
A time to be born, and a time to die;
a time to plant, and a time to
pluck up that which is planted;
A time to kill, and a time to heal;
a time to break down,
and a time to build up;
A time to weep, and a time to laugh;
a time to mourn,
and a time to dance;
A time to cast away stones,
and a time to
gather stones together;
A time to embrace,
and a time to
refrain from embracing;
A time to get, and a time to lose;
a time to keep,
and a time to cast away;
A time to rend, and a time to sew;
a time to keep silence,
and a time to speak;
A time to love, and a time to hate;
a time of war,
and a time of peace.

ECCLESIASTES
3:1-8

What Is Your Purpose in Life?

Everyone has a purpose in life. Very few people know what theirs is. What's yours?

A purpose can be summed up in just a few words. It usually begins, "I am. . . ." It's a simple but powerful statement about why you're here and what you are here to do.

In fact, it's what you've already been doing all along. You have been fulfilling your purpose your whole life, even if you don't consciously know what your purpose is.

A purpose is not a goal. A purpose can never be reached and checked off. A purpose is fulfilled, continuously, in every moment. Goals that can be defined, obtained and noted are but way stations along life's purpose.

Statements of purpose sound like, "I am a joyful explorer," "I am a lover of life," "I am a servant of spirit," "I am a giver of happiness," "I am a willing student of life," "I am a scout," "I am a servant of humanity," "I am a joyful giver," "I learn and I teach," "I know and I grow," "I am a silent contributor," "I am a cheerful disciple," "I am an intense appreciator," "I am a lighthearted creator," and so on. Get the idea?

A purpose is general enough to fit many situations at any point in life, but specific enough to fit you perfectly. "I am a student of life" might fit almost anyone. "I am a festive student of life" might be *you*.

You may *want* your life to go in a certain way. That's not necessarily your purpose. Statements about what you want in life are called affirmations. We'll talk about those later. Your purpose is what you are *already doing*. You can look back on your

*Nothing contributes
so much to
tranquilize the mind
as a steady purpose—
a point on which the soul
may fix its intellectual eye.*

MARY WOLLSTONECRAFT SHELLEY

life and say, "Yes, I've been doing that all along," and you can look ahead in your life and say, "Yes, that's what I'll be doing from now on."

The purpose also implies some directed action and movement. "I'm here" or "I'm a human" or "I am a child of God" may be accurate, but they don't indicate movement. A purpose includes both movement and direction.

To discover your purpose, begin by telling yourself, "I want to know my purpose." It may be immediately evident, or it may take a while to reveal itself.

Look back on your life. Write down the words (uplifting ones, please) that describe the activities and general thrust of your life thus far. As you write, a few may hit you as "right." You can also ask the people who know you well to suggest words (uplifting ones, please) that apply to you.

The words that seem right, write them on another sheet of paper. Experiment with them. Eventually the two or three that describe the thrust of your life will reveal themselves.

A purpose is not something you *create;* it's something you *discover.*

Once you know your purpose, it becomes a golden divining rod. When you're wondering, "Should I do this or should I do that?" look to your purpose. If one action is in line with your purpose and the other is not, the choice of which way to move becomes clear. If neither is in line with your purpose, look for more options. If both are in line with your purpose, it's dealer's choice.

It might be a good idea to keep your purpose to yourself. It can be your little secret. This keeps it powerful, prevents comments such as, "You don't act

*The secret of success
is constancy to purpose.*

BENJAMIN DISRAELI

much like a joyful giver with me," and keeps the discovery of your purpose from being a function of the ego. ("Let's see, what would sound *real good?*")

Once you discover your purpose, you've answered the time-honored question, "Why am I here?"

If you know your purpose, but haven't been fulfilling it as completely as you might, this could be a contributing factor to your discontent.

If you know your purpose is "I am a joyful giver," but you've been more of a begrudging giver or a joyful hoarder, that can cause blockages of energy, a sense of not belonging here, a feeling that "something's not right" (and all the negative thoughts that accompany that feeling)—that is, disease.

When you bring yourself more in line with your purpose—in an involved, doing, moving way—you may notice that your energy flows more freely, the blocks and the tensions in your body release, and you become more active, vibrant and alive—that is, healthier.

*I want death to find me
planting my cabbages.*

MICHEL EYQUEM DE MONTAIGNE
1533-92

What Do You Want?

Most people don't know what they really want. They think they know, but they really don't. An interview might sound something like this:

"What do you want?"

"I want a million dollars."

"What would you do with it?"

"I'd quit my job."

"Then what?"

"I'd buy things."

"Like what?"

"A car. A house. Furniture."

"Then what?"

"I'd travel."

"Where?"

"Uh, Europe, Hawaii."

"Then what?"

"I'd lie back and enjoy my life."

"Doing what?"

"Driving my car. Living in my house. Swimming in my pool. Watching TV."

"All the time?"

"Well, no. I'd travel some more."

"Where?"

"Uh, I don't know. What does it matter where? *Would you get off my back!?*"

*It is the chiefest
point of happiness
that a man is willing
to be what he is.*

DESIDERIUS ERASMUS
1465-1536

Most people don't really know what they want in life. They could not make a list—one through ten, in order of importance—of what they want to have, do or be.

Having such a list is invaluable. It helps us sort the opportunities that come our way. (Contrary to the popular belief, opportunity doesn't knock just once—it will knock you down.) It helps us set goals. It assists us in making plans. It answers that burning question, "What am I going to do the rest of my life?"

Avoid the inaccuracy people in loss situations tend to make. Don't say, "If I only had my health (or whatever else was recently lost), I wouldn't ask for anything ever again!" Don't kid yourself. If you had your health, you'd soon want other things. So, find out what those other things are. Sometimes by finding out what those things are and by doing them, you can have your health "mysteriously" return.

To make your list, you can begin by writing down everything you want to have, do or be. Free-associate. The sky's the limit. Write down all your desires, goals, wants and needs. Spend some time with it. Include material, mental, emotional, physical and spiritual goals. Make the list complete.

Now review the list. How many of the things do *you* really want, and how many did you write down because you think you *should* want them? Do you really want, say, a Rolls Royce, or is that just a symbol of something else? (Have you ever *driven* a Rolls Royce?) Remove from the list the things *you* don't really want.

Go through the list again and, with the ten steps from the chapter "You Can Have Anything You Want; You Just Can't Have Everything You Want" in mind (page 209), ask yourself about each item: "Am

*We must
cultivate our garden.*

VOLTAIRE

I willing to do the work required?" "Am I willing to make a plan and follow all ten steps to get this?" If you've discovered your purpose, ask yourself, "Is this in line with my purpose?" If the answer to any of those questions is no, cross it off and *let it go*. The next time you think about this one, tell yourself, "We thought about this and decided not to do it, remember?"

Now see if any remaining items on your list are in conflict with any others. "I want to own a candy factory and eat all the candy I want" may be in conflict with "I want a slim, trim, healthy body." "I want to be a concert pianist" may be in conflict with "I want to be an Olympic medalist." (Each requires a lot of daily practice.) "I want to party every night" and "I want a quiet home life" seem to conflict. (If you go out partying every night you might have a quiet home life—you won't be there, but your home will be quiet.) Between two conflicting desires, choose the one you want more and cross the other off your list.

Then do a first-pass prioritization. Mark each item on the list with "A" (I want this very, very much), "B" (I want this a lot), or "C" (I want this).

When you're done, count the number of A's, B's and C's. If you have more than ten A's, eliminate all the B's and C's. If you have ten A's and B's, eliminate the C's. (People seldom get to the C's anyway, so why pretend?) Keep eliminating until you have ten.

Rewrite the ten on a clean sheet of paper. Go through the list and pick the *one* that's most important. Write that on another sheet of paper and cross it off your second list. Then go through the remaining nine and ask, "What's the *most* important one?" Write that on the new list and cross it off the second list. Of the remaining eight, which do you

Put all your eggs
in one basket and—
WATCH THAT BASKET.

MARK TWAIN

want *most?* Continue until all ten are copied, in order, onto the new sheet.

Then copy them again, numbering from one to ten, elaborating on each. After each, answer one important question: "How will I know when I've reached this goal?" Be specific, so you'll know when to cross it off your list to make room for another.

Behold—Your Life Plan.

Given that we have only twenty-four hours in the day, 365 (or 366) days in the year and only so many more years on this planet, achieving this list may be all you'll have time for. Certain material items will be obtained and replaced by others, but some goals, such as being healthy, feeling happy and knowing God may take you the rest of your life— even if that's another ninety-nine years.

*When you get right down
to the root of the meaning
of the word "succeed,"
you find it simply means
to follow through.*

F. W. NICHOL

Do It

Now that you know what you want, make a plan, put it in motion, go about getting what you want, do what you have to do, get involved and take the necessary actions. If we didn't cringe at the overuse of a formerly vital expression, we'd say, "Go for it!"

The difference between efficiency and effectiveness is this: "Efficiency gets the job done right. Effectiveness gets the right job done." Now that you know what "the right job" is for you (your top-ten list), you're ready for effective action.

Here are some random thoughts on successful action:

1. Break each goal into do-able steps. If you want to be a lawyer but haven't gotten your high school diploma yet, your next do-able step might be "Call the board of education and find out where the next high-school equivalency test is being given." The next do-able step after that might be "Take the test." Based upon the results of the test, the next do-able steps will present themselves.

2. Make a plan. Once you have your goals in writing, and your next do-able steps for each goal, schedule them. Get a calendar or datebook or appointment book (if you don't already have one) and fill it up.

3. Be flexible. As you take next steps, you'll discover new information that may lead to changes in other next steps.

4. Be willing. Remember: "The willingness to do creates the ability to do."

5. Don't let how you feel about something stop you from doing what you know you need to

*Even if you're
on the right track,
you'll get run over
if you just sit there.*

WILL ROGERS

do. Feel the feeling (fear, boredom, resistance, etc.) and do it anyway. Move your body—physically—in the direction of your goals. Take your next steps. The feelings may complain. Expect them to. Thank them for their "advice" and move ahead.

6. *Turn fear into excitement.* As we said before, if you feel carefully, you'll notice that the physiological feeling we call "fear" and the physiological feeling we call "excitement" are the same feeling. One we label "bad," and the other we label "good." If you feel "that feeling" and automatically call it "fear," stop and call it "excitement" instead. Whenever you hear yourself saying (to yourself or to someone else) "I'm afraid," change it to "I'm excited." This much-maligned feeling is really a blessing. It's *preparation energy*. It keeps your mind focused, your energy up, your attention clear—just what you need to help you do new and "exciting" things.

7. *Turn stubbornness into determination.* Like fear and excitement, stubbornness and determination are the same energy. Both include steadfastness, constancy, power and drive. For most people, it's a matter of turning "won't power" (stubbornness) into "will power" (determination). When you find yourself being stubborn (I *don't* want this), find out what you *do* want and, using the same energy, move toward it. *Will* past your *won't*-ness. *Do* past your *don't*-ness.

8. *Do it as though you were teaching it to another.* Set a good example, even if no one else is around. Follow through with the precision, dedication, courage, kindness and persistence one would expect of a great teacher educating a beloved pupil. In a sense, that's exactly what you're doing—you are teaching various parts of you (your mind, your body and your emotions) how to live more fully.

The destiny of mankind
is not decided
by material computation.
We learn
that we are spirits,
not animals,
and that something
is going on
in space and time,
and beyond
space and time, which,
whether we like it or not,
spells duty.

WINSTON CHURCHILL

9. Be response-able. Be willing to respond to *whatever* happens along your path. Don't fall into the negative-thinking trap of labeling certain occurrences as "setbacks," "disappointments" or "letdowns." Consider them, instead, challenges. *Respond* to them in such a way that you get what you want. That's response-ability.

10. Ask. Learn to ask for what you want. Ask for assistance, help, guidance, instruction—whatever you need. The worst that people can do is not give you what you ask for—which is precisely where you were before you asked. As they used to say on TV, "You have everything to gain and nothing to lose." Also, don't expect people who've offered you help (especially ones close to you) to be mind readers. Let them know what you need as you need it. Don't assume they "should" know "if they really loved me." They can love you very much and still not know. Ask them.

11. Do it with love. Be gentle with yourself and others. Don't become so obsessed with the goal that the *process* is not enjoyable. Send the light of your own loving ahead of you. When you get there, the loving will have prepared a place for you. Be kind, gentle and enjoy the journey.

(The Insight Consulting Group teaches an excellent course called Managing Accelerated Productivity. It's about deciding what you want and specific techniques on how to go about getting it. It's taught in many cities in the U.S. and around the world. For more information, please call 213-829-2100.)

*We can endure
neither our evils
nor their cures.*

LIVY
59 B.C.- A.D. 17

If You're Not Actively Involved in Getting What You Want, You Don't Really Want It

Write that in big letters somewhere you can read it often. A lot of negative thinking, depression, frustration, illness, etc., stems from people *thinking* they want something they don't really want.

How do you know what you really want? Whatever you are *actively involved* in getting, that's what you really want. Everything else is just what you *think* you want. If you think you want something and you're not actively involved in getting it, you're just kidding yourself.

It's true that, in every moment, you can't be actively involved in doing something about *everything* you want. So how can you tell what you're actively involved in?

Here's where your calendar comes in handy. Have you scheduled activities that support each of the goals you want to accomplish? Are the "next doable steps" you know you need to take planned for some time in, say, the next two weeks? If not, ask yourself: "Is this goal becoming another one of my 'laters'?" ("I'll do it later, later, later," and it never gets done.)

We're a pragmatic pair. If someone tells us, "I'm dependable! You can count on me," we say, "Great," and then we wait and see. If she (in the last example we used *he*—let's use *she* this time) is late three times in a row, but continues to say she's dependable, we tend to base our opinion of her dependability more on her actions than on her words. Not that she means to intentionally deceive. She may, however, be deceiving herself.

*There is no failure
except in no longer trying.*

ELBERT HUBBARD

If people say they want health, we look to see what they are *doing* about it. Are they actively involved in their own healing? Are they doing everything they can to promote healthy ideas, healthy feelings and healthy actions? Are they exploring more and more options for greater health? If so, we'd say they really want health. If not, not.

Further, if they're involved in life-damaging activities—these are different for different illnesses and different individuals—we'd say that not only do they not have a desire for greater health, they have, in fact, a desire for lesser health.

We are more than our minds, more than our thinking process. We are also more than our feelings and more than our body. Most people have spent so much time in either thinking or feeling, they *think* that a thought or *feel* that a feeling is *them*. It's not. It's just a thought or a feeling. To *think* you want something or to *feel* you want something doesn't necessarily mean that's what *you* want.

What you want—what you *really* want—is that which you actively manifest in your life—what you make real through action.

If you think you want something but you're not really doing much to get it, you have three choices:

1. You can go on the way you've been: kidding yourself and pretending you really want this thing that you—based upon results—don't really want. This causes frustration ("Why can't I have what I want?"), hurt ("I never get what I want"), resentment ("Other people get what they want; why not me?") and unworthiness ("I guess I don't deserve it").

2. Give up the goal. Realize it's a nice idea, and if it were in the next room, you'd probably go to the next room and partake of it. It is, in fact, something you really don't want *more* than the *other things*

*I believe that
anyone can conquer fear
by doing the things
he fears to do,
provided he keeps doing
them until he gets a
record of successful
experiences behind him.*

ELEANOR ROOSEVELT

you are actively seeking. You recognize that your time is spent seeking other things; therefore, you must want them more than you want this; therefore—for the time being—you let this one go.

3. Do whatever is necessary to reach the goal. Eliminate from your schedule activities that support goals with lower priorities than the one in question. As you move toward your goal, certain mental, emotional and physical objections will be raised. No matter what complaints your mind, emotions and body bring forth, *if you know you need to do it, do it anyway*. Gently, lovingly—but firmly—teach the objecting parts of you that you have a new goal, a new priority, and that your actions will now be in alignment with achieving that goal.

Those are your choices. Most people choose by default—they "choose" number one by not choosing, and things carry on as they have in the past. We suggest you choose from options two or three. Either one will put you more actively in charge of your life, of your thoughts, feeling and actions.

One last point. If health, happiness, joy and/or loving are on your list of goals, you have a continual here-and-now barometer of whether you're moving toward those goals: where, in any given moment, you are placing your attention.

Are you focusing on what's not right, not good, not the way you want it? If so, health, happiness, joy and loving might be incompatible with that action.

If you're focusing on what's good, what's right, what's pleasant and what's worth appreciating around (and within) you, then we'd say you're doing a great deal to promote health, happiness, joy and loving.

*Faith is an excitement
and an enthusiasm:
it is a condition of
intellectual magnificence
to which we must cling
as to a treasure,
and not squander
in the small coin
of empty words.*

GEORGE SAND

Faithing

Faith, all by itself, can be a little passive. We like faith to be an *active* process—hence, our use of the word *faithing*.

Faithing is trusting that everything will work out for the highest good of all concerned. Beyond that, faithing is realizing that everything *already is* working out for the highest good of all concerned. We may not *like* it that way, but with faith we realize that our opinion and desire about how we think it should be aren't necessarily the way it will work out best.

Faithing is actively setting aside our personal shoulds, musts, opinions and beliefs and moving into the flow of *what's actually happening*. With faithing, we put acceptance above opinion.

Jesus said that if one has the faith of a mustard seed, one can move a mountain. What is the faith of a mustard seed? A mustard seed is a very small seed, but, when planted, it grows into a great tree, producing millions of mustard seeds.

The mustard seed doesn't have to *think,* "Oh, I'm really a tree and I know I can be one." The mustard seed has the faith of *action*. Contained within it *is* all that is necessary to grow a tree. Once planted—if properly nurtured—it will just *do it.*

If we have the faith that everything will turn out all right, it follows logically that everything already *is* all right. Where we are now is the "all right" we had faith about in some past moment of faithing.

Passive faith is used by some people to deny the moment. "As soon as this reality more closely matches my idea of how it should be, then everything will be OK." If you haven't already noticed,

*As the body
without the spirit is dead,
so faith without works
is dead also.*

JAMES
2:26

however, (to quote Roseanne Roseannadanna), "If it ain't one damn thing, it's another."

This moment is fine, just as it is.

Faithing works *here and now*. It acknowledges that there's a plan at work, and that the plan is unfolding perfectly. We may not like it, but it continues unfolding perfectly just the same. Faithing is flowing with what's going on, whatever that may be.

He that lives upon hope
will die fasting.

BENJAMIN FRANKLIN

The Two Sides of Hope

Remember the story of Pandora's Box?

Pandora was sort of the Eve of Greek Mythology—the First Woman, told not to do something by God (by Zeus, in this case), but she did it anyway.

Pandora was given a box (a jar, actually) and told not to open it because it contained all the evils of the world. She took the jar/box with her on her honeymoon. Being a dull honeymoon, she opened it.

Just as in *Raiders of the Lost Ark* when the Nazis opened the Ark and all the ghosts came wooshing out in Dolby SurroundSound, when Pandora opened the jar/box, all the evils of the world escaped. The last evil in the jar/box was hope. What happened to hope is not clear. Some stories say it remained inside; others say it got out. But all agree that hope was the last item in the jar/box.

Most people interpret this as good news—yes, evil has been added to the world, *however,* we've been given hope so that we can take care of all that evil.

Did you ever consider that hope can be one of the evils of the world? It's just that hope has a better PR agency than the others. (The other evils have to depend on word of mouth—and they do OK with it, too.)

If it weren't for hope, perhaps we would have cleaned up all the other evils long ago. We would have gotten sick and tired of being tired and sick and sent them packing—"Back to the jar/box!"

What we sometimes do instead is tolerate evil and *hope* it's going to go away. "Oh, I hope it will be better tomorrow," we sigh, never doing anything

Hope is a good breakfast,
but it is a bad supper.

FRANCIS BACON
1624

A gentleman
who had been
very unhappy in marriage,
married immediately
after his wife died:
Johnson said,
it was the triumph
of hope over experience.

BOSWELL

productive to get rid of "it" today. ("It" being whatever evil we happen to be currently sighing about.)

The hope we're talking about here is the kind of hope that inspires passivity, resignation and stagnation.

There are some people who use the word *hope* in a different way, almost as a prayer: "I hope it won't rain, but I'm bringing my umbrella anyway." As the saying goes, they hope for the best, prepare for the worst, and shoot down the middle.

If there's a situation in your life—be it a life-threatening illness or any other "evil"—and you're using hope to stimulate you to greater and greater depths of inaction, lethargy and torpor, the dark side of hope has gotten hold of you.

Shake it off. Become active. Do something to replace the evil with what you really want. Move toward a positive condition in which the evil cannot exist. (Don't "get rid" of evil—replace it with what you prefer and focus on the goodness of that.) Turn the evil around. *Evil* spelled backwards ("turned around") is *live*.

You can hope things will get better—as a form of holding a positive image of completion—and that's fine. But if you're not taking specific, energetic and frequent actions to make things better, you've got the wrong kind of hope working for you. (Or, more accurately, working against you.)

That the limiting kind of hope is almost epidemic in our culture is reflected by the frequent misuse of the word *hopefully*. As you may recall from Grammar 101, *hopefully* is an adverb (it ends in "ly"); therefore, it should be used to modify (describe) a verb.

*There is nothing
so well known as that we
should not expect
something for nothing—
but we all do
and call it Hope.*

EDGAR WATSON HOWE

*To travel hopefully
is better than to arrive.*

SIR JAMES JEANS

Verbs are, of course, action words—run, jump, skip, look, walk—words that describe movement. You can run hopefully, jump hopefully, skip hopefully, look hopefully and walk hopefully—which means you are running, jumping, skipping, looking, and walking *with hope*.

As the song goes, "Walk on, walk on, with hope in your heart." You are *walking,* and you're doing it with an attitude of *hope*.

All this is fine. It is correct English, and it is—to our way of thinking—correct living. You hope as you *do something*. You *take an action* while anticipating (hoping) the action will have a positive outcome. Well and good.

Most people, however, use the word *hopefully* as a replacement for the phrase "I hope."

"We will hopefully be going to the store" means, "We will, I hope, be going to the store." "This problem will go away, hopefully" means, "This problem will go away, I hope." "Hopefully, I'll be able to do it" means, "I hope I'll be able to do it."

Traditionally, this use of the word *hopefully* is incorrect—but so many people use it in this way that many grammarians are (reluctantly) conceding a second usage. We're not here to debate grammar. We're more interested in how the word went from the active "being hopeful while taking an action" to the more passive "I hope." Does that, we wonder, reflect a trend in our culture?

We look hopefully toward the day when people don't let hope stop them from doing what needs to be done. The combination of hope (anticipating a positive outcome) and action is a powerful way to get what one is hoping for.

It is natural for man to indulge
in the illusions of hope.
We are apt to shut our eyes
against a painful truth,
and listen to the song of that
siren till she
transforms us into beasts.
Is this the part of wise men,
engaged in a great and arduous
struggle for liberty?
Are we disposed to be the
number of those who,
having eyes, see not,
and having ears, hear not,
the things which so nearly
concern their temporal salvation?
For my part, whatever anguish
of spirit it may cost,
I am willing to know
the whole truth;
to know the worst,
and to provide for it.

PATRICK HENRY

Please use this information about hope for your upliftment and not as ammunition against others (or yourself). If someone says, "I hope you get better," don't say, "Yeah? Well, what are you *doing* about it?" Go to the essence of their communication —they are wishing you well—and thank them for it.

Do, however, listen to yourself. When you use the word *hope,* ask yourself, "Am I using it as a *replacement* for action or as an *adjunct* to action?" If it's a replacement, get moving. If it's an adjunct, keep moving.

Those who seek to satisfy
the mind of man
by hampering it with
ceremonies and music
and affecting charity
and devotion
have lost
their original nature.

CHUANG-TZU
368-286 B.C.

Poor Charity

Charity began as such a wonderful word. To quote from *The Dictionary of Word Origins:* "Charity was first an inner love; then a sign of this feeling; then an action or an act." The roots of *charity* include the Greek *chayrs,* meaning "thanks, grace," and the Latin *caritas,* "love, regard, affection," and *carus,* "to hold dear." *(Carus* is also the root of such words as *caress* and *cherish.)*

And what does *charity* mean today? The first three definitions in *The American Heritage Dictionary* read "1. The provision of help or relief to the poor; almsgiving. 2. Something that is given to help the needy; alms. 3. An institution, organization, or fund established to help the needy."

To give charity under this definition produces an immediate rift between giver and receiver. Although the material needs of the recipient may be met, both giver and receiver suffer separation. "I—superior and blessed among people—give proudly to you, poor, needy person." "I—poor, needy person—accept humbly this gift from you—magnificent, benevolent, rich person."

We certainly aren't knocking charities or charitable feelings. It's just that a perfectly good word—one that started out meaning love, regard and affection—has, for many people, come to mean pity.

This stigma on the word affects people who are, as the phrase goes, "forced to take charity." (Note the implied destitution and helplessness in that.) Sometimes people need whatever it is a given charity provides, just as we daily need water from the water company and power from the power company.

*Charity degrades
those who receive it
and hardens
those who dispense it.*

GEORGE SAND
1842

*Charity creates
a multitude of sins.*

OSCAR WILDE

The onus of having to go to a charity, because of the popular misdefinition of the word, can strike deeply at one's sense of self-worth—precisely what one does not need when in need.

Ironically, most charities—providing they have the means—are more than happy to provide help to people who can truly use it. That's why the charity was formed in the first place. And the people who work for most charities were drawn there by a genuine desire to help others.

The latter dictionary definitions of *charity* are more up our avenue: "4. An act or feeling of benevolence, good will, or affection. 5. Indulgence or forbearance in judging others; leniency. 6. *Theol. a.* The benevolence of God toward man. *b.* The love of man for his fellow men; brotherly love."

The trouble is, the latter definitions in the dictionary are not the common perceptions of the word. We're afraid *charity* is a word that will forever be associated with the sort of human condition described in Emma Lazarus' inscription on the Statue of Liberty:

Give me your tired, your poor,
Your huddled masses yearning to breathe free,
The wretched refuse of your teeming shore,
Send these, the homeless,
    tempest-tossed, to me:
I lift my lamp beside the golden door.

This, of course, hasn't been the philosophy of the Immigration Service for many years (if, indeed, it ever was). It is, however, the way in which any number of charities portray others when asking for money. It's a successful tactic. It works. It will no doubt continue.

Charity begins at home.

TERENCE
190-159 B.C.

But how shall we expect
charity towards others,
when we are
uncharitable to ourselves?
Charity begins at home,
is the voice of the world;
yet is every man
his greatest enemy, and,
as it were,
his own executioner.

SIR THOMAS BROWNE
1642

We're all in favor of the good works charities do. What we're concerned about is the image of "the privileged" helping "the needy." We *all* need help from each other on one level or another.

Rather than rehabilitate the word *charity*, let us introduce an alternate word—*service*.

Do all the good you can,
By all the means you can,
In all the ways you can,
In all the places you can,
At all the times you can,
To all the people you can,
As long as ever you can.

JOHN WESLEY

The Joy of Service

Ironically, the word *service*—which has its roots in the words *serf, servile, servitude* and *slave*—seems today to indicate a more freely given exchange between equals. "May I be of service to you?" has a very different slant to it than "Would you accept my charity?"

Service, as we define it here, is the art of taking such good care of yourself that you cannot help but take good care of others. When you fill yourself with love, happiness and compassion, the desire to share the overflow of these with others is automatic.

It's one of the great open secrets of the world that by serving others you serve yourself. As Emerson said, "It is one of the beautiful compensations of this life that no one can sincerely try to help another without helping himself." Those who have given to others for the joy of giving know that the reward is just that—joy.

Service is a self-ish thing—in the truest sense of *self*-ish. We do it because it *feels good*. And because it feels good, we want to do more. As a poet once wrote, "The greatest gift is to fill a need unnoticed." The gift is given, simultaneously, to both the giver and to the receiver. "The love I give you is secondhand: I feel it first."

Those who have given to others and found it depleting have not taken the time to give fully to themselves first. Always give to others of the overflow, and if you're giving to yourself unconditionally, the overflow will always be more than enough.

In true service, the person serving and the person being served are one. They are equals. By allowing others to serve you, you serve. By serving

*Lord, make me an
instrument of Your peace.
Where there is hatred
let me sow
love;
where there is injury,
pardon;
where there is doubt,
faith;
where there is despair,
hope;
where there is darkness,
light;
and where there is sadness,
joy.*

ST. FRANCIS OF ASSISI

others, you are serving yourself. It's the most wonderful cycle of giving and receiving. Soon it's hard to tell who's giving and who's receiving. It becomes a flow.

Besides feeling good and knowing that you have done good for others, service is physiologically good for you.

A study in Tecumseh, Michigan, for example, showed that doing regular volunteer work—more than any other factor—dramatically increased life expectancy. "Men who did no volunteer work were two and a half times as likely to die during the study as men who volunteered at least once a week."

Doing good for others enhances the immune system, lowers cholesterol levels, strengthens the heart, decreases chest pains and generally reduces stress. One interesting study at Harvard showed that even *thinking* about doing service produced positive physiological results.

Service can be done in any number of ways. Even from bed. The phone is a marvelous tool of service with which you can—to quote Ma Bell— reach out and touch someone.

So long as we love
we serve;
so long as we are loved
by others,
I would almost say that
we are indispensable;
and no man is useless
while he has a friend.

ROBERT LOUIS STEVENSON

Let Others Serve You

One of the greatest forms of service is allowing others to serve you. Their giving might be of the "charitable" sort at first, but gradually they may learn the joy of giving, and, in allowing them to give, you have been their teacher.

Giving to others feels good; it strengthens the physiology and enhances self-worth. When you let others give to you, you are giving them the gift of good feelings, strengthened physiology and enhanced self-worth.

Each time someone does something for you, remind yourself, "I am worthy of this." If you weren't worthy, it wouldn't be taking place. (Pragmatism 101.) You *are* worthy. Accept the service.

When, through your own service, you see how much there is to be gained by being of service, you will gladly let others serve you. Or, you can learn how much there is to be gained by watching the faces of the people as they serve you.

They may arrive, pressured from a day of "getting while the getting is good," and, within a few minutes of giving freely with no thought of return, transform. Faces relax, breathing slows, tension eases; love, joy and laughter flow. And all because you're there, accepting the gift of their giving.

One of the greatest myths of our culture is that of the "rugged individualist"—independent, "I can do it myself." Hardly. Imagine what your life would be like if you had to meet *every* need yourself.

Did you make your own clothes? Did you weave your own cloth? Did you grow your own cotton? Did you chop the trees to make the loom and mine the ore to make the needles? Did you make the tools

*Independence? That's
middle-class blasphemy.
We are all dependent
on one another,
every soul of us on earth.*

GEORGE BERNARD SHAW

you used to chop the trees and mine the ore? Did you invent all these?

If we take it back just a few levels, the myth of "independence" quickly falls apart. We are, in fact, inextricably *interdependent*. We depend on something someone has done—or is doing—for almost everything in our lives. And, other people are depending upon what we do and have done.

If you can assist others, without overtaxing or overextending yourself, do so. If you want assistance from others, ask for—and receive—it. It's all part of the flow, the interaction, the interdependence, the interconnectedness of life.

The superfluous,
a very necessary thing.

VOLTAIRE

Get Off the
Excitement Treadmill

Some people become addicted to excitement, to mental-emotional-physical intensity of any kind. Some of it is "positive," some of it is "negative," but all of it is *exciting*.

Excitement addiction, like any other addiction, requires that future levels of excitement be greater, and greater, and greater still.

The results of this are graphically illustrated in a film we saw that featured an unfortunate mouse. (No, not one of those Disney antidrug films—this was a movie about a real mouse.)

The mouse had been surgically wired so that the pleasure center of the brain was stimulated by an electric current each time the mouse touched a switch in its cage. The mouse would touch the switch, an electric current would stimulate its pleasure center, and the mouse would fall on its back, writhing in ecstasy.

At first, one "hit" was sufficient for quite a while. The mouse would lie there, smoke a cigarette, wonder if it would respect itself in the morning, get something to eat, and see who was on *The Tonight Show*.

As time went on, however, the interval between lever hits grew shorter, and the amount of time the mouse could hold down the lever grew longer. Eventually, the mouse abandoned all nourishment and sat, spasmodically pushing the switch several hundred times per minute.

In Rome
you long for the country;
in the country
—oh inconstant!—
you praise the distant city
to the stars.

HORACE
65-8 B.C.

In the valleys you
look for the mountains
In the mountains you've
searched for the rivers
There is no where to go
You are where you belong
You can live
the life you dreamed.

JUDY COLLINS

Humans who become addicted to excitement do approximately the same thing. More and more they need more and more and enjoy it less and less.

If you find yourself on this treadmill, get off. Slow down. Take it easy. Learn to appreciate the quieter, subtler, simpler pleasures of life.

The process is the same as we discussed before—focusing on the positive. The positive is not necessarily what will get you excited: "Oh, boy!" The positive is sometimes contemplating the wonder of a plant or reflecting on the amount of time and attention that went into making even the most common of objects, say, a drinking glass.

Replace the idea of "excitement" with that of "enjoyment." When you feel the need for excitement, see if you can find something *enjoyable* instead. Too much excitement strains the body. Enjoyment, in its own quiet way, strengthens.

(An excellent book on getting off the excitement treadmill—and the physiological importance of doing so—is *Treating Type A Behavior and Your Heart* by Meyer Friedman, M.D. and Diane Ulmer, R.N., M.S. Their earlier book, *Type A Behavior and Your Heart,* was a landmark on the relationship between negative thinking and cardiovascular disease. *Treating Type A Behavior and Your Heart* tells what to do about it—how to "cure" Type A behavior. Both are available in paperback from Fawcett Books, New York.)

*Do not take life
too seriously.
You will never
get out of it alive.*

ELBERT HUBBARD

Take It Easier

Be easier on yourself, on everyone and everything. As much as you can, suspend your judgment of the way things "should" be, "must" be and "ought to" be. These judgments may contribute to any disease that's in your life. Suspending them gives you greater ease.

Consider ease the antidote for disease.

Do things that bring you ease—quiet walks, resting, hot baths, being with friends, meditating, contemplating, reading, writing.

Approach life with new attitudes—acceptance, patience, flowing, giving, grace, effortlessness, simplicity, allowing, acquiescing, permitting, forgiving.

Write these words—and others like them—on separate cards and put them in places you will see them. Pick one of these attitudes each day and, all day, no matter what happens, meet it with that attitude.

It often happens
that I wake at night
and begin to think about
a serious problem
and decide I must tell
the Pope about it.
Then I wake up
completely and remember
that I am the Pope.

POPE JOHN XXIII

What Would a Master Do?

When challenged by a situation you're not quite sure how to respond to, ask yourself, "How would a Master handle this?" or "How would the perfect _____ respond to this?" (Fill in the blank with whatever "role" you happen to be playing—the perfect *friend,* the perfect *boss,* the perfect *employee,* the perfect *lover,* the perfect *patient,* etc.)

If you have religious or spiritual beliefs, ask yourself how the One you worship would respond to the situation. If you admire certain leaders—masters—in their chosen fields, ask yourself what they would do.

You'll probably get an answer. You're not obliged to *follow* that answer, but it will, at least, give you another option.

For the most part, Masters don't get upset. They have, as the sayings go, "the wisdom of Solomon," "the patience of Job," and "the love of the Christ." If you have this kind of wisdom, patience and love, what is there to be upset about?

We believe that, within us, we *all* have that kind of wisdom, patience and love. It's just a matter of calling upon it and using it.

You call upon it by asking, "How would the perfect _____ do it?" or "How would the Master respond?" and then following through on the answer.

Life is too short to waste
In critic peep
or cynic bark,
Quarrel or reprimand:
'Twill soon be dark;
Up! Mind thine own aim,
and God speed the mark!

RALPH WALDO EMERSON

Complaining

Some people are extremely good at knowing not only what's wrong, but also who to tell about it, and how. These people we call "the effective complainers." Their complaints often result in some measurable improvement.

Most people, however, are ineffective complainers. They moan, groan, kvetch and complain to anyone who will listen.

This phenomenon can be seen from 4 p.m. until 7 p.m. every working day. It's the daily National Convention of the "Ain't It Awful? Club." The Club Motto is *Miseria Libere Companio* ("Misery Loves Company"). Bars and cocktail lounges all over the country serve drinks at half-price, and, for the price of a drink, people tell each other their troubles. For some unknown reason, this period of time is known as The Happy Hour.

Conversations between many people consist of nothing but a litany of how unfair it all is. When some people ask their friends, "What's new?" what they may mean is, "Any news of fresh disasters?"

In the spirit of focusing on the positive, it's obvious that the habit of complaining is, to mix metaphors, not flowing with the river in the direction the horse is riding. That is, if you're looking for things to complain about, you'll find them—and you'll also find the consequences of negative thinking as well.

To reverse this habit, we have two suggestions:

1. Only complain to someone who can do something about it. If your water bill seems too high, there's no point in telling anyone but the water company. If your reception on cable TV is not up to par, telling a friend will do no good unless

Some of you young folks have been saying to me, "Eh, Pops, what do you mean, what a wonderful world? How about all those wars all over the place? You call them wonderful? And how about hunger and pollution? That ain't so wonderful either." How about listening to old Pops for a minute? Seems to me it ain't the world that's so bad but what we're doing to it. And all I'm saying is see what a wonderful world it would be if we only gave it a chance. Love, baby, love—that's the secret. Yeeeaaahhh. If lots more of us loved each other, we'd solve lots more problems. And then this world would be a gasser.

LOUIS ARMSTRONG

that friend happens to work for the cable company. This helps keep your conversations on the positive side of the street. With some people, you may find you have nothing to talk about.

2. Compliment at least as often as you complain. If you're a complainer who knows how to get things done through Creative Complaining, well and good. Knowing whom to complain to and in what manner is a good thing to know. We suggest, however, that you add a step to each negative communication—compliment at least as often as you complain.

For every letter you write grumbling about something, write a letter of tribute as well. (It need not be to the same person or company.) Each time you ask the maitre d' over to condemn the food, invite the same maitre d' to your table to praise something.

If, in fact, you find something to praise *before* giving your complaint, (A) you may find the person receiving the complaint more open to hearing it (and doing something about it), and—more importantly—(B) you will be learning to look for the positive even in situations worthy of complaints.

*You grow up the day you
have the first real laugh
—at yourself.*

ETHEL BARRYMORE

If It'll Be Funny Later, It's Funny Now

Probably some of the best anecdotes in your personal repertoire are stories of how disaster befell you. With the passage of time, most tragedies have a way of becoming comedies.

J-R: Once I was traveling to give a lecture. The plane was late, and everyone else's luggage came off before ours. Somewhere across town, there were several hundred people in a rented hall waiting for me to give a talk—perhaps on the importance of being on time—and it was getting later and later.

Finally our luggage started to arrive. (We were carrying our own sound equipment, so it wouldn't have done much good to go on ahead.) One suitcase had sprung open, and clothes were spread all over the conveyer belt. Another piece of luggage was obviously damaged. The people traveling with me were getting more and more upset.

Finally I said, "Relax, this is funny. In a few weeks we'll be telling stories about tonight and laughing about it. If it'll be funny then, it's funny now." And we started looking at the situation as if it were a Woody Allen movie. When some of the luggage didn't arrive, we smiled. When the car rental company didn't have our reservation (or cars), we laughed. When we heard there was a taxi strike, we howled.

We cherish our friends
not for their ability
to amuse us,
but for ours
to amuse them.

EVELYN WAUGH

Sure, everybody thought we were crazy, but we were having a wonderful time. When we finally got to the lecture, I had a great "opening monologue."

Start looking at "bad" situations in life as raw material for your "opening monologue." Ever notice how much humor is based on misfortune? What's the difference between laughing about something and crying about it? Attitude. Which would you rather do?

Yes, sometimes crying is appropriate. We don't want you to turn laughter into a form of denial. But often, laughter is the best response to those slings and arrows of outrageous fortune. As the tribulations mount, tell yourself, "This is great! I can't wait to tell so-and-so!"

The people you know who laugh easily, talk to them often.

*The growth
of the human mind
is still high adventure,
in many ways the highest
adventure on earth.*

NORMAN COUSINS

Laugh

Many years ago, Norman Cousins was diagnosed as being "terminally ill." He was given six months to live. His chance for recovery was one in five hundred.

He could see that the worry, depression and anger in his life contributed to, and perhaps helped cause, his disease. He wondered, "If illness can be caused by negativity, can wellness be created by positivity?"

He decided to make an experiment of himself. Laughter was one of the most positive activities he knew. He rented all the comedy movies he could find. (This was before the advent of VCR's, so he had to rent the actual films.) He read, and had friends read him, funny stories. His friends were asked to call him whenever they said, heard or did anything funny.

He was in enormous pain, so great that he could not sleep. Laughing for five solid minutes, he found, relieved the pain for several hours, and he could sleep.

He fully recovered from his illness; and lived another twenty happy, healthy and productive years. (His journey is detailed in his book, *Anatomy of an Illness.*) He credits visualization, the love of his family and friends, and laughter for his recovery.

Some people think laughter is "a waste of time." It's a luxury, they say, a frivolity, something to be indulged in only every so often.

Nothing could be further from the truth. Laughter is essential to our equilibrium, to our well-being, to our aliveness. If we're not well, laughter helps us

*I have never made
but one prayer to God,
a very short one:
"O Lord,
make my enemies
ridiculous."
And God granted it.*

VOLTAIRE

get well. If we are well, laughter helps us stay that way.

Since Cousins' ground-breaking subjective work, scientific studies have shown that laughter has a curative effect on the body, the mind and the emotions.

So, if you like laughter, consider this *carte blanche* to indulge in it as often as you can. If you don't like laughter, then take your medicine: laugh anyway.

Use whatever makes you laugh—movies, sitcoms, *Monty Python,* records, books, *New Yorker* cartoons, jokes, friends. Give yourself permission to laugh—long and loud and out loud—whenever anything strikes you as funny. The people around you may think you're strange, but sooner or later they'll join in—even if they don't know what they're laughing about.

Some diseases may be contagious, but none is as contagious as the cure—laughter.

No man is a failure
who is enjoying life.

WILLIAM FEATHER

Do Things
That Make You Happy

Whatever makes you happy—as long as it doesn't hurt you or hurt someone else—do it.

Schedule pleasurable activities into your life with the same dedication, precision and priority you give less-than-pleasurable ones.

Some people think that happiness just happens, and, yes, to a degree that's true. But happiness has a better chance of happening in situations you generally find enjoyable. Experienced positive focusers *can* find happiness in a garbage pile, but even experienced positive focusers find it easier to find happiness at a museum (or reading a good book, or watching a good TV show, or at the beach, or . . .).

Make a list of the things you enjoy doing. Do these things often. Actively pursuing happiness may be the same as actively pursuing health.

*Know you what it is
to be a child?
It is to be something
very different from
the man of today.
It is to have a spirit
yet streaming from
the waters of baptism;
it is to believe in love,
to believe in loveliness,
to believe in belief;
it is to be so little
that the elves can reach to whisper
in your ear;
it is to turn pumpkins into coaches,
and mice into horses,
lowness into loftiness,
and nothing into everything,
for each child has
its fairy godmother in its soul.*

FRANCIS THOMPSON SHELLEY

Learn to Play Again

Did you ever watch children at play? They can create enormous amounts of fun, enthusiasm and joy with anything that's at hand. A stick becomes a scepter. A stone, a throne. Two minutes later, the stick is a magic wand and the stone a pet dragon.

Somewhere along the way, we "serious adults" forgot how to play. Recapture that sense of being in the moment with whatever the moment has to offer.

One way is to play with young children—five, six, seven. They'll stretch your imagination while rekindling in you the sense of wonder you, too, once had.

You might even get yourself some toys you played with—or wanted to play with—as a child: finger paints, Erector sets, crayons, dolls. Take a trip to a toy store and *buy yourself* whatever seems like fun.

Be your own nurturing parent. Give yourself permission to play.

*If I had to define
life in a word,
it would be:
Life is creation.*

CLAUDE BERNARD

From The Bulletin of
New York Academy of Medicine

Be Creative

One of the great joys of life is creativity. Information goes in, gets shuffled about, and comes out in new and interesting ways.

Whatever it is of a creative nature you've always wanted to do—do it now. Writing, painting, sculpting, cooking, gardening, sewing, knitting, singing, playing an instrument, composing, dancing, choreographing, designing, photographing, acting, directing—the list is endless.

It doesn't matter if you don't know how to do it "perfectly." It doesn't matter how "good" you are. What matters is the process. Does it give you joy? Does it give you satisfaction? Is it fun? Does it make you feel more in touch with the creative flow of life? If the answer to any of these is yes, then do it.

Letting creativity flow through you can be therapeutic. "Energy flowing through a system acts to organize that system," as the *Whole Earth Catalog* reminds us.

Give yourself plenty of creative time, and plenty of opportunities to create.

*A noble person
attracts noble people,
and knows how to
hold on to them.*

GOETHE

Choose Well Your Fellow Travelers

Be with people who are headed in the same direction you are. If you know people who have a positive direction to their lives—or who are working on one—you may find them more rewarding to be around.

Conversely, the people who are addicted to their negative thinking—and who refuse to recognize that that's what they're doing—can be a downright (and downward) drag. They will feed you negativity and criticize every positive move you take.

Negative thinkers can be a great challenge. If possible, avoid the challenge.

Populate your life with those who applaud each positive thought, feeling and action you have, who encourage you toward more and better, who know how to praise the good and the beautiful.

As we said before, you don't *have* to spend time with people you don't want to. If you choose to spend time with them, you're entitled to set certain parameters: "I don't want to discuss negative things." If they don't like it (and they probably won't), they're entitled to go elsewhere and spend time with people who do.

If there are people you feel you *must* spend time with (usually relatives), (A) try to do it on the phone, and (B) use the time with them to learn something about yourself. Watching how other people negate and sabotage themselves can provide you with a blueprint of how you may do it to yourself.

You don't have to be negative about their negativity.

I love tranquil solitude
And such society
As is quiet,
wise, and good.

SHELLEY

The idea that it's better to spend time with up-lifting people is also true of books, movies, TV shows, records—everything. Not that you have to watch *The Sound of Music* three times a day—it's just that certain sources of information enforce the notion that "life is terrible," while other sources of information uphold the idea that "life is wonderful." (Try watching *Field of Dreams.)*

Which of those sources you surround yourself with is entirely up to you. As you may have guessed, we suggest the wonderful.

Some patients,
though conscious that
their condition is perilous,
recover their health
simply through their
contentment with the
goodness of the physician.

HIPPOCRATES
460-400 B.C.

The Miracle of
Modern Medicine

That sounds like an article from *Reader's Digest,* doesn't it? The fact is, modern medicine routinely does things that would have been considered truly miraculous only a century ago.

In some cases, far less than a century ago: Before the discovery of stable penicillin in 1941 and its widespread manufacture after World War II, pneumonia killed more people than any other complication. People would have a simple disease or accident and die from pneumonia. Alexander the Great, the most powerful man of his day, died of pneumonia. King Henry VIII, the most powerful man of his day, died of syphilis. Since penicillin, deaths in the Western world from pneumonia have dropped significantly and syphilis deaths are almost not measurable. (According to *The World Almanac,* 0.0 percent.)

Although the remarkably expanded life expectancy of human beings over the past two hundred years is more thanks to plumbing and transportation than medicine (the carrying away of refuse and the addition of fresh fruits and vegetables to the daily diet have done more to lengthen the average life-span than anything else), any number of formerly "incurable" diseases and maladies are now routinely cured.

It's interesting to sit with a group of people and ask, "Would you be alive today if medicine were only as advanced as it was one hundred years ago?" Most people who had syphilis, pneumonia, any other usually fatal bacterial disease, a severe accident, or almost any operation—including appendicitis and Caesarean section—would have to say no.

Honor a physician
with the honor
due unto him
for the uses which ye may
have of him:
for the Lord hath
created him.

ECCLESIASTICUS
38:1

The discovery of just The Big Three—anesthesia, antiseptics and antibiotics—directly accounts for the saving of tens of millions of lives each year.

There are miracles happening every day in medicine. You—or someone you know well—is still alive because of them. When you think of medicine, don't just think of sterile science, lab coats and test tubes. Ponder the wonder of medicine, the marvel of how far it has come—and how quickly. Consider the magic of it.

The history of modern medicine is less the story of predictable, plodding advances than it is a chronicle of miracles.

And the miracles continue still.

*The man who is
tenacious of purpose
in a rightful cause
is not shaken from
his firm resolve
by the frenzy of his fellow
citizens clamoring for
what is wrong,
or by the tyrant's
threatening countenance.*

HORACE
65-8 B.C.

Explore Every Medical Option

As we mentioned at the start of this book, nothing in this book is designed to replace proper medical treatment. The ideas in this book are designed to augment whatever treatment program you're on, or—like indoor plumbing and fresh vegetables— keep diseases away so treatment won't be necessary.

If you have a life-threatening illness, explore every possibility of treatment, of cure, or of delaying the progress of the disease.

*All interest
in disease and death
is only another expression
of interest in life.*

THOMAS MANN

Know the Disease

Your doctor has hundreds of diseases to learn and keep current on—you have just one. Know it. It is, after all, a visitor. Even an unwelcome visitor you'd probably spend some time getting to know. And the better you know it, the more ways you'll have of getting it to leave.

Ask your doctor about the disease, its treatment, its cure. When you've reached the limits of your doctor's knowledge (or patience), do some research. Read about the disease. Talk to other people who have it or, better still, who no longer have it.

Become a co-creator of your own cure. Work *with* your doctor on the best course of treatment for you. Don't be the passive patient, taking pills and paying bills. Become involved.

As any good doctor will tell you, diagnosis and treatment of many illnesses are as much an art as they are a science.

Justice is
the only worship.
Love is
the only priest.
Ignorance is
the only slavery.
Happiness is
the only good.
The time to be happy
is now,
The place to be happy
is here,
The way to be happy
is to make others so.

ROBERT GREEN INGERSOLL

Focus on the Cure

The reason for knowing your disease is so that you can cure it. Keep that always in mind as you do your studying.

No matter how clever, powerful or tenacious a disease may be (and some of them are remarkable), keep reminding yourself, "I'm smarter than that," "I'm more powerful than that," "I'm more persistent than that."

Because you are.

MARTIANS BUILD TWO IMMENSE CANALS IN TWO YEARS

Vast Engineering Works Accomplished in an Incredibly Short Time by Our Planetary Neighbors

NEW YORK TIMES

Front-Page Headline
August 27, 1911

Don't Believe Everything You Read in the Papers (Magazines, TV, etc.)

Knowing the disease can not only help you work toward the cure, it can also keep you from getting worse due to fear. Once you know the disease, media accounts that once might have caused you to panic now only produce a smile and a sigh. (Although the temptation will be great, don't let your reaction get more negative than a sigh.)

The news media are, for the most part, the bringers of bad news. That statement, of course, is no longer news. And it's not entirely the media's fault—bad news gets higher ratings and sells more papers than good news. ("Three Americans Shot by Mad Gunman!" sells papers. "258,829,439 Americans Not Shot by Mad Gunman!" doesn't.)

When your disease is reported in the media, remember that the reporting is apt to (A) focus on the negative, and (B) be superficial enough to appeal to everyone. Because you have a vested interest in knowing about the disease, you may know more about it than the reporter who reported it. (The reporter probably has to cover every other known disease and Space Shuttle launchings, too.)

The media often fall into the "Is the glass half-full or half-empty?" trap. If a disease has a fifty-fifty survivability rate, the media tend to say, "Fifty percent of all people with this disease die," rather than, "Half the people diagnosed with this illness are cured." Same information, different slant.

Sometimes the reporting is so general it blurs the issue. Because the media only report that so-

*The French army
is still the best all-around
fighting machine
in Europe.*

*TIME**

June 12, 1939

---

*Speaking of time, have we told you about our *You Can't Afford
the Luxury of a Negative Thought* <u>watches</u>? Upset when you (or
other people, or planes, or trains, or busses) are late? Now,
every time you look at your watch, it can remind you that you
can't afford the luxury of a negative thought. Gold-plated, bat-
tery operated, quartz movement, black leather band, and only
$35. Please specify men's or women's size when ordering. Think
we're kidding? Send us $35 and you'll see. Money back if you're
not delighted. Call 1-800-LIFE-101 or send check or money
order for $35 to Prelude Press, 8165 Mannix Drive, L.A., CA.
90046.

---

and-so "died of cancer," many people don't know, for example, that "cancer" is not one always-fatal illness, but a term describing a whole collection of illnesses, the majority of which are now considered curable.

When people—who for years have read that even rich and famous people die from "cancer"—learn they have cancer, naturally they panic. The cancer they have may have a high rate of survivability, and the doctor may let them know this, but inside they've been trained to believe—by years of generalized, superficial reporting—"I have cancer. I'm going to die."

Also, diseases in the media tend to follow a trend—they have their day in the spotlight and fade into obscurity. In the early eighties, herpes had its day. Now, although people still get and have herpes, you don't hear much about it. Now AIDS has the spotlight.

The problem with this kind of "fad reporting" is three-fold:

First, it tends to report rumors, speculations and projections as facts. These are more, well, *sensational*. How do they do this? By quoting some "expert." Experts seldom agree, especially at the early stages of studying a disease, and you can always find some expert who will say something hopelessly hopeless about anything.

Second, most of the curative work is done after a disease has fallen out of media favor. When a cure—which usually happens in gradual stages of treatment and prevention—is found, the disease is by then in media exile, and the report of the cure is often relegated to a small article next to the supermarket ads—if reported at all.

*Comet Kohoutek
promises to be the
celestial extravaganza
of the century.*

NEWSWEEK

November 5, 1973

Third, if the horrifying projections turn out to be, shall we say, exaggerated, no one bothers to report, "Five years ago we made a big mistake. Hope we didn't frighten you folks too much." (Remember during the herpes scare when experts were predicting that the virus would eventually attack the spinal column and people would die horrible deaths? How many retractions of this misinformation have you seen?)

In the media, good news must, alas, also be taken with a grain of salt. If going against the popular grain and reporting the opinion of an overly optimistic "expert" will make a good headline, so be it.

As any reporter will tell you, when writing for the mass media on an intricate subject such as disease, the instructions are, "Generalize, simplify, and don't take up too much space (or time)." "All the news that's fit to print" too often becomes "All the news that fits."

On the brighter side, the scare tactics of the media often make available more time, money and resources for treatment and cure than might otherwise have been available. We just wish there was a way to do it without all that fear—especially for the people who have to deal with not only the disease and their own fear of the disease, but everyone else's fear as well.

*The principles
of Washington's farewell
address are still
sources of wisdom
when cures for social ills
are sought.
The methods
of Washington's physicians,
however, are
no longer studied.*

THURMAN ARNOLD

Learn to Separate "Opinion" and "Projection" from Fact

The Experts Speak is must-reading for anyone who listens to "experts" make predictions about their lives. (Any time someone tells you that you only have so long to live, how much pain you will go through or what you'll be able to do between now and your demise—it's a *prediction*, an *opinion* based upon a statistical norm. Nothing more.)

The Experts Speak (by Christopher Cerf and Victor Navasky, Pantheon Books, New York) is 392 pages, in small type, of noted experts being wrong about almost every major event, discovery and human endeavor of the past seven thousand years. According to the "experts," all of Beethoven's symphonies were trash, World Wars I and II could not happen, and *Gone With The Wind* wouldn't make a nickel.

A general sampling. Edison: "The talking picture will not supplant the regular silent motion picture." Aristotle: "Women may be said to be an inferior man." Edison: "The phonograph is not of any commercial value." *Business Week,* 1968: "With over 50 foreign cars already on sale here, the Japanese auto industry isn't likely to carve out a big slice of the U.S. market for itself." Edison: "The radio craze will soon die out."

Here are a few of the quotes that concern us most directly, from the chapter "The Annals of Medicine: Man's War Against Disease."

"The abolishment of pain in surgery is a chimera. It is absurd to go on seeking it. . . . <u>Knife</u> and <u>pain</u> are two words in surgery that must forever be associated in the consciousness of the patient. To this compulsory combination we shall have to adjust ourselves."

—*Dr. Alfred Velpeau*

(French surgeon,
professor at the Paris Faculty of Medicine)
1839

"The abdomen, the chest, and the brain will be forever shut from the intrusion of the wise and humane surgeon."

—*Sir John Eric Erichsen*

(British surgeon, later appointed
Surgeon-Extraordinary to Queen Victoria)
1873

"Louis Pasteur's theory of germs is ridiculous fiction."

—*Pierre Pachet*
(Professor of Physiology at Toulouse)
1872

"One-half of the children born die before their eighth year. This is nature's law; why try to contradict it?"

—*Jean-Jacques Rousseau*
(Author of the most widely read
child-rearing manual of its day)
1762

"Every man who has sexual relations with two women at the same time risks syphilis, even if the two women are faithful to him, for all libertine behavior spontaneously incites this disease."

—*Alexandre Weill*
The Laws and Mysteries of Love
1891

"A genuine kiss generates so much heat it destroys germs."

—*Dr. S. L. Katzoff*

(faculty member, San Francisco
Institute of Human Relations)
1940

"If excessive smoking actually plays a role in the production of lung cancer, it seems to be a minor one."

—*Dr. W. C. Heuper*

(National Cancer Institute)
quoted in *The New York Times,*
April 14, 1954

"For the majority of people, smoking has a beneficial effect."

—*Dr. Ian G. Macdonald*

(Los Angeles surgeon),
quoted in *Newsweek,*
November 18, 1963

We quote these—and there are many, many more—to show that experts—even doctor experts—are human, and humans make mistakes. There are certain medical *facts,* but predictions about how long someone will live are just that—predictions, opinions.

Unfortunately, when some people are told by a doctor—Authority Figure Extraordinary—"Your disease is incurable; you only have six months to live," they may believe it so faithfully they—with their own thoughts, feelings and actions—may sentence themselves to die within six months. And they do.

We believe that if they were given years, they would have lived years, and if the doctor had said, "There's a condition here, and if you work with me, together we can beat this," they would have—given a fully cooperative patient ready to do "whatever it takes"—beaten it.

When a disease is officially deemed "incurable," the incurability of it becomes a self-fulfilling prophecy. When people cure themselves, they are usually told, "Ah, we made a mistake in diagnosis." "How do you know you made a mistake in diagnosis?" "Because the disease we first diagnosed is incurable, and since you no longer have any signs of it, it must not have been that disease, because that disease is incurable."

A dear friend of ours went through this. In 1971, she was diagnosed as having leukemia and "given" three years to live. She went to work on herself, and within a year all signs of leukemia were gone. She was told there had been a misdiagnosis. To this day, she is still doing fine. (That is something of an understatement.)

Some doctors don't like to admit that they misdiagnosed. They just call the healing a "spontaneous

*The art of medicine
consists of
amusing the patient
while nature
cures the disease.*

VOLTAIRE

remission" and leave it at that. There's no rhyme or reason to the cure, they claim. It was "spontaneous." Besides, you're not "cured." The disease is just "in remission." It could flare up at any time. You were lucky, nothing more. Go home.

Other doctors, however, ask, "What did you do? How did you do it? Let's see what it was, and maybe it will help others." We loudly applaud this ever-growing group of medical practitioners.

AIDS, for example, is currently thought to be "incurable" and "always fatal" by most experts. The problem is, some people who have had AIDS before AIDS even had a name are still alive. Until *everyone* dies, we don't understand how it can be called "*always* fatal."

The Center for Disease Control studied 5,833 New York City people with AIDS. They found that 15 percent were still alive five years (or more) after diagnosis. When the black and Hispanic IV (intravenous) drug users (who tended to die much more quickly; more about this, however, in the next section) were factored out, it was shown that 30.9 percent of the gay white males diagnosed with Kaposi's sarcoma (one of the diseases indicating AIDS) were alive five years after diagnosis.

These are, of course, sobering statistics. But, to us, it certainly pokes a rather sizable hole in the generally held belief that AIDS is "always fatal." From that point of view, these figures are encouraging (unless you're a black or Hispanic IV drug user), especially considering the fact that all the survivors in this study lived through "the dark age of AIDS," when medical treatment for people with AIDS was nowhere near as advanced as it is today, or will be tomorrow.

We have not lost faith,
but we have transferred it
from God
to the medical profession.

GEORGE BERNARD SHAW

Another recent prediction—now reported as fact by most of the media—is that 99 percent of all people who currently test positive for the HIV antibody will die of AIDS complications. (One doesn't die of AIDS; one dies of the complications from opportunistic infections the AIDS-suppressed immune system can't fight off.)

This is devastating information for anyone who's ever taken "an AIDS test" and had a positive result. (There is no "AIDS test." The test is for the *antibody* to the HIV virus, the virus most experts believe causes AIDS. All the test shows is that the *antibody* to the virus is in the bloodstream. It does not show the *presence* of the AIDS virus or of the disease AIDS.)

Before taking this 99 percent figure too much to heart (or head, and thinking negatively about it), consider the facts.

We'll go into detail on this as an example of how important it is to look beneath the well-circulated doomsday predictions about any disease and to find something closer to the truth.

In 1978, at a sexually transmitted disease clinic in San Francisco, blood was taken from thousands of patients and stored as part of a study on hepatitis. When, in 1984, the test for the HIV antibody was discovered, an experiment was begun on 5,000 primarily gay men whose 1978 stored blood showed the presence of the HIV antibody.

By 1988, 48 percent of the people who had the HIV antibody in their blood in 1978 had developed AIDS.

These are tragic figures, but *this is all that is currently known*. Scientific fact stops here. Expert projection and opinion take over.

*Public opinion
is compounded of folly,
weakness, prejudice,
wrong feeling,
right feeling, obstinacy,
and newspaper paragraphs.*

SIR ROBERT PEEL
1788-1850

Some experts looked at the graph and projected the rise of AIDS cases in the future based upon what had happened in the past. Based upon this *assumption,* they predicted that, by the year 2000, nearly everyone in the study would have AIDS.

Based upon *this* projection, they further projected that 99 percent of *all people* who are HIV antibody-positive will die of complications arising from AIDS.

This series of assumptions and projections upon projections fails to take into account the following:

1. A disease tends to affect the weakest and/or most susceptible portions of a population first. If these same experts had graphed the bubonic plague (which wiped out half of Europe from 1348 to 1350) or the flu epidemic of 1918 (which killed more than twice as many people as World War I—20,000,000 worldwide, 548,000 in the United States), Europe would have had no human life by 1352, and the whole of the world's population would have been history sometime in the 1920s. This, of course, is not what happened. The diseases ran their course and eventually died out without a "cure" ever being found. It's as reasonable to predict that the same thing will happen to the people in the test group as it is to predict that they are all doomed.

2. The people in the study were coming to a public clinic for sexually transmitted diseases. The majority of them had a history of syphilis, gonorrhea, parasites, herpes and/or hepatitis. This brings up certain questions: (A) Were these people more susceptible to diseases than an "average" group of gay males? (B) Was the immune system, prior to exposure to AIDS, already suppressed by repeated exposure to other diseases, and, if so, did that give the AIDS virus a stronger foothold? (C) Was the health

The biggest liar
in the world
is They Say.

DOUGLAS MALLOCH

care they were given at a public clinic as good as the care other gay males received from private treatment?

3. The chances are very high that many of the men in this population would have had, through multiple sexual contacts, repeated exposure to the AIDS virus. There is no evidence on this specifically relating to the HIV virus, but multiple exposure to most viruses tends to bring on a stronger case of the disease and to bring it on more quickly. The people in the study were already HIV positive by 1978, and the guidelines for "safe sex" were not announced for another six years.

4. Drug use was higher than average among this population.

5. The number and frequency of sexual partners in this population were higher than average.

6. Many of the gay males in San Francisco in the late 1970s practiced a great deal of sex that was not just "unsafe" (in terms of AIDS transmission) but downright acrobatic. Some of the activities could, from a transmission-of-AIDS point of view, be considered *very* unsafe.

7. The study only goes as far back as 1978. The AIDS virus, in its current form (HIV), is believed to have been around at least twenty-five years, probably longer. Some of the people in the study may have been infected for twenty years or more.

8. The people in the study have known since 1984 that they've had antibodies to HIV in their blood since at least 1978, and probably before. They've read reports about the study, as well as heard experts "predict" the grim state of their life expectancy. They may have watched friends who were in the study die from AIDS, or even friends infected *after* 1978. Can you imagine the kind of negative

*Do not put your faith
in what statistics say
until you have carefully
considered what
they do not say.*

WILLIAM W. WATT

thinking this can induce among this dwindling population of volunteers?

In making this list, we do not for a moment cast a "moral" judgment on the actions of the members of this group, or anyone who practiced a life-style similar to theirs. (We, in fact, want to praise the people in the test group for their willingness and courage to serve others by taking part in the experiment.) It's just that, from what we now know about the transmission of AIDS and using the 20/20 vision of hindsight, we can see that these people may have had more contributing AIDS factors than the general population—probably even more than the general population of people who currently test HIV antibody-positive.

Taking these eight factors into account, we don't see how the experts made the "99 percent prediction" for even the remaining members of the test group, much less the entire population. (And why 99 percent? Why not 98 percent? Or 100 percent? Or 99-44/100 percent?)

This shows that, before believing what you read, or even what you are told by a professional, you'd do well to find out (A) if the information is *fact* or *projection,* (B) where the study was done and under what conditions, and (C) who took part in the study and what's the difference between your life and theirs.

And remember, according to the experts, man can't fly, the sun goes around the earth and the *Titanic* is unsinkable.

≈

*We should always
presume the disease
to be curable,
until its own nature
prove it otherwise.*

PETER MERE LATHAM

This chapter was originally written in 1988. In 1991, we revised the book. There was little to change in this chapter, except to say that the alarmists were wrong—once again. For example, the statistics from the San Francisco study—far from getting increasingly grave and horrifying—have gotten no worse at all. The percentage of people in that study who developed AIDS has stayed virtually the same since 1988. Did this make the front page of any newspaper? Did an evening television newscast open its broadcast with this wonderful information? We don't even need to answer that one.

We saw an article about a year ago. The headline read: "AIDS INFECTION RATE LESS THAN ORIGINALLY THOUGHT." The article went on to say that the number of people "infected with AIDS" (as the press likes to misrepresent HIV-antibody positive) is not 1.5 million, as originally thought, but closer to one million. The article was three paragraphs long and printed on page 22. The original scare projections were off by *one-third,* the number of infected people *500,000 less* than the blaring front-page headlines first proclaimed. Where do we find this corrected information? Page 22, next to ads for office supplies and FAX machines.

The studies of otherwise healthy people who happen to have HIV antibodies in their systems have been—uniformly and universally—encouraging. In other words, the news about being HIV antibody positive is positive. Far from a death sentence, HIV antibody positive status is yet another of life's wake-up calls. "Watch your diet; do what you love; monitor your attitude; exercise; reduce stress; don't worry, be happy," seem to be its message. Those who heed the message seem to have the same chances of living a long, full life as almost anyone else.

The "HIV-POSITIVE equals AIDS equals DEATH in a few years" falsehood will probably be looked upon as one of the most inaccurate—and cruelest—myths of the latter part of the Twentieth Century.

*The mind of man
is capable of anything—
because everything is in it,
all the past
as well as all the future.*

JOSEPH CONRAD

If One Has Done It,
You Can Be Two.

If None Has Done It,
You Can Be One.

In the last section we gave the Center for Disease Control statistics from a study of New York City people with AIDS. According to the CDC, black and Hispanic IV (intravenous) drug users had a much greater chance of dying from AIDS within the first five years of diagnosis than white, gay males.

Does that mean if you're a black or Hispanic IV drug user living in New York City, recently diagnosed as having AIDS, you should give up? Not at all. As long as *one* black or Hispanic New York City IV drug user has survived more than five years, *you* can be number two. If *no* black or Hispanic IV drug users have survived for more than five years, you can be number one.

Whatever your disease, there are statistical tables telling you your odds of surviving the illness. Remember, however—you are a human being, not a statistic. You can do anything you want, as long as you're willing to do whatever it takes to get it. If getting over the illness is what you want above all else, you can have it. The tables give statistical averages, not facts about your life.

The insurance industry's life-expectancy tables are an example of this. No matter what your age, they will tell you—to the month—when you will die. Of course, they do nothing of the kind. But *statistically*, they're accurate. The absurdity of this is

*There are
three kinds of lies:
lies, damn lies,
and statistics.*

BENJAMIN DISRAELI

reflected in the insurance salesperson who was looking up the life expectancy of an elderly client. The salesperson looked and looked and finally said, "I'm sorry. I can't sell you insurance. You're already dead."

Let's say you have a disease with a very low rate of survivability—95 percent of all people who have your disease die within a certain length of time. Don't look at the percentages and say, "Oh, 95 percent of the people who have this die. Of course, I'm one of the 95 percent." Ninety-five percent of the people hearing that information would say just that. It's probably what makes them part of the 95 percent.

Tell yourself instead, "Five percent make it. Great. I'm in that 5 percent."

Five percent may seem like a small number, but when you multiply it times the number of people who have ever had that particular disease, it's usually a sizable number of people.

If the disease affects, say, 10,000 people each year, that means, statistically, 500 people will make it. You might find it hard to think of yourself as being part of 5 percent, but being one of 500—that's easier. After all, you only have to be *one* of those 500. And there's room for 499 others as well.

Even if only *one* other person survived the life-threatening illness currently visiting you, you can be number two. And if no one else survived it, you can be the first. You've probably always wanted to be first at something. Here's your chance.

Die, my dear doctor,
that's the last thing
I shall do.

LORD PALMERSTON

Be the Perfect Patient

What your doctors want more than anything else is your recovery. Give your doctors what they want. Get well.

While doing that, follow your doctor's orders to the letter. (If you're rebellious, just think of "orders" as "kindly suggestions." If you're competitive, think of them as "challenges.") Take the pills, avoid the foods, do the exercises, take the rest, practice the therapy and be, in a word, cooperative.

In addition to all the things your doctor asks, you can do whatever you like from this book. There is probably nothing in this book that would interfere or conflict with anything a doctor would ask of you. Use the suggestions given here as an adjunct to your regular medical treatment.

Follow your doctor's advice as though it were an affirmation. Do everything he or she asks, no matter what. If you want to make a change in treatment, ask permission first. If the doctor says no, don't make the change. If you're not happy with the care you're getting, change doctors. Don't take it upon yourself to make the change.

Ask your doctor what each pill and procedure is for. As you take the pill or do the procedure, tell yourself, "This pill *will* heal my _____." "This exercise *will* strengthen my _____." "Not partaking in this *will* make my _____ better." Don't just blindly take pills. Add your own energy to each pill, such that—even if it were only a sugar pill—it would still do the intended job.

Following your doctor's orders, to the letter, is a discipline. Doing it with a will to be well will make you well.

*To whom
can I speak today?
I am heavy-laden
with trouble
Through lack of
an intimate friend.*

THE MAN WHO WAS TIRED OF LIFE
1990 B.C.

Consider Therapy

There is a book that neither of us has read—we don't even know if it's still in print. It was popular about twenty years ago, entitled *Psychotherapy: The Purchase of Friendship.*

Consider all the things you classically think a friend to be. (Coleridge: "Flowers are lovely; love is flower-like; Friendship is a sheltering tree.") Alas, as with all rare things, true friendship can be hard to find.

However, the qualities of a willing ear, enduring patience, sound advice, and the knowledge that "someone's in your corner" can be found in a good therapist.

If you have a life-threatening illness, you may find it invaluable to have someone you can just be yourself with, someone with whom you can openly discuss your fears and concerns (especially the ones you're afraid and concerned might frighten and concern your friends and loved ones), someone you can trust. Such a relationship can be—you'll excuse the expression—a lifesaver.

Whether you have a life-threatening illness or not, the goal of conquering a habitual pattern of negative thinking (or any other bad habit) can often use the support, compassion and guidance of a qualified therapist.

Select a therapist as you would anyone you plan to work closely with. Just because they're "A Therapist" doesn't necessarily mean they can help you. Not all therapists are right for all people. We suggest shopping around. Have initial sessions with several. Choose the one you feel most comfortable

*A faithful friend
is the medicine of life.*

ECCLESIASTICUS
6:16

with, a natural empathy for, and, above all, one you can trust.

One guideline in working with a therapist: be honest at all times about all things, including how you feel about the therapist. You can con and make nice and play games and spare the feelings and try to win the approval of everyone else in your life, but with your therapist, just be *you*. Don't pretend or cover up or conceal. Give yourself the freedom to feel, think and express whatever happens to be there.

Therapy is a place to explore yourself, express yourself, and experiment with new behaviors as well as to gain the comfort, support, love, caring and experience of another.

It's a special relationship, one you're worthy of.

There is nothing so powerful as truth— and often nothing so strange.

DANIEL WEBSTER

Consider Alternative Therapies

In addition to the cornucopia offered by the "established" medical community, there is a vast body of healers, chiropractors, nutritionists, massage therapists, herbologists, naturopaths, body workers, acupuncturists, prayer therapists (and on and on and on) available to you.

Once all the medical doctor's advice has been followed, you will probably find time in the day in which you can explore "the other side."

As you do, keep this in mind: the traditional medical establishment and the alternative practitioners do not, for the most part, see eye to eye. Along the borders of their frontiers are, at some places, an uneasy truce and, at others, open warfare. If you choose to go from one camp to another in search of health, know that you will from time to time be in No-Man's-Land.

Both sides may take potshots, at best, and mount major attacks, at worst, on your dalliance with "those other people."

The attitude of the alternative practitioner might be, "Don't take that poison (your prescription medications) your doctor gives you. *That's* what's killing you. Stop it at once!"

The attitude of the established medical doctor is sometimes more benign—he or she has, after all, won the battle of who's best with the vast majority of the public and can afford to be magnanimous. The established doctor may dismiss the entire field of alternative healing with a comment such as, "It's a complete waste of your time and money."

We have found enormous value in each camp. When ill, we wouldn't dream of being without lavish

*The only medicine
for suffering, crime,
and all the other woes
of mankind,
is wisdom.*

THOMAS HENRY HUXLEY

attention from both. Some things, traditional medical science can cure with a bottle of pills. We take the pills. Other things have traditional medical science stumped, but for the natural healer, they are no problem. In those cases, we visit the alternative practitioner.

At some places the lines begin to blur. Traditional medicine begins incorporating alternative medicine, and alternative medicine begins including the traditional. Acupuncture, for example, once pooh-poohed by the traditionalists, is now used and accepted by more and more doctors. Dietary changes—once thought to have no significant effect on one's health as long as one was getting the daily minimum allotment of nutrients—are now, with many illnesses, standard medical practice.

More and more M.D.s are using alternative medicine in their practices, and more and more natural healers are saying, "A good shot of penicillin will clear this up faster than anything else," or, "Have you tried aspirin?"

We applaud this "meeting of the minds." It may be some time before there is One Medicine. The day, frankly, may never come. Even if it never comes, use whatever things work for you from either world and incorporate them in your plan for wellness.

Don't be duplicitous: let each health-care provider—traditional or alternative—know what you're doing with all the others. Some may throw up their hands and shriek, others may shake their heads in disapproval, but let each know you plan to continue. "What can you do for me *in addition* to this?" is what you want to know. If they say, "Nothing," move on. There are plenty of healers on both sides who are flexible enough to augment.

The philosophies
of one age
have become the
absurdities of the next,
and the foolishness
of yesterday
has become the wisdom
of tomorrow.

SIR WILLIAM OSLER
Montreal Medical Journal
1902

What you want is a cure. Where it comes from doesn't matter. Maybe it will be from this, and maybe it will be from that, and maybe it will be from everything together, and maybe it will be from none of those, but your attitude and enthusiasm ("being one with the energy of God") will heal you anyway.

It doesn't matter. Be healed. Be well. That's what all healers worth their salt want.

Two very good—and very different—books on health are Larry King's *Mr. King, You're Having a Heart Attack* and Wesley J. Smith's *The Doctor Book* (with an introduction by Ralph Nader). Mr. King's book tells, in a fascinating first-hand account, what it was like recovering from a heart attack (his recovery included bypass surgery). Mr. Smith's book is an easy-to-read guide to the often-confusing traditional medical community. Mr. King's book is available at all bookstores, Mr. Smith's by calling 800-227-8801 or 213-657-6100.

Avoid what is evil;
do what is good;
purify the mind—
this is the teaching
of the Awakened One.

THE PALI CANON
500-250 B.C.

Take Good Care of Yourself

This may seem redundant—not of what was in the book before, but of what you were taught as a child.

There are certain common-sense guidelines for taking care of yourself—and particularly your body —that we will list here. Most medical types will assume you're doing these things already. Maybe you are; maybe you're not. We won't go into much detail. A part of you will say, "I know what they mean." Compare that inner knowledge with what you are doing and, if necessary, make alterations.

- ◆*Get Sufficient Rest.* How much sleep do you need? Go to sleep. When you wake up, that was enough. Use earplugs if noises bother you.

- ◆*Take Vitamins.* You may need more vitamins than you are getting. Check with your health care practitioner about which ones you need. Minerals, too.

- ◆*Eat Sensibly.* Remember the Four Basic Food Groups? Eat some of each every day. Especially raw vegetables, the food group most Americans omit from their diet. But eating only raw vegetables is not the answer, either. Take the time to enjoy eating your food so that (A) it's fun, and (B) it's properly assimilated.

- ◆*Avoid Fad Diets.* What's wonderful in Asia may not work here. Listen to your body. It will tell you what it needs. Learn to distinguish between wants and needs.

*I have had a good many
more uplifting thoughts,
creative and expansive
visions while soaking
in comfortable baths
in well-equipped
American bathrooms
than I have ever had
in any cathedral.*

EDMUND WILSON

♦*Maintain a Reasonable Weight.* Not too fat, not too thin, but *just right.* Some people, faced with a life-threatening illness, will try to put on weight to "see me through the rough times." Extra weight just creates "rough times" for the body here and now. Maintain a reasonable weight.

♦*Get Some Exercise.* Because this book will find its way to people in all sorts of conditions, we're not going to give any specifics. Check with your doctor.

♦*Get Massaged.* OK, so maybe you didn't learn this as a child, but it's one that will awaken the child within you. Massage releases tensions, frees energy, removes physical blocks and, perhaps most important of all, feels *good.* Indulge yourself. Often. You deserve it.

♦*Take Hot Baths.* In this rush-rush, stand-up world, most people take showers. They're faster. More efficient. Some people haven't been in a hot bath for years. Too bad. They don't know what they're missing. Soaking in hot water, even for a few minutes, relaxes the body and soothes the mind faster than almost anything we know. So take a hot bath every day—whether you need it or not. And more often if you do.

How many cares
one loses
when one decides
not to be something
but to be someone.

COCO GABRIELLE CHANEL

Part II: THE CURE

TWO:

E-LIM-I-NATE

THE

NEGATIVE

We sandwiched this section on eliminating negativity between two sections on adding positivity. We did this for a reason. We firmly believe that the way to more health, wealth and happiness is to *focus on health, wealth and happiness*. This may sound simplistic, but many people try to obtain health, wealth and happiness only by trying to *eliminate* disease, poverty and unhappiness.

One problem with this approach is that the lack of disease is not necessarily health, the lack of poverty is not necessarily wealth and the lack of unhappiness is not necessarily happiness. Sometimes we successfully eliminate a negative and discover we still don't have what we want. "After all that work!" we sigh. And, discouraged, sometimes we return to the negative.

*Give me chastity
and continence,
but not just now.*

ST. AUGUSTINE
354-430

Another problem with trying to get rid of something negative is that we must pay attention to the negative thing we're trying to eliminate. This attention gives it more energy—*our* energy—and sometimes makes the thing seem too great to overcome.

The elimination of negation—and nothing else—to get what you really want can be the long way 'round. If there were one hundred objects on a table, and we wanted you to pick up object 27, we could tell you, as you randomly selected items, "No, don't pick up object 34. No, don't pick up object 29. No, don't pick up object 63."

Eventually, you would get to object 27, and we wouldn't say anything. You might, however, after twenty or thirty "Don'ts," give up. We could hardly blame you. It would have been much easier for us to simply tell you, "Pick up object 27."

That's why we asked you earlier to make a list of the things you *want* in life (your "top-ten" list). Going directly for what you want is a much easier and more effective way of getting what you want than *not* going after what you *don't* want.

You may find "negative" things opposing your goal, however; things that must be sacrificed in order to get what you want. If you want happiness, for example, you must sacrifice unhappiness. Some of these opposing activities may be easy to give up; others may have become bad habits.

When eliminating the bad habits, always keep in mind *why* you are eliminating them. Focus on your *goal*. Rather than saying, "I want to lose weight," tell yourself, "I want a slim, vibrant, healthy body." Rather than, "I want to give up negative thinking," tell yourself, "I want to enjoy all the positive things in my life."

Habit is habit,
and not to be flung
out of the window,
but coaxed downstairs
a step at a time.

MARK TWAIN

Breaking bad habits can be difficult, but it's easier if you remember that what you're adding to your life (the goal) is more valuable than what you're eliminating (the habit).

In releasing yourself from the bondage of bad habits, don't try to eliminate all of them at once. Usually that's just inviting failure. Take them one or two at a time, starting with the ones that will be easier for you to change. When these are under control, take on a few others that may be a bit more challenging. Build upon the strength of each victory. As the saying goes, "It's a cinch by the inch, but it's hard by the yard."

*Over the piano
was printed a notice:
Please do not shoot
the pianist.
He is doing his best.*

OSCAR WILDE

Separate "Noticing the Negative" from "Negative Thinking"

We're not responsible for every thought that passes through our brain, only the ones we hold there. The thought, "What an inconsiderate person," may float through our mind and probably do little harm. It's when we *add to* that thought ("And furthermore. . . .") that we get into trouble.

Maybe the person *was* being inconsiderate. That might be an accurate observation. We noticed him or her do something we would consider inconsiderate. We start the cycle of negative thinking when we add some variation of "and I don't like that" to whatever we observe.

It's important to keep this distinction in mind when breaking the habit of negative thinking. Merely noticing that something is a certain way, and that that way might fall into the negative spectrum of expression, is not necessarily a "negative thought."

To notice a houseplant is withering is an observation, and not necessarily a positive one. From that observation, we have two ways in which we can go.

One, the negative-thinking route: "Oh, the plant is dying. How many times have I told so-and-so to water the plants? Plants always die on me. I must have some plant-killing energy," etc.

Two, the positive-action route: "I'd better water the plant. Apparently I'm not doing enough to impress upon so-and-so the importance of watering the plant; I'll write a note now. Plants don't seem to do

*The first idea
that the child
must acquire,
in order to be
actively disciplined,
is that of the difference
between good and evil;
and the task
of the educator
lies in seeing that the
child does not confound
good with immobility,
and evil
with activity.*

MARIA MONTESSORI

well in that location. Maybe I should get a hardier plant," etc.

Every time we see something and think it might be better another way, we are not necessarily having negative thoughts. It's when we *get negative* and demand that things and people be different from what they are that we get into trouble. This is especially true of areas in which we have the authority or the responsibility to make changes.

You're entitled to have your house or apartment the way you want it—keeping in mind the current limitations of your time, abilities and budget. If you're not willing to invest the time, activity and money in making something the way you want it, then you might as well change the "want." (Once you get good at it, changing "wants" takes less than a second, consumes almost no energy and costs absolutely nothing.)

If you're a parent or a boss, you have certain guidelines within which you can reasonably expect your "charges" to "behave." If you didn't keep them within these guidelines, you wouldn't be doing your job. The challenge is not to get negative while asking others to take corrective actions.

We live in a negative-feedback world. Often, the signal that tells us something needs attention is a negative one. *Noticing* these signals is not negative thinking. *Doing* something corrective about them is positive action. *Getting upset* about them is negative thinking.

The latter method of responding to "negative feedback" is what we're suggesting you keep to a minimum.

*He who has begun
has half done.
Dare to be wise;
begin!*

HORACE
65-8 B.C.

Freedom from Addiction

Negative thinking is a bad habit. For many people it's an addiction. An addiction means something's on automatic—it has control over you; you do not have control over it.

If you think you're not addicted to negative thinking, give yourself a challenge—don't think a negative thought for the next twenty-four hours. Starting now. Not one negative thought. Go.

Don't kid yourself by saying, "Oh, I'm only *noticing* the negative. You said that was OK." Is that all you did? Did you start to get upset about any of the negativity you noticed? If you did, you were doing more than noticing. You were adding to the noticing. What you were adding was negative thinking.

If you were unable to meet that challenge, you might want to take a good, honest look at how much control negative thinking has over your life.

Addictions are not always bad. We're addicted to breathing, for example. We would never suggest breathing be an addiction you might want to eliminate. If you're addicted to negative thinking, it's up to you to decide if negative thinking is, for you, a positive addiction or a negative one.

If you realize you're addicted, and realize it's a negative addiction, you also must decide whether you want to be free from the addiction. Some people must scrape bottom a few times before coming to this point. As the saying goes, "When you're sick and tired of being tired and sick, you'll change."

Others see the value of being free and don't have to plummet the depths before exploring the heights. These people are either blessed or charmed, depending upon your theology.

*If at first
you don't succeed
you're running
about average.*

M. H. ALDERSON

Breaking addictions is not necessarily an easy process. If it were, it wouldn't be an addiction. For the non-smoker to give up cigarettes is easy; for the two-pack-a-day smoker, it's not. One is addicted; the other is not.

For some, giving up negative thinking may be a snap. They've been thinking negatively just because they somehow thought they *should,* that there was some *good* to be gotten from it. Upon learning they can get along marvelously without negative thoughts, they just walk away from it. All they needed was permission.

For others, moving from automatic negative thinking to manual positive focusing and, eventually, to automatic positive focusing is going to be a challenge—maybe the greatest challenge of their lives. And perhaps the challenge of life itself.

It's going to take time, perseverance, patience, forgiveness, determination, discipline, fortitude, enthusiasm, support, endurance and, above all, love. Love for yourself, love for the process, love for what you're creating in place of the addiction and, yes, even love for the addiction itself.

By perseverance
the snail reached the ark.

CHARLES HADDON SPURGEON

Take It Easy, But Take It

Going "cold turkey" on negative thoughts may be too much for some people. The nature of their thinking may be so negative that to attempt a total stoppage all at once would leave them nothing to think about.

In such cases, replacing negative thoughts with a positive focus can be done in more gradual stages. Such a plan consists of two stages—first, taking the new steps and, second, maintaining the progress of the previously taken steps.

The following is not a definitive plan—it's more of a sample one. You can modify the ideas listed here to suit your personal recovery program.

1. Start by simply noticing when you are thinking negatively. You don't have to do anything about it; just observe that it's going on. Rather than saying, "I'm *justifiably upset* over what's happening," say, "I'm sure reacting negatively to this." Begin to notice that it's not *what's happening* but *how you're reacting* that's causing the problem.

2. Pause before thinking negatively. When you notice yourself starting to get agitated about something, tell yourself, "I'm going to wait two minutes before getting upset." Think about something else—something uplifting—for two minutes, *then* get flustered. Gradually work up to three minutes, then four, then five. Even if you start by putting just a few seconds between your automatic reaction and your postponed reaction, you are starting to take conscious control over the response. (It helps to have a prepared list of uplifting thoughts to focus on. Keep your "book of good things" close at hand.)

I know of no more
encouraging fact
than the unquestionable
ability of man
to elevate his life
by conscious endeavor.

THOREAU

3. Declare "negative-free zones" throughout the day. Plan two-minute segments of time throughout the day in which you entertain not a single negative thought. For these brief moments, focus so intently on the positive that negative thoughts have no place to exist. Increase the duration and frequency of these positive periods.

4. Pick minor areas you won't think negatively about anymore. Choose certain categories of thought you simply refuse to think negatively about. Start with areas that are not of critical importance to you. If you only occasionally get upset about, say, television commercials, tell yourself, "No matter how dumb, stupid, boring, condescending or misleading I find a television commercial, I will not get upset about it." Gradually expand your list until it includes all the nonessential areas of your life. Make lists. If you find yourself thinking negatively about an area on your list, stop.

5. Increase the duration of "negative-free zones." Add a minute each day to your positive periods so that, eventually, you only have to think negatively a few times per day. Set aside, say, four periods of fifteen minutes each in which you will think *only* negatively. Postpone all negative thinking until one of these times. Make a list of what you have to think negatively about so you won't forget. Do not add to the agenda items from areas you decided not to think negatively about anymore. Those are off limits, even during "the negative hour." If you don't get to everything on your list within one period, table it until your next meeting. Allow yourself to schedule one "emergency session" per day.

6. Add more central areas of your life to the "verboten" list. Decide you'll do no more negative thinking about, say, an important relationship; then extend it to all relationships. Gradually fold in

Perseverance is more
prevailing than violence;
and many things
which cannot be overcome
when they are together,
yield themselves up
when taken little by little.

PLUTARCH
46-120 A.D.

business, money, health, death. Focus only on the positive aspects of these areas.

Plan it so that everything in your life winds up on the "think only positive" list at the same time the scheduled "negative hours" are reduced to nothing.

Congratulations. You are now free of the addiction of negative thinking.

Will you still have negative thoughts? Sure. But, as time goes on, you'll catch yourself sooner and the periods of negative thinking will be shorter. Also, the influx of positive focusing will lessen the intensity of the negative periods. A situation that would have had you fuming for days now lasts only an hour. Something that would have had you terrified for several hours now has you worried for only a few minutes.

The goal, "I'm going to focus more and more on the positive aspects of life," is a never-ending lifelong adventure.

*Personally I'm always
ready to learn,
although I do not always
like being taught.*

WINSTON CHURCHILL

The Tester

When we're breaking an addiction or overcoming a bad habit, there are times in which the willpower loses its will. Temptation becomes stronger than resolve. Our discipline seems suddenly exhausted, and the habit returns with renewed energy. All the good energy we generated seems to reverse itself. This is known as the Law of Reversibility.

Fortunately, the Law of Reversibility has a predictable pattern. When we know the pattern, we know when to be extra watchful. Our potential for failure is greatest during these periods. Knowing this, we can be particularly vigilant at these times.

When you first consider giving up something you are addicted to, there is often a wavering. "Maybe yes, maybe no. I'm not sure." "I'll try it for a while and see what happens." "I'll do it if it's not too hard." When working with addictions, such attitudes almost always lead to failure. As soon as the first wave of habitual desire comes along, these half-resolves are washed away.

Eventually we say, "This is it. No matter what, this is it. I'm through with this thing that's dragging me down." At that point, the Law of Reversibility begins.

The Law of Reversibility is not the enemy. Far from it. It is the Tester. It tests us to see how strong we have become. It tests us to make sure we have overcome that which we said we would overcome. The tester not only tests; it also awards the diploma of freedom.

The initial enthusiasm of a firm declaration of independence from a bad habit usually lasts about three weeks. Then it's time for the first test. If you

The control
man has secured
over nature
has far outrun his control
over himself.

ERNEST JONES

get through the three-week test, things settle down until about three months after you started. Then another test. If you pass the three-month test, things go along relatively smoothly until six months. Then it's time for mid-term exams.

The mid-terms can be rough. You may find some of the most powerful—and tricky—testing to date. If you succeed at the six-month shakedown cruise, it's generally clear sailing for another six months. Then —one year from when you started—it's time for final exams.

When the Law of Reversibility tests, it's not necessarily a major frontal challenge—some people are better at confronting the big challenges than the hundred daily little ones. The Law of Reversibility can be subtle. In the area of negative thinking, for example, it may tempt you with a dozen only slightly tainted thoughts, progressively building up to a clearly negative one. The negative thought is one you're sure you wouldn't have thought, but, since you're now only a small step away from it, it's much easier to indulge in.

Here are some thoughts that often come during the periods of testing (which are also, by the way, the periods of strengthening). They're followed by a few comments on where the thoughts come from and possible ways to deal with them.

"I can take this, but I'm afraid if it gets any worse I won't be able to take it, so I'll do it just to keep it from getting any worse."

This is fear of fear—we're afraid we're going to get more afraid, so we give in. What we're giving in to, however, will only cause us more fear. Better to face the fear about the fear than face a lifetime of fearful negative thinking.

*Life is like playing
a violin in public
and learning
the instrument
as one goes on.*

SAMUEL BUTLER

"I've had it. I've done enough. If I haven't mastered it by now, the hell with it."

Notice fear's older brother, anger, in there? When being tested, we'll often get angry at our anger, impatient with our impatience and irritable with our irritability. As with being afraid of fear, getting angry at anger is a powerful opponent. If you can, see the humor of the situation. Imagine getting angry at being angry at being angry on into infinity. That's kind of funny—except, of course, when you're in it. The best thing to do is to *move*, to do something physical unrelated to the anger. (More tips on dealing with anger's "dynamic duo" — guilt and resentment — later.)

"I know I'm going to fail—I always do—so I might as well quit now."

Here unworthiness rears its ugly and familiar head. It becomes a self-fulfilling prophecy—I always fail, so why bother trying, therefore I'll fail, therefore I was right: I always fail. Note, too, the fear of failing and the self-anger contained in that sentence. Solution? Tell yourself over and over, "I am worthy of success." If it gets really bad, say it out loud in front of a mirror looking into your eyes. Go through the feeling of unworthiness. Persevere. Endure. On the other side is the worthiness that you truly are.

"I'll regret not doing this later."

You'll probably regret *not* not doing it even more. This one often combines with unworthiness and says, "I'm going to fail sooner or later, so it might as well be sooner because I don't want to miss out on this," "this" being temptation. Keep your goal in mind. Realize you really want your goal more than you want the negative habit—although it may not seem so at the time.

"This is too much work. I'm tired. I give up."

*The condition
upon which God
hath given liberty to man
is eternal vigilance.*

JOHN PHILPOT CURRAN

Getting a little cranky, are we? The price of freedom is whatever it costs, and it's a bargain at twice the price. Therefore, there is never "too much" work. How do we know how much work is enough? When we've achieved the goal, that was enough. Then we *maintain* the goal through vigilance.

"I'm bored."

Boredom is a subtle form of negative thinking that can encompass both anger and fear. Stewart Emery defined boredom as "Hostility without enthusiasm." Fritz Perls called it "The step just before terror." There's a dulling quality about boredom, as though we were numbing something we didn't want to look at. We find that people often experience boredom just before they take a step they don't want to take, but know they must take. It's usually a step of growth, of movement into their own magnificence. But the step may have fear ("I'm going into uncharted territory") or anger ("Why do I have to do this?"), or both, attached. If this is the case, boredom is a welcome sign. All you have to do is find the step toward your own greatness you are reluctant to take, and take it. The boredom goes, and more of your resplendence is revealed.

The Law of Reversibility is nothing to be feared. As all clever students know, it's good to prepare for tests. Knowing when the tests are coming—three weeks, three months, six months, one year—helps you prepare.

When you decide about a certain area of negative thinking, "No more," write it in your calendar. For example, "I'm not going to get upset about TV commercials anymore." Make a note to yourself a week later, "TV commercials?" That means, review what you've done about anger at TV commercials during the week. Have you really monitored your

Perhaps the most
valuable result
of all education
is the ability
to make yourself
do the thing
you have to do,
when it ought to be done,
whether you like it or not.

THOMAS HENRY HUXLEY

displeasure at televised Madison Avenue, or was the decision to do that just "another good idea"?

If you meant it—based upon results—make a note in your calendar three weeks from the time you started. This is a testing period. Be particularly vigilant when watching TV, especially when commercials are pending. If you get past the three-week test without major mishap (no vases thrown at the TV), then make a note in your calendar for three months from the date you began.

When three months rolls around, be extra vigilant several days before and after the actual three-month date. If your TV and patience are both intact after three months, make a note—in red ink—for three months hence, six months from the time of the original launching.

At six months, expect the television commercials to be louder, noisier, more disruptive and deceptive than ever. Expect them to interrupt your favorite movie at your favorite moment. Expect the worst. That way, if you're disappointed, it will be pleasantly so.

Then mark the one-year anniversary of your declaration of freedom. Again, be vigilant. Once passed, reward yourself with a gift—a VCR, say, so you can fast-forward through commercials from now on.

Do this with each of the areas about which you declare "No More Negative Thinking." Your calendar can start to look a little funny. A typical week might include, "TV commercials," "neighbor's dog," "lines," "selfish drivers," "junk mail," "junk phone calls," "answering machines," and "the weather." Someone looking at your calendar might think you were crazy.

Freedom has many costs.

*If we open a quarrel
between the past
and the present,
we shall find that we
have lost the future.*

WINSTON CHURCHILL

Keep Track
of Negative Thoughts

If there's an area of negative thinking causing you trouble, keep track of it. Every time you have a negative thought in that area, make a tick mark on an index card reserved especially for that purpose.

At the end of the day you'll have a good idea how many times you thought negatively about that area. The number may surprise you. Sometimes seeing in black and white how much time we're wasting and how much harm we're doing to ourselves sparks a realization that enough is enough.

You can continue to keep a card a day on that area of thinking. It will chart your progress. You can look back over a month of cards and see how you're doing. It's a good feedback system. If the tick marks are increasing or staying about the same, maybe you need to do more to eliminate them. If the tick marks are decreasing (as they probably will be— simple awareness can be curative), congratulations are in order.

You can keep multiple cards if you like—one for each area of negative thinking.

Watching the number of tick marks decrease is a wonderful reminder that not only *can* you do it, but *you've already done it*. If you can do it in one area, you can do it in any area.

*One's friends
are that part
of the human race
with which
one can be human.*

GEORGE SANTAYANA

The Power of Partnership

Let's face it—taking dominion over one's thought process (the mind is a wonderful servant, but it can be a terrible master) is not only challenging but, well, unusual.

If a friend asks, "What new?" and you answer, "Oh, I'm breaking my addiction to negative thinking so I can be more healthy, wealthy and happy," you may not be met with comprehension—much less enthusiasm. (On the other hand, your friend may say, "It's about time!")

When starting something that's both challenging and unusual, it helps to have support. We've already discussed how helpful a good therapist can be. Later we'll be taking a closer look at the value of groups.

Now we'd like to explore the power of partnerships. Find one or two or three people you can form a close alliance with, people who are moving in the direction of a more positive focus. Form a contractual relationship to support each other unconditionally.

Speak with these people at regular, agreed-upon intervals—daily, if possible. It's sometimes best if at least one of them is not part of your regular circle of family and friends. That way you can be totally candid without fear of offending or of anything being repeated, however unintentionally, to others.

These people are your "buddies." Don't gather too many—you're going for depth of relationship here, not quantity. It is good, however, to have two or three just in case one decides to "drop out." (The road to enlightenment is strewn with the abandoned vehicles of the faint-hearted.)

What do you talk about in your daily or thrice-weekly discussions? Why, the thrill of victory and

*Each friend
represents a world in us,
a world possibly not born
until they arrive,
and it is only
by this meeting that
a new world is born.*

ANAIS NIN

the agony of defeat, of course. "I'm so proud about. . . ." "I really blew it when. . . ." "I can't find a way out of this. . . ." "Well, I found it helpful to. . . ."

Chatter, laughter, swapping war stories, sharing secrets, giving and receiving support—all done in an atmosphere of non-judgment, unconditional caring and the knowledge that "we may not have come here on the same ship, but we're all in the same boat."

Two important points:

One, talk to each of your buddies at least three times a week. This gives a sense of continuity, of flow. You can discuss the details of life that are often forgotten in less-frequent talks. It's the difference between the daytime soap operas and the nighttime soaps.

Two, keep your agreements with each other. If you say, "Tuesday at four," mean it. Keep it. This creates a foundation of trust upon which the partnership can build.

In addition, you may want to take it a step further and gather several people into a regular support group. These can meet less often—every week, say—and have remarkable results.

Tell him to live by
yes and no—
yes to everything good,
no to everything bad.

WILLIAM JAMES

Just Say No

How do you control negative thoughts? One way is just to say, "No," or "Stop." When a negative thought enters your mind, just say, "Stop." When it re-enters—and it will—say, "Stop." When it re-re-enters, "Stop."

It's not a struggle. It's *your* brain, *your* mind, and you have every right to think the thoughts you choose. If a negative habit of thinking has taken over some part of your mind—especially if it's become an addiction—it may take a constant repetition of "Stop" to let it know you're reclaiming your mind for the thoughts you want to think.

Don't let the negative thought even finish its sentence. "Stop" it in its tracks. When it starts up, "Stop" it again. And again, and again and again. Some mental dialogues may sound like a succession of "Stops," and that's fine. You can get to the point where you can anticipate a negative thought entering your mind. Tell it to "Stop" before it can even say the first syllable.

If saying "Stop" mentally isn't enough, say it out loud.

How many "Stops" are enough? As many as it takes. When the troublesome negative thought stops, that was enough.

Necessary,
forever necessary,
to burn out false shames
and smelt the heaviest ore
of the body
into purity.

D. H. LAWRENCE

Burn 'Em

If one area of thought seems to be troubling you more than others, here's a good technique for lessening the power the thoughts have over you.

Get a clean sheet of paper and write down everything terrible about the situation. No one else will read it, not even you, so be as candid as you can. Don't worry about grammar or spelling or penmanship (penpersonship?).

Include all the loaded words you can find. Get *really* negative. Add invectives, insults, profanity, abuses, railings, billingsgates, contumelies, obloquies, revilements, scurrilities, vituperations, curses, oaths, epithets, blasphemies, expletives and swearwords. (Aren't thesauruses wonderful?) Get it all *out* of you and *onto* the paper.

Then burn it.

Don't reread it. Don't make a copy for your files (no matter how eloquently you expressed your plight). Just burn it.

We hope we don't have to drag out Smokey the Bear or Sparkey the Fire Dog to tell you how to do this safely. Over the toilet bowl is a good place. When it gets too close to your fingers, you can safely drop it—and then have the extra satisfaction of flushing it.

As it burns, imagine all those negative thoughts you've ever had about the troublesome situation going up in flames. Feel purified by the flames. As you watch the ashes swirl down the drain, be purified by the water.

If burning is not workable for you, tearing the paper into little pieces works just as well. If you

Burn, burn,
burn like fabulous yellow
roman candles
exploding like spiders
across the stars
and in the middle you see
the blue centerlight pop
and everybody goes
"Awww!"

JACK KEROUAC

can't write, dictating to someone you trust and having them burn it or tear it up works, too. Or tape record whatever's bothering you and destroy the tape.

This process does two things—it gets the negative thoughts *outside* and *away* from you. Then it destroys them.

Don't *think about* whether this will work. *Try it* once and see.

A variation on this is to get a package of cigarette papers. Each time a negative thought appears from your "trouble area," write it on the cigarette paper and burn it over a large ash tray.

It's a good idea to use tweezers or tongs to hold the paper—cigarette paper burns rather quickly, and you've already been burned enough by your negative thoughts.

To save matches, you can have a candle burning in the ash tray. Let the flame represent the Light of who you are, eliminating the darkness of your addiction.

*I do not want people
to be very agreeable,
as it saves me
the trouble of
liking them a great deal.*

JANE AUSTEN

Aversion Therapy

There may be some areas of negative thinking—commonly referred to as "pet peeves" or "Achilles' heels"—that, no matter what you do, seem to evoke either anger or fear or both. We'll just call them your problem areas.

For those areas, it's time to drag out The Big Guns. Here are two Big Guns.

The Rubber Band. Yes. The Rubber Band. One of The Big Guns. Place a rubber band on your wrist. Make sure it fits loosely enough not to restrict circulation, but snugly enough so it won't fall off. Every time you think a negative thought from your problem area, snap the rubber band.

Snap it firmly so that it stings, but not so hard that it leaves welts. We're looking for aversion here, not abuse. Every time you realize you're thinking negatively about the problem area, SNAP!

Yes, this may look silly—especially if you're combining it with other techniques here. Can you imagine what someone would think watching you say "Stop" out loud, snap the rubber band on your wrist, find and make a tick on the proper index card, add the thought to a list of thoughts you will consider during your "negative hour," write the thought on a piece of cigarette paper and then burn it using tongs? Loony Tunes.

But it works.

Exhaust the Response. Here we have our second Big Gun. It's for those problem areas you just can't seem to "get out of your mind." Schedule some time in which you won't be disturbed, an hour or two at least.

Exhaust
the little moment.
Soon it dies.
And be it gash or gold
it will not come
Again in this
identical disguise.

GWENDOLYN BROOKS

Close your eyes. Imagine yourself surrounded, filled and protected by a pure, white light. Know that only that which is for your highest good will take place during this process.

Then think about *nothing* but the problem area. Really get into it. Project ahead to your worst possible scenario; then make it even worse. Growl, scream, cry, tremble. Use all your creativity. Write a horror film and you're the star—the poor, helpless hero or heroine to whom all these nasty things keep happening.

Don't let it get funny. Keep it awful. Your habit wants to think negatively about this, so let it. Give your habit what it wants. Make it nasty. Make it terrifying. Make it horrible. Make it infuriating. Let the villain win over and over. And get away with it. And get rewarded for it.

Don't let any other thoughts come in. Dismiss any uplifting thought, any positive direction, any semblance of reality. Keep it bad, terrible, awful. Don't stray into other problem areas—stay within the one you started on.

After a while, you will finally say, "This is enough!" Open your eyes and see how much time you spent thinking negatively. Fifteen minutes? Half an hour? An hour? However much time it was, close your eyes and *do it for that much longer*.

Force yourself to go over the same rancid thoughts again and again. Play out every imagined terrible outcome, but this time make it even worse. Don't think about something else negative—stay in the original problem area. Don't think positive thoughts. *And don't quit.* You're stronger than the negative thought that's trying to convince you to quit.

Let us train our minds
to desire what
the situation demands.

SENECA
4 B.C.-A.D. 65

After the allotted time, stop. Close your eyes again. Imagine yourself surrounded by a white light. Take a deep breath. Relax. Let this white light fill the area where the problem area was.

This technique fights negativity with negativity. There's an old Hindu saying: "It takes a thorn to remove a thorn." What you're doing is making the negative thoughts about a certain area so negative and so exhausting you won't want to think negatively about it ever again.

During this process you're also experiencing, directly, the results of negative thinking. Some people get physical symptoms—aches, pains, nausea. They see—sometimes for the first time—the direct relationship between negative thinking and emotional and physical misery.

This is not an easy process to do, especially if you really *do it*. As with anything, half-hearted attempts produce half-baked results. It's a powerful process. It should be reserved for those areas of negative thinking that don't seem to be responding to other techniques.

Please, don't attempt this process until you've read the next section, "Latch On to the Affirmative." There you will find additional techniques to protect and heal you before, during and after the process.

I'm glad I don't have to
explain to
a man from Mars
why each day I set fire to
dozens of little pieces
of paper,
and then put them
in my mouth.

MIGNON MCLAUGHLIN

Activities That Contribute
to Negative Thinking

Anything you abuse or overindulge in contributes to your negative thinking. It reaffirms unworthiness. It is a physical affirmation, "I'm not worthy to have control over my life."

We don't have to tell you what those things are for you. You know. They're the ones about which you've said, "I know this is a bad habit, but . . ." and "I wish I didn't do this, but . . ." and "I know this isn't good for me, but. . . ."

It's time to get off your buts.

We'll list some of the popular ones. Yours may or may not be among them, but you'll get the idea. The idea? Stop doing them. Knock it off. It may be killing you. That's the negative way of putting it.

The positive way? You have authority and dominion over your life. You have the power, the right and, yes, the obligation to do only those things you know to be uplifting, life-enhancing and elevating. You are stronger than anything that gets in the way of your achieving this goal.

Smoking. Every smoker knows the multiple health dangers associated with smoking. To continue smoking, then, is an ongoing affirmation of illness. Every time smokers light up, the message they're giving themselves is, "I'm not worthy of health. I'm not able to control my hands, much less myself." Smokers admit by the very action of lighting up that tobacco is a more powerful influence on their lives than they themselves are. This admission may do more harm than the physiological effects of the smoke. Stopping smoking is easy. You simply

*Gluttony is not
a secret vice.*

ORSON WELLES

never put a lit cigarette in your mouth ever again. Period. It's getting to that point that's difficult.

Overeating. You can look at the process as "overeating" or "underdoing" or a combination of the two. The result of putting more energy into your body than you use is overweight. The health risks associated with being overweight are well-known. Carrying around excess baggage puts a strain on just about every muscle and organ in the body. Also, aside from a few "chubby chasers," overweight is not considered generally attractive. Each time too much food goes in, the overweight person is saying, "I'm not worthy of a slim, healthy, attractive body. I'm out of control." Think of the extra weight on your body as stored energy—that's exactly what it is. All that energy is there for you to accomplish what you want. Don't think of the process as *losing* weight but of *using* weight.

Drug and Alcohol Abuse. If you automatically turn to drugs and/or alcohol in times of trouble, or if you find the use of them negatively affecting your work, your relationships, or your general well-being, you're abusing them. The abuse of drugs and alcohol has physiological effects that make it difficult to hold positive thoughts. The residual toxicity of the chemicals in the body makes toxic thinking very easy. This is why drug and alcohol dependence often needs dramatic, outside support—joining AA or checking into a treatment hospital such as The Betty Ford Clinic. The cure, however, is easier than the primary problem—fully realizing that there's a problem in the first place.

Hanging Out with Negative People. Negative thinking is one of the most contagious diseases around. As George Herbert pointed out in 1651, "He that lies with the dogs, riseth with fleas." If you spend time with negative people, sooner or later

*A great many people
have asked how I manage
to get so much work done
and still keep looking
so dissipated.*

ROBERT BENCHLEY

you'll probably be thinking negative thoughts. People often gravitate toward similar people to support their own weaknesses. "But everyone I know _____." You can fill in the blank with the addictive behavior of your choice. "We can't *all* be wrong!" Every lemming thinks that about every other lemming as they head for the cliff. As you change your thinking, you may have to change some of your "friends." We put "friends" in quotes because the severity with which some negative people criticize the positive movement of those around them we would hardly call "friendly." And, by "changing" friends we mean "finding new ones," not "changing the thinking of the ones you have." If they want to change their thinking, they will. Give them a copy of this book. If they're ready, they'll act on it. If they're not, they probably won't even read it. If so, let it go. Changing your own thinking is a full-time occupation.

Compulsive Sex. Some people seek sexual highs the same way drug and alcohol abusers seek chemical highs. Just because sex is "natural" (nonchemical) doesn't mean it can't be abused. It can. *What* you do sexually is not the issue. *Why* you do it is. Is it an expression of love for another, or is it a way of avoiding some inner feeling—loneliness, for example? Compulsive sex, like any lust, carries the following message: "I'm not enough as I am. I need something or someone *out there* to make me happy. Without *that,* I'm worthless."

Workaholic. Is your work an expression of who you are, or is it the only place in your life you feel "in control"? People who work too much often do so from a desperate need to prove they are worthy. "I've done all this—see? I am worthy." The problem is, nothing is ever good enough. As one goal is about to be reached, a new, more difficult goal replaces it. The real problem, however, is that these people never believe they

Life means
to have something
definite to do
—a mission to fulfill—
and in the measure
in which we avoid setting
our life to something,
we make it empty.
Human life,
by its very nature,
has to be dedicated
to something.

JOSE ORTEGA Y GASSET

are worthwhile just as they are. Worthiness is; it doesn't have to be earned or proven. If your work is your play and also your personal expression of life, then spending long hours at it is fine. So many people, however, hide from themselves in work that the term "workaholic" is now part of the language. Everyone knows what it means. Does it apply to you?

Complacency. Chronic inaction in areas of your life you know need attention can be an addiction. Some people become habitually lethargic. Not taking an action becomes an automatic response. This stems from the belief, "I can't do it." Not doing anything "proves" the belief to be true, thereby strengthening the response that there's no reason to respond. The habit of complacency is solved through action—physically moving and doing something. If the habit is strong, it may feel at first as though you're moving through Jell-O—every motion in every direction seems to have something pulling against it. That's the habit. You're stronger than it is. Keep moving. Set yourself a reasonable task and complete it. Then another. Then another. Show yourself you *can* do it, because you can.

PETER: One of the organizations John-Roger founded has two marvelous audio-cassette and book packages especially designed for overcoming bad habits. One is called *Body Balance,* for people with overeating habits, and the other is *Freedom from Smoking.* I've used the *Body Balance* program for the past two months, and I've gone from 178 to 150 pounds "Without Hunger or Any Sense of Deprivation!" as they say in those ads in *The National Enquirer.* These cassette/book programs are $30 each, plus $4 each for postage and handling. You can also have a personal tape made just for you. Make a list of five things you want less of in your life, and five things you want more of. Send them the list, along with $75, and tell them you want "one of those tapes" mentioned in this book. You can order from Mandeville Press, Box 3935, Los Angeles, California, 90051; 213-737-4055. Checks, VISA or MasterCard is fine.

Thanks be to God,
since my leaving
drinking of wine,
I do find myself
much better,
and do mind
my business better,
and do spend less money,
and less time lost
in idle company.

SAMUEL PEPYS
1660

The Twelve Steps

While exploring addictions, we would be remiss if we didn't discuss what is probably the most successful program ever for overcoming addiction—Alcoholics Anonymous.

For more than fifty years, through the AA program, millions of people have found freedom from their addiction to alcohol. The Twelve Steps—as the AA program is called—are so successful that more than 150 other organizations use them to overcome addictions to such things as overeating, compulsive sex, drug abuse and negative emotions.

The core of the AA program is described in the book *Alcoholics Anonymous* (also known as The Big Book). Here are the Twelve Steps, along with the three paragraphs preceding and the one paragraph following them. If you don't have a problem with alcohol, just substitute "negative thinking" (or whatever you feel your addiction to be) for "alcohol."

Remember that we are dealing with alcohol—cunning, baffling, powerful! Without help it is too much for us. But there is One who has all power—that One is God. May you find Him now!

Half measures availed us nothing. We stood at the turning point. We asked His protection and care with complete abandon.

Here are the steps we took, which are suggested as a program of recovery:

1. We admitted we were powerless over our addiction—that our lives had become unmanageable.

2. Came to believe that a Power greater than ourselves could restore us to sanity.

*Some people
have greatness
thrust upon them.
Very few have excellence
thrust upon them.*

JOHN GARDNER

3. Made a decision to turn our will and our lives over to the care of this Higher Power, *as we understood Him, Her, or It.*

4. Made a searching and fearless moral inventory of ourselves.

5. Admitted to our Higher Power, to ourselves, and to another human being the exact nature of our wrongs.

6. Were entirely ready to have our Higher Power remove all these defects of character.

7. Humbly asked our Higher Power to remove our shortcomings.

8. Made a list of all persons we had harmed, and became willing to make amends to them all.

9. Made direct amends to such people wherever possible, except when to do so would injure them or others.

10. Continued to take personal inventory and when we were wrong, promptly admitted it.

11. Sought, through prayer and meditation, to improve our conscious contact with our Higher Power *as we understood Him, Her, or It,* praying only for knowledge of our Higher Power's will for us and the power to carry that out.

12. Having had a spiritual awakening as the result of these steps, we tried to carry this message to others and to practice these principles in all our affairs.

Many of us exclaimed, "What an order! I can't go through with it." Do not be discouraged. No one among us has been able to maintain anything like perfect adherence to these principles. We are not saints. The point is, that we are willing to grow along spiritual lines. The principles we have set down are guides to progress. We

*The best thing
about the future
is that it comes only
one day at a time.*

ABRAHAM LINCOLN

claim spiritual progress rather than spiritual perfection.

No, *You Can't Afford the Luxury of a Negative Thought* is not an AA book, nor are we saying these twelve steps are the *only* way to break addictions. We just wanted to offer them as a way millions of people have found successful.

As far as we know, there is no Negaholics Anonymous (NA) for people who realize they are powerless over their negative thoughts. The closest we've found is Emotions Anonymous. If you consider that a negative thought is usually the step just before a negative emotion, then the goal of EA and the goal of overcoming negative thinking seem in alignment.

One of the advantages of AA and EA and all the other organizations that end with "Anonymous" is the availability of meetings. These meetings provide support, camaraderie and the knowledge "I'm not alone in this."

For more information on AA or EA, call telephone information and ask for the number in your area. Or, write for meeting times and places in your area. (Emotions Anonymous, Box 4245, St. Paul, Minnesota 55104. Alcoholics Anonymous, Box 459, Grand Central Station, New York, New York 10163.)

EA has a book entitled *EA: Emotions Anonymous*. AA has, in addition to *Alcoholics Anonymous,* a long list of publications. Write to the above addresses for information.

*No man chooses evil
because it is evil;
he only mistakes it
for happiness,
the good he seeks.*

MARY WOLLSTONECRAFT SHELLEY

What Are You
Getting from This?

Pain hurts. We as human beings seem prepared to do almost anything to avoid pain. So why do we persist in doing things we know will bring us mental, emotional and/or physical pain?

We've already discussed the role of unworthiness in this seeming paradox—we do unworthy things to prove to ourselves we are indeed "right" about our unworthiness. But there's something else we get, too—a *seeming* benefit, some kind of "payoff."

Return with us now to those thrilling days of yesteryear—childhood. Most children find that when something bad happens to them—an illness, an accident—they get an extra measure of care, understanding, sympathy and love. "Oh, you hurt your finger! Let me kiss it and make it better." Injuries and illness seem to bring a great outpouring of affection.

Given this scenario, it's not difficult for a child to conclude, "Injury and illness get me love." Some children then create accidents and sicknesses because they want the love, the cuddling, the pampering. The payoff.

It's not necessarily a conscious creation—although we'd bet just about everyone at one time or another faked an illness in order to stay home from school. Some part of us learns that illness and accidents bring extra loving, so, if we want some extra loving, one way to get it is to get sick or get hurt. It can become the start of a lifelong pattern.

For the children unwilling to go through physical trauma to get attention, there are other ways.

*I always keep a supply
of stimulant handy in
case I see a snake—
which I also keep handy.*

W. C. FIELDS

Children who get their way by throwing tantrums sometimes grow up to be "rageaholics." When they don't get what they want, they get mad. Even in adulthood, getting angry sometimes gets them what they want. And probably quite a bit of what they don't want.

Some children misbehave to get attention, and even negative attention is better than no attention at all. These children can grow to be adults who go through life causing problems just to be noticed.

Actually, however, all of these payoffs are just *symbols* of loving, not the genuine article. But, when the real thing's not around—and people haven't yet learned how to give loving to themselves—a symbol will have to do.

Some of the popular payoffs people receive from indulging in negative behavior include attention, sympathy, avoidance, excuses, protection, acceptance, approval, martyrdom, deception, control, manipulation and a false sense of strength, security, closeness and accomplishment.

Other seeming benefits are avoiding responsibility, not having to risk, appearing to be right, self-justification, and attempting to prove worthiness. People even boast about their negativity, "I'm working out my problems," "I'm learning," "I'm getting a good emotional release," "Pain equals growth," and "I can handle pain."

You might want to take an honest look at what you're getting—or seeming to get—from whatever negative thoughts, feelings or physical manifestations you put yourself through. If you want attention, for example, that's a good thing to know. If you can find a way of getting attention without having to go through all the negativity, wouldn't that be easier? (Not to mention less painful.)

*There is luxury
in self-reproach.
When we blame ourselves
we feel no one else
has the right to blame us.*

OSCAR WILDE

There's a simple way of getting payoffs directly—asking. "Would you please pay attention to me for a few minutes?" "Could I have some support?" "Tell me you love me." Yes, there's risk involved—you might not get it. But—as you may have discovered—negative behavior doesn't always get it, either.

Make a list of what you're getting from your illness—the payoffs. Work on getting those things more directly. Maybe a part of you long ago learned that illness was the way to get certain things. If you're getting those things anyway, you may be able to let the illness go.

Making such a list requires unflinching honesty. The idea that we're doing something as drastic as a life-threatening illness just to get attention or sympathy or love is a tough realization for some people to have. We're not saying it's true in all cases. Yours may or may not be one. Only you really know.

Maybe you'll look at your list of payoffs and decide you don't need some of them after all. Then cross them off the list and tell yourself, "I don't need _____ anymore. I can let that one go." The part of you that's creating the illness because it thinks you still want those things will listen and respond. This part of you only wants you to have what you want!

Of the remaining things—the things you really do want— give them to yourself. Love yourself. Pay attention to yourself. Nurture yourself. Cuddle yourself. Pamper yourself. Give to yourself so fully that whatever anyone else gives will be just extra icing on the cake.

When you are filled full by your own nurturing, there's no need to seek payoffs "out there." If there's no need to seek payoffs, maybe the illness that's seeking them for you will have no need to stick around.

*People are always
blaming their
circumstances for
what they are.
I don't believe
in circumstances.
The people who get on
in this world
are the people who get up
and look for the
circumstances they want,
and, if they
can't find them,
make them.*

GEORGE BERNARD SHAW

Accountability

This is one of the most misunderstood concepts in modern psychology. If we even hint that maybe people have more to do with creating, allowing or promoting what happens to them than they ordinarily think, some people immediately take the defensive. "You mean this is *my fault?!* Is *that* what you're trying to tell me?"

No, that's not what we're trying to tell anyone. That's the dark side of accountability—fault, blame, guilt. It's also the inaccurate side, a misuse of the concept. It's as though we gave someone a hammer and, instead of using it to hang pictures, the person used it to smash frames. We're then told, "This hammer was a lousy thing to give me." It was not used in the way we intended.

The light side of account-ability is realizing a simple fact—we are far more powerful than we generally like to admit. If we can see, for example, that we had a hand in creating, allowing or promoting something we don't like in our life—even a life-threatening illness—we can also see how we have the power to get rid of it.

The word *accountability* is an ancient Roman term, which meant "to stand forth and be counted." We're merely suggesting you might want to stand forth and be more counted (account-able) in your life.

Take a look at what you're happy with in your life—the people, the things, what you've learned, all you've accomplished. The idea of accountability says you had a hand in all that—that you created, promoted or allowed all of the good in your life. Let's take a look at creating, promoting and allowing.

*It is the commonest
of mistakes to consider
that the limit of our
power of perception
is also the limit of all
there is to perceive.*

C. W. LEADBEATER

Create. You saw it, you wanted it, you went out and got it. Simple creation. Maybe after you got it you didn't want it as much, but you got it nonetheless. It was your doing. If you saw, say, a Picasso reproduction and wanted it for your living room—you saw it, you bought it, you hung it in your living room. Creation.

Promote. Here you were a co-creator. Someone or something else was involved and together you created it, but it might not have happened if you did not have some outside influence. A friend has a Picasso hanging in her living room and offers to sell it to you. You think, "Not bad. Sure, I'll buy it." It ends up in your living room.

Allow. More subtle still. In these situations, you could have said "Stop" or done something earlier on to avoid it, but you didn't. The same friend gives you the Picasso for your birthday. You think it's all right, but not what you would have chosen for the living room. You do, however, have that bare spot on the wall. It's been bare for months. You can't say you don't like it, because that's not entirely true. Besides, it might hurt your friend's feelings. And you can't say you have no place to hang it, because that's obviously not true either. So, accompanied by feigned squeals of delight, the Picasso ends up in your living room. And, over time, you've grown to like it there.

If you look at everything you like in your life, you'll find you had something to do with getting it—even if it was the passive act of allowing it to happen.

Now, apply these same concepts to *small* things in your life you *don't* like. Start small, now. Don't immediately go for the greatest tragedies. That's one of the best ways of dismissing a new idea without having to fully explore it: apply it to the most challenging situation you can think of and see if the

*When a man blames
others for his failures,
it's a good idea to credit
others with his successes.*

HOWARD W. NEWTON

concept holds up. It probably won't. It's as though we were newly introduced to math and suddenly given a problem in trigonometry: "Here. See if your math can solve *this*." Eventually it can, but right now we're at nine minus six equals three.

So start with, maybe, the pictures on the walls you *don't* like. How did they get there, and why are they still there? You probably participated to some degree in creating, promoting or at least allowing them to be there. If it's your apartment and the pictures are still there five minutes from now, you are *allowing* them to remain by not taking them down.

Every so often we like to pretend we are the victim. We had nothing to do with it. We didn't want it. It just happened. That, in fact, is a good definition of a victim: a person to whom life happens. As someone said, "There are three kinds of people in the world: the ones who make life happen, the ones to whom life happens, and the ones who wonder, 'What happened?' " Victims fall (after slipping on a banana peel) into the latter two categories.

Being a victim can become a habit—also the source of some of our best anecdotes. Most stand-up comics make a living from it. Stand-up comedy is mostly one "victim story" after another. Rodney Dangerfield has gained enormous respect telling stories of how little respect he gets.

Victim stories can be fun—although not usually to the person they're happening to until much later. Here are some victim stories, taken from actual auto insurance reports:

> "Coming home I drove into the wrong house and collided with a tree I don't have."

> "The guy was all over the road. I had to swerve a number of times before I hit him."

*Faced with the choice
between changing one's
mind and proving there
is no need to do so,
almost everyone gets busy
on the proof.*

JOHN KENNETH GALBRAITH

"In my attempt to kill a fly, I drove into the telephone pole."

"I had been driving for forty years when I fell asleep at the wheel and had the accident."

"To avoid hitting the bumper of the car in front, I hit the pedestrian."

"An invisible car came out of nowhere, struck my vehicle, and vanished."

"The indirect cause of this accident was a little guy in a small car with a big mouth."

"The telephone pole was approaching. I was attempting to swerve out of its way when it struck my front end."

"The pedestrian had no idea which way to run, so I ran over him."

"I pulled away from the side of the road, glanced at my mother-in-law, and headed over the embankment."

Funny, sure. But also note the lack of accountability in these. That may be one reason they're so funny—we remember the lame excuses we've invented in the past. "The telephone pole was approaching," indeed.

It's fine to tell victim stories, but when we start to *believe* them we get into trouble. Inherent within that belief are the underlying beliefs, "I have no control over my life," "I can't have things the way I want them," and "I'm not worthy of what I want."

Take a look at something—small, now—that you felt victimized by. Tell yourself the story as

*I have been
a selfish being
all my life,
in practice,
though not in principle.*

JANE AUSTEN

though you were telling it to a sympathetic friend, with all the bitter details.

Then take a look at the same story, and see if you can find some areas in which you were accountable—areas in which you helped, even in some small way, to create it, promote it or allow it. You'll probably start seeing little glimmers of, "Well, if I had done this—and somehow I knew it would be best if I did—it might not have happened." Or, "I made it even worse by. . . . " Or, "I could have left half an hour before."

To help find greater areas of response-ability in the story, here are some clues:

1. Go back in time. Usually we start a victim story at the point we can claim to be The Innocent. "I was just standing there, minding my own business when. . . ." If we go back in time, we often find the innocence fades. "I was all ready to go when Paul called and said he couldn't make it." If we go back in time, we might discover we canceled an appointment at the last minute with Paul the week before, or Paul had a history of being unreliable, or Paul mentioned something else might come up—you get the idea. When we go back, we usually find we had some information or experience that takes the bloom off our innocence.

2. What were you pretending not to know? We all have an inner voice that gives us direction. Some people are more in touch with it than others. It's not necessarily the loudest voice "in there," but it's consistent, and usually correct. (We call it the Master Teacher.) Often when something bad happens, people will spontaneously say, "I knew it!"—a highly accountable statement—then they may immediately revert to blame, accusations and other forms of playing victim. What did our Master

*Anytime you don't
want a thing,
you get it.*

CALVIN COOLIDGE

Teacher tell us about the situation? It might have been "Don't go" or "Be careful" and we went and we weren't careful and—*voilà*—a victim story. Not that you should follow every voice inside your head. If, however, you get a message from yourself, it's certainly worth checking out. Also, as you learn to listen to your Master Teacher, you'll be able to distinguish it from the voice of your lust, the voice of your discontent, the voice of your fear and so on. (More on how to call upon this helpful inner voice later.)

3. What thoughts did you have about the situation? Did you, perhaps, through worry or doubt or unwillingness or some other negative thinking, contribute to what happened? Let's use the example of Paul canceling at the last moment. Maybe you had some thoughts: "I'm not sure I want to go to this place," or "I don't know if I want to spend time with Paul," or "I don't feel like going out," or "I wish I could watch TV tonight." Sometimes we think something, our wish is granted, and then we complain because we got the thing we wanted. The same is true of wanting to do something *so much* that our unworthiness surfaces. "I *really want* to go with Paul, but maybe I won't be good enough company for him," or "I never get to go to places with people I really want to, like Paul," or "If I were Paul, I wouldn't go there with me." Remember: what we fear can come upon us.

The more you can look at all the incidents of your life—good or bad—from an accountable point of view, the more you'll reclaim the power you've given to the illusion of "random" situations "out there."

Remember the three magic words: Create, Promote, Allow—C.P.A.—Account-ability.

Continue looking at more and more important situations in your life with the question, "How did I

*The price of greatness
is responsibility.*

WINSTON CHURCHILL

create, promote or allow what's happening here?" And, as things are taking place, step back in your awareness and ask, "How am I creating, promoting or allowing what's happening *right now?*" and "How can I create, promote or allow more of what I really want to take place?"

If you have trouble, consider it a creative puzzle—*"What if* I were accountable?" Also, be *willing* to know. The willingness to know creates the opportunities to know.

There are three aspects to accountability.

1. Act-knowledgment. We simply acknowledge that we had *something* to do with the situation. We "act knowingly." We may not know all that we did—consciously or unconsciously—to set it up, but we're willing to take a look and, when we find something, to acknowledge our part in it. This is not blame, burden, criticism, condemnation, denunciation, censure, reprehension, reprobation or guilt. (We'll get to guilt soon.) It's making a simple statement —"This happened to me, so I must have had something to do with it. I wonder what that was?"—and then exploring and answering the question for yourself.

2. Response-ability. The ability to respond. How could you have more effectively responded to the situation? What effective responses can you take now? Realize that in *any* situation there are response options that will either lift you higher or drag you lower. Why not take the uplifting ones? Sometimes the response is physical, sometimes it's a change of attitude, and sometimes it's both. You always have the ability to respond in an elevating way. Response-ability is not blame. People often ask, "Who's responsible for this?" in tones that clearly mean, "Who's to blame for this? Who can we punish?" That's not how we use it here. Response-ability

*I will not steep
my speech in lies;
the test of any man
lies in action.*

PINDAR
522-433 B.C.

is simply looking at the response options available, and the willingness to choose an uplifting one.

3. Corrective Action. If we learn something, but it doesn't lead to a change in behavior, then we haven't really learned it. It's still a concept. It may be a nice concept, a well-thought-out and brilliantly described concept—but a concept nonetheless. When genuine learning takes place, so does a corrective action. If we say, "Yes, we understand hammers are to be used for hanging pictures, not smashing frames," and we continue to smash frames, we haven't learned. We just comprehend. To become truly accountable, one must be willing to take corrective action. We don't make plans with Paul, or, the next time we make plans with Paul, we have alternate plans in mind. Either of these would be corrective action.

To make plans with Paul and fully expect him to be there is—how shall we put this? We'll give you a choice: (A) unreasonable, (B) dumb, (C) an indication we haven't learned, (D) evidence we're not being accountable to ourselves in our relationship to Paul, (E) all of the above. If you chose (E), you've got the concept down.

Corrective action incorporates forgiving yourself and others. It also includes, if appropriate, making amends. If we spill milk on a friend's floor, we can acknowledge we did it, we can take responsibility for it, but—for it to be true accountability—a corrective action is in order: cleaning up the milk.

≈

As you continue to examine more and more important and "impossible" ("I couldn't *possibly* have

*You'll get no laurel crown
for outrunning a burro.*

MARTIAL
40-104 A.D.

had *anything* to do with that!") areas of your life from an accountable point of view, perhaps you'll start to get a sense of how powerful you truly are.

We use that enormous power to create—consciously and unconsciously, positively and negatively. As we look at our role in creating our life to date and see how much more we had to do with it than we ever thought, we can start to bring more and more of that creative action into conscious awareness. From there, we can direct it in more and more positive ways.

Accountability is a major key in discovering and reclaiming this power.

The good
that I would
I do not:
but the evil
which I would not,
that I do.

ROMANS 7:19

Guilt

Guilt is a miserable game we play with ourselves. It's the price we pay for not taking an honest, compassionate, realistic, forgiving look at the reality of our lives. It's a game of make-believe with bitter consequences.

Guilt is anger directed at ourselves. We get angry with ourselves for something we should have done or shouldn't have done. It accumulates over time. Our self-punishment becomes worse with each repeated occurrence. ("I should have known better!")

Fear steps in. We become afraid of situations in which we might fail to live up to our personal expectations. We're afraid of what we might do to ourselves if we fail again. We're afraid of our own anger.

We avoid new people, situations, activities. We enter into a predictable rut, and then feel guilty we aren't doing more for ourselves. Some people become immobilized with guilt, afraid of doing anything lest they let themselves down again.

This cycle of negative energy—from ourselves to ourselves—can have devastating effects. It poisons relationships, inhibits growth, stifles expansion. It hurts. It can create a feeling not just of unworthiness but of self-hatred. It puts enormous stress on the mind, the emotions and the body.

Over time, it can kill.

Perhaps the most tragic part about guilt is that it is completely, totally and thoroughly unnecessary.

That's the bad news. Now, let's lighten up a bit and discuss the good news: after reading this chapter you'll never have to feel guilty again. You probably

When lovely woman
stoops to folly,
And finds too late
that men betray,
What charm can soothe
her melancholy?
What art can wash
her guilt away?

The only art
her guilt to cover,
To hide her shame
from every eye,
To give repentance
to her lover,
And wring his bosom,
is—to die.

OLIVER GOLDSMITH
1776

will, but you won't have to. Once you understand how guilt works, you don't have to let it do its dirty work on you.

We all have images, beliefs and expectations about ourselves. They usually begin, "I am a good person, and good people. . . ." Most of them are cultural and were "sold" to us when our sales resistance was particularly low—when we were children. We, however, bought them. And we reconfirm the sale every time we feel guilt.

To illustrate, let's take a fairly common example. Say we're on a diet. We want to lose some weight. Chocolate cake is not on our diet. We eat the cake. We feel guilty.

What images or beliefs about ourselves might have been violated by eating the cake?

"I am a good person, and good people take care of their body, keep commitments with themselves, have willpower, only eat things that are good for them, care about how they look, follow through on plans, meet goals, set a good example for others and care about their loved ones." Something along those lines.

This is what good people do, but what did we do? When we describe our guilty actions to ourselves, we tend to exaggerate. Remember the fast-talking, bad-mouthing vulture? It has a field day. Squawk, squawk, squawk. Negative, negative, negative. Bad, bad, bad. Shame, shame, shame. It might sound something like this:

"I'm getting big as a house, and still I ate the fattening, empty-caloried piece of cake after having too much to eat at dinner anyway. I ignored all inner guidance to the contrary. I broke a solemn agreement with myself not to eat fattening foods. I have no willpower. I damaged my body by adding extra fat to it. I already look terrible, but now I'll

*The New England
conscience doesn't stop
you from doing
what you shouldn't;
it just keeps you
from enjoying it.*

CLEVELAND AMORY

look worse. I can't accomplish anything. I never do what I tell myself I'm going to do. I hurt my loved ones by setting a bad example of how to diet after I told them I was going to lose weight. If I don't care about myself, at least I could care about the people I love." And that's just round one.

The pristine image we have of ourselves is repeatedly violated by our despicable actions.

What to do? Well, the small print at the bottom of the "I am a good person . . ." contract reads, "And when I'm not, I'll feel *guilty.*" Feeling guilty lets us prove we're still a good person.

After all, who feels bad about doing bad things, good people or bad people? Good people, of course. Bad people *enjoy* doing bad things! Bad people feel *wonderful* doing bad things.

To prove we're good, we punish ourselves with guilt. This allows us to maintain the image that we *are* all of those wonderful things. By feeling guilty, we're saying, "I did it this time, but I'll never ever do it again. See how much this hurts me? I don't want to hurt this bad again. So I promise, cross my heart and hope to die, I'll never ever do it again."

What guilt does is allow us to pretend something is true about ourselves that, based upon results, *simply isn't true.* It lets us maintain an inaccurate image about ourselves, an image that does not match our actions.

Are we saying we're not good people? Not at all. That part's true. The falsity begins with ". . . and good people. . . ." Do good people always, only and exclusively do those things? Of course not.

Do good people sometimes not take care of their bodies? Sure. Do good people sometimes break commitments with themselves? Yes. Do good people

I have,
all my life long,
been lying till noon;
yet I tell all young men,
and tell them
with great sincerity,
that nobody
who does not rise early
will ever do any good.

SAMUEL JOHNSON

sometimes lack willpower? Absolutely. Do they always only eat things that are good for them? Ha! Do they always care about how they look? Hardly. Do they always follow through with their plans, always meeting their goals? Nonsense. Do they always set a good example for others? Of course not. And do they always care about their loved ones? Afraid not.

The truth is, good people *do* do all those good things *and sometimes they don't.*

The further truth is, you *are* a good person. You do a lot of good things. And sometimes you don't. Does that alter the fact that you're good? Not at all. It merely confirms the fact that you're *a human being.*

Guilt not only protects an erroneous gilt-edged image we have about ourselves, it also *lets us do the thing we felt guilty about doing again.* When we've "paid the price" for our "crime," we're free to do it again *as long as we're willing to pay the price again.* The price? More guilt. "How badly do I want the cake? Is it worth two hours of guilt? No. I'll take a smaller piece and only feel guilty for an hour."

We plea-bargain with ourselves before we even commit the crime.

So, guilt as it's popularly practiced in our culture (A) feels lousy, (B) has devastating effects on our mind, emotions and body, (C) maintains an inaccurate image of what "good people" are and do, (D) allows us to believe one thing about ourselves while doing something completely contradictory, and (E) lets us continue doing things that may not be in our best interests.

Talk about your nonproductive activities. And what good is there in guilt? Guilt is anger at ourselves. Anger is the energy for change. Therefore,

MAE WEST: For a long time
I was ashamed
of the way I lived.

"Did you reform?"

MAE WEST: No;
I'm not ashamed anymore.

guilt can be used as the energy for personal change. We can use the energy to change the image of how we should be, or change the action we felt guilty about.

There is also the *twinge* of guilt we feel before taking part in the contrary action. That's a much quieter sensation. Easy on the mind, body and emotions. That twinge of guilt is our friend. Just as the warning light in the car reminds us to get gas, this twinge of guilt tells us when we're about to trigger the more painful form of guilt.

When you're about to do something—or even contemplating something—and feel that twinge of guilt, stop. The twinge of guilt is telling you you're getting off balance. You are about to take an action that would violate an image you have about yourself.

At this point, rather than plea-bargain or blindly rush ahead, do one of two things—*change the image or the action*. You can change the image you have about yourself, bringing it up to present-day reality, *or* you can not take the action that violates your image.

If you do one or the other, you will not have the punitive, painful, lasting guilt.

Take chocolate cake, for example. You have lots of options for changing the image. You could change your belief to include occasional forays into cake-dom, or you could decide your weight is fine as it is and call off the diet, or you could promise to take a long walk after dinner, or any other alteration of the image that currently says, "Chocolate cake is *verboten*." Changing the action is simple: don't eat the chocolate cake. (Once again: simple, but not necessarily easy.)

If you do one of those two things—change the image or the action—you will not feel guilty about

*If error is corrected
whenever it is recognized
as such,
the path of error
is the path of truth.*

HANS REICHENBACH

eating the chocolate cake. If you don't change the image or the action, it's back to the old cycle of crime and punishment.

In addition to the obvious physical, emotional and mental benefits of breaking the cycle of guilt, here are three others:

1. It gives us a more realistic view of ourselves and humanity in general. One of the values of the recent popularity of "tell-all" biographies is that they let us see that good people—great people—who have accomplished laudable, extraordinary things, are human beings, too. We all have a full complement of quirks, foibles, preferences, habits, lusts and temptations. Sometimes they serve us; sometimes they don't. And so what? It's the human condition. Nothing to get upset about.

2. It lets us set more reasonable goals. So we eat a piece of chocolate cake now and again. So we don't lose three pounds a week. Maybe we lose only one pound a week. That's still 52 pounds a year. We can take it easier on ourselves, taking time for what we once called "failure" and now call "diversion."

3. It lets us do the things that are truly important. By not kidding ourselves and cluttering up the daily "agenda for action" with pipe dreams, we can focus more clearly and with greater determination on the truly important tasks at hand. If our mind is not cluttered with twenty or thirty things we "should" be doing, it's easier to do the two or three things that really must be done.

Freeing yourself from guilt is a gradual progression. Guilt, for most people, is an automatic response. When it goes off—and it will—don't feel guilty about feeling guilty. And if you do feel guilty about feeling guilty, don't feel guilty about feeling

*Life teaches us to be less
harsh with ourselves
and with others.*

GOETHE

guilty about feeling guilty. And if you do feel guilty about feeling guilty about . . .

Some people create a New Enlightened Image of themselves that says, "I am a good person and I no longer feel guilt." Please, change that image before you even create it. Probably the most accurate one you can have is, "I am a good person and I feel what I feel," because that's the way it seems to go. Sometimes it's guilt and sometimes it's glory.

If you're in a cycle of guilt, there are ways out. But first, let's talk about resentment.

Man must evolve
for all human conflict
a method
which rejects revenge,
aggression and retaliation.
The foundation
of such a method
is love.

MARTIN LUTHER KING, JR.

Resentment

Resentment is a miserable game we play with ourselves and others. It's the price we pay for not taking an honest, compassionate, realistic, forgiving look at the reality of other people's lives. It's a game of make-believe with bitter consequences.

Resentment is anger directed at others. We get angry with others for something they should have done or shouldn't have done. It accumulates over time. Our punishment becomes worse with each repeated occurrence. ("They should have known better!")

Fear steps in. We become afraid of situations in which people might fail to live up to our personal expectations. We're afraid of what we might do to others if they fail again. We're afraid of our own anger. We avoid new people, situations, activities. We enter into a predictable rut, and then feel resentful because we aren't doing more for ourselves. Some people become immobilized with resentment, afraid of doing anything lest they "let others have it" again.

This cycle of negative energy—from ourselves to others—can have devastating effects. It poisons relationships, inhibits growth, stifles expansion. It hurts. It can create a feeling not just of unworthiness but of hatred. It puts enormous stress on the mind, the emotions and the body. Eventually, it can kill.

Perhaps the most tragic part about resentment is that it is completely, totally and thoroughly unnecessary.

Sound familiar? No, you weren't having an attack of *déjà vu*. What we just said about resentment is the same thing we said about guilt a few pages ago.

Hating people
is like burning
your own house down
to get rid of a rat.

HARRY EMERSON FOSDICK

I never hated a man
enough to give him
his diamonds back.

ZSA ZSA GABOR

Resentment and guilt are the same process. The difference is, with guilt, *we* don't live up to the images we have about how *we* should be, and with resentment, *other people* don't live up to our images about how *they* should be.

The images are ours. The anger is ours. We're judge, jury and executioner. With guilt, the judgment goes against us. With resentment, the judgment goes against others. (All that we're about to say about resenting *people* works for *things*, too—cars, stereos, weather, nature, food, TV commercials. For the sake of clarity we'll just talk about people. Please add "and things" at key points.)

When we resent others, we are protecting our image of how they should behave. Based upon results, the image is false. But we protect the image because, after all, it's easier to keep our image and resent them for not measuring up than it is for us to change our image.

We have a lot invested in our image of how others should behave. We inherited the basic plan from our parents and teachers. Then we spent years refining it. Now that all the variables are in place, why should we change our shoulds, musts and have-tos about others just because some inconsiderate people are too lazy to measure up?

The problem is, of course, the anger. Almost invariably, it does more harm to us than to the people we're feeling it about. Earlier we quoted, "The love I give you is secondhand—I feel it first." The same is true of hate. From a cardiovascular point of view, the most dangerous and damaging emotion to have is anger. It's one of the most unpleasant emotions, too.

The solution? Once again, the six magic words—change the image or the action. Except this time it's shortened to three—*change the image*.

*It is easier to fight
for one's principles
than to live up to them.*

ALFRED ADLER

With anger at ourselves, we have an option. We have, after all, the right to change our actions if we so choose. We do *not*, however, have the right to change anyone else's actions. We, therefore, have only one solution—change the image.

There are two situations in which you have the right to change another's actions—when you're the parent or when you're the boss. In those situations, you may have not only the right but the obligation to change behavior. You will find, however, that if you change your image of how they should be behaving before attempting to change their behavior, you will get better results and feel better in the process.

With resentment, *always* change the image, and *only* if you're the parent or the boss do you have a right to change the action.

(Some people add an exception to the above list: "If I'm in a relationship, I get to change the other person's behavior." No. Especially no. That's the cause of more disastrous relationships than probably anything else. Accept your loved ones; don't change them.)

To eliminate resentment, we add ". . .and sometimes they're not" to all the images we have about other people. "Friends are always honest, and sometimes they're not." "Doctors are always meticulous, and sometimes they're not." "Waiters are always friendly, and sometimes they're not." When you feel resentment, you know the other person is behaving in the ". . . and sometimes they're not" area of your images.

Why do you suppose Jesus told his followers, "Love your enemies, bless them that curse you, do good to them that hate you, and pray for them which despitefully use you, and persecute you"? (Matthew 5:44) Do you suppose he said it primarily

*He that is
without sin among you,
let him first cast
a stone at her.*

JOHN 8:7

Fifty-four-year-old Ellsworth Donald Griffith told a Des Moines, Iowa judge that he was too old to go to prison, and asked instead for a public stoning for his conviction for terrorizing his former employer. His one condition was that only those without sin be allowed to cast stones. The judge sentenced him to 5 years in prison.

THE WORLD ALMANAC
& BOOK OF FACTS

so those nasty persecuting people could enjoy the benefit of his disciples' love, blessings, goodness and prayers? Maybe, maybe not.

We think he advised his disciples to love their enemies because it was good for *the disciples.* That way, no matter *what* happened to them, they would always be loving, blessing, doing good and praying—not a bad life.

That the people around you will feel better when you stop resenting them is a secondary benefit. That *you* will feel better when you're not resenting others is the primary gain.

Again, we have an inner friend to tell us when it's time to change our images. It's a twinge of resentment. The twinge of resentment is quiet, like the twinge of guilt. It will gently tug and remind you, "It's time to change your image about. . . ."

If you don't change the image at that point, you'll probably be off on resentment, running the gamut from ticked off to seething. That's OK. As soon as you find yourself doing it, back off, take a deep breath, and take one (or all) of the steps listed in the next chapter.

When you realize that your resentment is based not on others' *actions,* but on your *reactions* to their actions, it's a day for celebration. Yet another "bad thing" you thought happened "out there" comes directly under your influence. You reclaim even more of your power. You have more mastery, more control over your life. Not because you can control others' actions, but because you're learning to modify your own re-actions.

Another word for it is freedom.

*BELINDA: Ay, but you
know we must return
good for evil.*

*LADY BRUTE: That may be
a mistake in the translation.*

SIR JOHN VANBRUGH
1698

Ways Out of Guilt and Resentment

Whenever you're caught in the cycle of guilt or resentment, here are a few techniques to help get you back on track. We'll be discussing most of these points in detail later, but here's a capsule summary.

1. Change the Image. We know we said this several times, but it bears repeating. Ask yourself, "What am I upset about?" and let whatever it is be OK. Accept it. Give yourself and others permission to do what you or they *have already done.* Allow your image to adjust to reality. You don't have to *like* it, but you don't have to hate it either.

2. Forgive. Forgive the others and forgive yourself. Forgive yourself for whatever you did. Forgive the others for whatever they did. Then forgive yourself for judging yourself and others.

3. What's the Payoff? Are you *enjoying* the intensity of it all? Are you feeling "right"? What are you getting from this?

4. Move. Do something physical. Run around the block. Clean a closet. Do aerobics. If you're in bed, move your arms a lot. Get the energy moving.

5. Refocus. Yes, once again we suggest: focus on something positive.

6. Is It Worth Dying For? If you had a choice—defending that inaccurate image or your life—which would you choose?

7. Be Grateful. Find something to be grateful for—anything.

8. Observe. Observe the anger or resentment. Observe the *feeling*. Don't do anything to it or with it.

*Humor is
a prelude to faith and
Laughter is
the beginning of prayer.*

REINHOLD NIEBUHR

Don't pay attention to the thoughts feeding the feeling. Pay attention to the feeling itself.

9. *Breathe*. Resentment and anger are usually felt in the stomach, abdomen or chest. Take slow, deep breaths into these areas. Stretch the area as you breathe in. Imagine a white light going in with each breath and filling the area.

10. *Surrender*. Let go of the struggle. Don't *try* to get rid of the feeling. Just surrender. Flow with it.

11. *Sacrifice*. Give it up. You thought sacrifice meant giving up the good things? It can also mean giving up the not-so-good things. Sacrifice your guilt and resentment. Give them up.

Use any or all of these techniques, in any order, when you feel "stuck" in guilt or resentment. If these don't work, declare an emergency session of "exhaust the response." (See "Aversion Therapy.")

The important thing is not getting rid of guilt and resentment as quickly as possible. The important thing is *learning* about yourself. What "shoulds," "musts" and "have tos" hold the most control over you? Where did they come from? What can you do about them? What are you getting out of the guilt and resentment? What are the payoffs?

Guilt and resentment are the primary expressions of anger. Anger and fear are the primary "negative" emotions. Learning to master them can take time. Be patient with yourself. Tell yourself you're doing a wonderful job.

You are.

Nothing is so certain
as that the evils of
idleness can be shaken off
by hard work.

SENECA
4 B.C. - A.D. 65

Depression

We're not going to discuss "clinical depression" here. That's a medical condition and is best treated by a doctor. If you feel you may be clinically depressed, by all means discuss it with your doctor and/or therapist.

The depression we're talking about is the run-of-the-mill depression—the blues, the blahs, the sort of feeling people refer to when they sigh and say, "I'm depressed."

There's a certain heaviness to depression. A lethargy. A sluggishness. You feel as though you've been transported to a planet with six times the gravitational pull of Earth.

The easiest cure for that kind of depression is movement—active, physical movement. Get up and do something. Wash the car. Do the laundry. Exercise. Take a walk. Anything.

Get your energy moving—it's been stagnant for too long. Getting the energy moving helps. Doing something that could be considered even remotely productive will help even more. You'll get the physical boost of the movement and the psychological boost of the accomplishment.

Don't wait until you "feel" you have enough energy to move—start moving and the energy will be there. Energy follows demand. When we demand of the energy by taking a physical motion, it's there.

Depression? Move it to lose it.

*If you can't say anything
good about someone,
sit right here by me.*

ALICE ROOSEVELT LONGWORTH

Watch What You Say

Don't we have a funny language? We say, "Watch What You Say," and everybody knows what we mean. In fact, it's very hard to *watch* what you say, unless you're standing in front of a mirror. The idea we want to convey is *monitor* what you say.

Listen to yourself as you speak. Note especially any time you (A) let your words limit you, or (B) set something in motion you might not want in motion. Sentences along the lines of "I can't take this anymore," "I'll never get it right," "This is killing me," or even "It's to die for!"

We are powerful creators. What we speak can become reality. When it comes to pass, we say, "Now, I *know* I didn't create this!" Oh no? Remember six months ago when you said, "I need to lose ten pounds; I don't care how, but I need to lose ten pounds"? The "how" is extensive dental work that will keep you from eating very much for a few weeks. By the time it's over, you'll have lost ten pounds. "But I didn't want it *this* way!" "I don't care how," you said. This is the how.

If you find yourself saying something you don't necessarily want to take place, quickly say, "Cancel," or "Deflect," or any other word you understand to mean, "Cancel that order," or "Don't put what I just said in motion." Then say what you really want.

Put yourself on a one-minute time delay. Remember Yul Brynner as the Pharaoh in *The Ten Commandments*? Remember when he gave a command? "So let it be written," he would say in deep, pharaonic tones, "so let it be done." Give yourself sixty seconds to cancel an order before the scribe within you hears, "So let it be written, so let it be done."

Elysium is as far as to
The very nearest Room
If in that Room a Friend await
Felicity or Doom—
What Fortitude the Soul contains,
That it can so endure
The accent of a coming Foot—
The opening of a Door—

EMILY DICKINSON

Yes, as my swift days
near their goal,
'Tis all that I implore:
In life and death
a chainless soul,
With courage to endure.

EMILY BRONTE

Endurance

If something can't be removed, ask for the strength to endure it. There is an old saying, "That which doesn't destroy us makes us stronger." A life-threatening illness can be a strengthener, not necessarily to the body—maybe so, maybe not—but certainly to the character and to the spirit.

Robert Louis Stevenson prayed: "Give us grace and strength to forbear and to persevere. Give us courage and gaiety and the quiet mind."

If all of our tribulations were taken from us, we would never grow. It would be crippling. As Oscar Wilde said, "When the gods choose to punish us, they merely answer our prayers."

When we learned to walk, we stumbled, fell, struggled, fell again, bumped our heads—it went on for months. Our parents, who could easily have lifted us and carried us, instead encouraged us. They comforted us when we fell, but put us back on our feet and stepped back, saying, "Come on, we know you can do it."

We may have wondered, "Why are they doing this to me? Why are they putting me through this torture? Why don't they just pick me up and take me with them?" Without this "torture," however, we never would have learned how to walk.

Perhaps there's a new level of "walking" ahead of us, one that requires this new "torture." If that be the case, then all we can ask for is the strength to endure—not just physically, but in wisdom, too. The wisdom that knows, as written in Psalm 40:5,

"Weeping may endure for a night, but joy cometh in the morning."

*Alas, I know if I ever
became truly humble,
I would be proud of it.*

BENJAMIN FRANKLIN

Part II: THE CURE

THREE:

LATCH ON TO THE

A-FIRM-A-TIVE

Ah, now we're ready for the really good stuff—the affirmations of living, of loving, of health, wealth, happiness and joy.

We're not quite sure what Johnny Mercer meant by "latch on to" in the lyric of his song. We doubt if he meant "become attached to." *We* certainly don't mean it that way. If joy, loving and happiness become new "shoulds," "musts," and "have-tos," we are, once again, "doomed before we even take the vow."

Humans have a natural ability to want things, to desire, to aspire, yearn, and long for. Any attempt to diminish this natural desire, we find, is (A) counterproductive, (B) frustrating, and (C) so improbable it borders on the impossible.

Some people desire desirelessness with such a passion that they actually *increase* their ability to desire. What we do we become stronger in, you'll remember, and these people yearn so much and so

Ah, but a man's reach
should exceed his grasp,
Or what's a heaven for?

ROBERT BROWNING

often to have no more yearning that their ability to yearn becomes astronomical.

We see nothing wrong with the human trait to desire. In fact, we consider it part of our success mechanism. Becoming *attached* to what we desire is what hurts. If you *must have it* in order to be happy, then you are denying the happiness of the present moment.

If, however, you're focusing on the positive aspects of the reality around you while traveling in the direction of what you want, we see no problem in that at all. It sounds to us like a good way to live.

Rather than trying to diminish desire, we suggest you desire what you really want more of. *Desire* happiness. *Aspire to* gratitude. *Long for* health. *Crave* compassion. *Seek* satisfaction. *Lust after* God (however and whatever you perceive God to be). *Want* to love yourself, others and everything around you more and more each day.

These are laudable goals. They're also fun, challenging, exciting, and not only within your grasp but also within your reach.

All nature is but art
unknown to thee,
All chance,
direction which thou
canst not see;
All discord,
harmony not understood;
All partial evil,
universal good;
And, spite of pride,
in erring reason's spite,
One truth is clear,
Whatever is, is right.

ALEXANDER POPE

A Is for Acceptance

Acceptance is such an important part of happiness, contentment, health and growth that some people have called it "the first law of personal growth."

The world goes on, people do what they do, things do what they do, and, for the most part, our only choice in all this is, "Do I accept it or not?" If we accept it, we flow with it. We allow life to do what it's already doing.

If we refuse to accept it, we usually feel pressure, pain, frustration, anxiety and dis-ease. We struggle with what is. The struggle, for the most part, takes place within us—where it also does the most harm.

Acceptance is not the same as *liking* or *being happy about* or even *condoning*. It is simply seeing something the way it is and saying, "That's the way it is." It's seeing what's going on and saying, "That's what's going on." It's looking at something that's happening and saying, "That's what's happening."

Acceptance is realizing that to do *other* than accept is (A) painful and (B) futile. Through non-acceptance we try to control the world. We want our "shoulds," "musts," and demands to somehow rule the world. It doesn't work. It simply does not work.

To prove how futile the struggle to control the world is, get up tomorrow at 4 a.m. and try to keep the sun from rising. Do *everything* you can to keep it from coming up. Struggle like mad. You won't be able to delay its scheduled ascension for so much as a fraction of a second.

Maybe you don't want to control the turning of the earth; you just want to control the world around

*The more
the marble wastes,
the more the statue grows.*

MICHELANGELO

you. Good luck on that, too. The truth is, we sometimes can't even control ourselves—that part of the universe we have the most direct authority over. If we can't control our own thoughts, feelings and physical reactions, how can we hope to control others?

Nature goes on being nature in its own natural way. We have very little control over it. What do we have control over? Ourselves. The space contained within the skin of our body. We can work to make that environment as loving, joyful, peaceful and wonderful as we like. That in itself is a lifelong project, and a worthy one at that.

The rest—the outer environment—does what it does. There's not much more to do than say, "It's doing what it's doing."

If we do want to change something, one of the best starting points is acceptance. The sculptor begins by accepting the block of marble as it is, and then removes everything that isn't a statue. When asked how to sculpt a horse, one artist explained, "I see the horse in the stone; then I take away everything that's not the horse."

Michelangelo's *David* was carved from a flawed block of marble. Another sculptor had begun work on the block and abandoned it. There was a deep gash in the side, making the stone "unacceptable" to sculptors for decades. Michelangelo, however, accepted the marble—gash and all—and created one of the marvels of humankind.

We begin with acceptance and move from there. This includes acceptance of ourselves. We are, please remember, a part of nature. We can be as contrary as a thunderstorm on a picnic. That "natural" part of us has its own rhythms, its own

There is no good
in arguing
with the inevitable.
The only argument
available with an east wind
is to put on your overcoat.

JAMES RUSSELL LOWELL

timelines and its own agenda. While bringing this "animal" under control, we must learn to accept.

This "natural" part of us most people call the body, and that's accurate, providing that you remember the body includes the brain that thinks the thoughts and the nerves that feel the feelings. Thoughts and feelings are a necessary part of the human animal.

The "natural" part of us thinks the Fight or Flight Response is *terrific*. Eons of genetics have told it so. We now must gradually convince "it" that the Love and Acceptance Response is more valuable for its survival as an animal. It also feels better.

This "convincing" we call *education*. The source of the word is *educare*, "to lead forth from within." It's the gradual process of leading from within rather than being led from without.

In that process of *teaching* acceptance, we must *practice* acceptance. Set a good example for yourself. Learn to accept whatever you do. This, of course, is not *carte blanche* to run roughshod over others or to hurt yourself. It's just a realization that, being human, we're going to do things we're not going to like (and by "doing," we mean *all* levels of doing, including thoughts and feelings), and we might as well accept those, too.

Learn to accept even your lack of acceptance. When you're not accepting something, accept your nonacceptance of it. Can't accept your nonacceptance? Then accept the fact that you can't accept your nonacceptance. If the bad stuff like guilt can pile up in layers (feeling guilty about feeling guilty about feeling guilty), so can the good stuff (accepting the fact that you can't accept your nonacceptance).

I travel light; as light,
That is, as a man can
travel who will
Still carry his body
around because
Of its sentimental value.

CHRISTOPHER FRY

Yes, it gets funny, and it certainly can be fun. That's one of the keynotes of acceptance: a certain sense of lightness. As you accept the heaviness, you begin to feel "the unbearable lightness of being." Accept that, too.

With acceptance, you can't set some things aside and say, "I'll accept these, but not those." Acceptance is unconditional. You can *like* one thing more than another—that's preference, and that's fine—but acceptance is not excepting anything. (Actually, it's easier that way. You don't have to *remember* what to and what not to accept. If it's there, accept it. Simple.)

Schedule acceptance breaks throughout the day. Give yourself an acceptance break right now. Accept *everything* around you, everything inside you, everything everything. Accept your thoughts. Accept your thoughts about your thoughts. Accept your thoughts about your thoughts about your thoughts. Accept whatever feelings you have, whatever sensations are in your body. Don't try to change any of it—*trying* to change is a form of nonacceptance.

Accept your surroundings, your physical environment. Accept the room, its furnishings, the smells, the sounds, and the occupants. Accept your thoughts about whatever's not there, too. (If it's not there, it's a thought: a memory or a fantasy.) Accept your memories and your fantasies and your demands and your musts about how it should be.

Accept all the things you did but wish you didn't do, and all the things you didn't do but wish you did. Notice that these decisions about what's hot and what's not about an activity (or inactivity) are thoughts, too. Accepting thoughts—including the negative ones—is an important step toward greater joy.

And greater health.

*To be conscious that we are
perceiving or thinking
is to be conscious
of our own existence.*

ARISTOTLE

*To become the spectator
of one's own life is to
escape the suffering of life.*

OSCAR WILDE

Learn to Observe

Observation is a tool of acceptance. To observe is to think, feel, taste, smell, see and hear without attachment, without attempting to manipulate the outcome, without taking sides.

All you do is observe. Simply "be with" whatever information your senses present to you. If your mind goes off on judgments and evaluations, observe that. Don't get involved with the thoughts; don't try to change them; just observe them.

As you learn to observe, you become more and more in touch with that part of you that's *you*—the part beyond the body, beyond the mind and beyond the emotions. When you stand back and observe, you'll begin to experience a *you* that isn't your mind and its thoughts, isn't the emotions and their feelings, and isn't the body and its sensations.

This is a strange thing to write about, because we're communicating it through *words,* which are part of the mental process. And the mind does not like to relinquish its authority or to admit that there's something more basic to you than it.

You'll understand by doing. After fifteen or so minutes of consciously observing, you may begin to notice the part that's doing the observing. Give yourself a period of time in which you won't be disturbed. Decide for that period of time to do nothing but observe. Sit or lie comfortably. Now, be still and be.

The mind will present "good ideas" to do something else. Don't do anything about them; just observe them. The feelings will want something more exciting to feel about. Don't fulfill them; observe them. The body will demand attention. Don't attend to it; just observe the demands.

I am a camera
with its shutter open,
quite passive, recording,
not thinking.
Recording the man shaving
at the window opposite
and the woman in the
kimono washing her hair.

CHRISTOPHER ISHERWOOD

If you want to change positions, don't. Just observe the desire to change positions. If you have an itch, don't scratch it. Observe the itch. Your mind, body and emotions may throw little—and sometimes not so little—temper tantrums. Observe the tantrums. Observe the inner kicking and screaming. These may be what has controlled you for some time now. Gain authority over them. You gain authority by doing nothing. Just sitting and observing.

The game is this: The mind, body and emotions say, "I'm going to get you to move before the fifteen minutes (or whatever time you set for yourself) is over." *You* say, "No, I'm not." And the game begins. You may say, "Oh, it's easy not to move for fifteen minutes." Most games look easy from the sidelines. Play the game and see.

If it's easy, congratulations! If it's not, don't be surprised. The same things that trouble you during this process are probably the same things that trouble you in life: the "shoulds," "musts," "have-tos," and the demands of your mind, body and emotions.

The solution? Observation. Simply observe. You'll learn a lot about yourself. And, you'll learn a lot about the parts of yourself that aren't your self.

You can, if you like, extend the "sitting observation" to "moving observation." As you move through life, observe everything. Observe your reactions to everything. Observation is a primary tool of awareness. The more you observe what you're now unconscious of, the more conscious you become.

Behold: Consciousness.

Thinking to get at once
all the gold
the goose could give,
he killed it and opened it
only to find
—nothing.

AESOP

Patience

There is a saying that has found its way onto plaques, posters, buttons, bumper stickers, mugs, T-shirts and balloons. Any idea with such universal appeal must have more than a modicum of truth in it. This saying does.

Be patient. God isn't finished with me yet.

Patience is the compassion we have for the distance between what we are now and what we know we can be.

Because we have such fertile imaginations, we can envision ourselves scaling mountains one moment and swimming oceans the next. To get from the mountain top to the beach, however, takes a certain amount of time. If we're on the mountain and want to go to the ocean, that's fine. But if we strike against ourselves for not being in the ocean *right now,* we're practicing impatience.

Most people reading this book have already formed a mental image of what the "perfect, healthy, positively focusing" person "should" be. You may have formed such an image, and you also may have cast yourself as the star of the production. This is great. It's how we get from where we are to where we want to be.

If, however, you're putting undue pressure on yourself to achieve these goals of perfection, health and positivity, then impatience has crept in.

Relax. Life is a lifelong journey. You're fine just as you are. You're not finished with yourself yet, and probably never will be. We've yet to meet a person who has said, for any length of time, "I'm done!" Humans have desires, dreams and goals beyond

No thing great
is created suddenly,
any more than
a bunch of grapes
or a fig.
If you tell me
that you desire a fig,
I answer you
that there must be time.
Let it first blossom,
then bear fruit, then ripen.

EPICTETUS
50-120

Dear God,
I pray for patience.
And I want it <u>right now</u>!

OREN ARNOLD

their current reality, no matter how marvelous that reality might be. It's part of the human condition.

Realize, then, that the journey from here to there will never be over; on some level or another you will always be traveling. Such is life. Have compassion for the distance between where you are now and where you're going next. (Where you are now, remember, is the goal of some former moment in time.)

Patience is enjoying the journey. It's not climbing the mountain to get to the top; it's climbing the mountain to enjoy the climb. Enjoy the *process* of your own life. As the travel ads claim, "Getting there is half the fun."

The other side of that is, if you don't have fun while getting there, you probably won't have much fun when you arrive. Your fun muscles will have atrophied. You will have learned to postpone fun so well that you'll postpone it until your *next* destination. ("Oh, I can't wait to take a vacation. Oh, I can't wait to get home.")

Another saying, popular on posters (etc.), is, "Let go and let God." Letting go is relaxing. Letting God is being patient. Relax and be patient. What a wonderful prescription for enjoying life.

When you learn patience with yourself, it's easy to extend it to others. When you learn patience with others, be sure to extend it to yourself.

Realize that, right now, everything is the way it "should" be. And when later comes, everything will be "perfect" then, too.

What is patience? Enjoying the moment. How does one enjoy the moment? By being patient. An endless loop? Sure. And you can jump in at any point. Come on in—the ocean's fine.

Paradise is where I am.

VOLTAIRE

Altitude and Attitude

Another "closed loop" (we like to think of them as *upward spirals)* is the one of altitude and attitude. When "stuck" in something you don't like, you can either change the altitude or the attitude and, as Peter Pan would say, "U-u-u-u-up you'll go!"

Altitude is our viewing point, the perspective we have. The higher our viewing point, the more we can see. The more we can see, the more information we have. The more information we have, the better we can make a well-informed decision.

The question that needs deciding is, "Shall I think negatively about this moment or not?" We maintain that, with enough altitude, your spontaneous response will be "or not."

Have you ever been in a situation that seemed awful at the time, but eventually led to something wonderful? If you knew, at the time, that the bad situation would eventually lead to a much better one, would you have wasted all that energy feeling bad about it? Probably not.

What if *all* situations in life were like that? What if there was a *reason* behind all movement, a *plan* behind the action? What if, with sufficient altitude, you could see the plan? Not necessarily the way in which every detail will come to pass—what a dull life it would be if we knew precisely what the future held—but more a general sense that "something good will come from this."

Attitude is the way we approach things—our point of view. Do you look at life as an adventure to be enjoyed or a problem to be solved? There are infinite possibilities for living in either Adventureland or Problem City. The choice, as we've pointed out

It is possible that our race
may be an accident,
in a meaningless universe,
living its brief life uncared for,
on this dark, cooling star:
but even so
—and all the more—
what marvelous creatures we are!
What fairy story,
what tale from the Arabian
Nights of the jinns,
is a hundredth part as
wonderful as this true
fairy story of simians!
It is so much more heartening,
too, than the tales we invent.
A universe capable of giving
birth to many such accidents is
—blind or not—
a good world to live in,
a promising universe.
We once thought we lived on
God's footstool;
it may be a throne.

CLARENCE DAY

numerous times before, is yours. The key is your attitude.

The connection between attitude and altitude is easy to see. If we have a good attitude, our altitude will lift, and if we have an elevated altitude, our attitude will rise. (The reverse, by the way, is also true. Spirals go up or down, and seem to be infinite in either direction.)

You can add upward momentum by raising either your attitude or your altitude.

Altitude is raised through meditation, contemplation, prayer, spiritual exercises, creativity, service —connecting directly in some way with the uplifting energy of life.

Attitude is lifted through inspiring lectures, reading, seminars, therapy, support groups, books, movies, TV shows—learning concepts and techniques that naturally lead to an enlightened approach.

If you lift the attitude, the altitude will lift. If you raise the altitude, the attitude will lift. Either way, *comme tu veux* (it's up to you).

Of course, doing things to lift both attitude *and* altitude will put you on what is technically known as an *upward hyper-spiral,* or, as it's more commonly known, joy.

*My religion consists of
a humble admiration of
the illimitable superior spirit
who reveals himself
in the slight details
we are able to perceive with
our frail and feeble minds.*

ALBERT EINSTEIN

I could prove God statistically.

GEORGE GALLUP

Reach for God

We've dropped God's name quite a number of times in these last few chapters. Maybe it's time to talk directly about the Deity.

We're going to suggest you reach for God in two ways.

First, whatever your concept of God currently is, reach a little higher. Whatever you believe or perceive God to be is fine with us—from the bearded, omnipotent Father on the throne to the creative flowing of Mother Nature. Whatever it is, see if you can expand it just a little bit more.

Second, reach for God, in whatever way you choose, toward whatever form you feel God to be. If God is the power that grows plants and moves planets, fine. If God is the creator behind all that, fine. If God is the part of us that beats our heart and breathes our breath, fine. Reach into that power, energy and spirit for support, solace and love.

Relate to God in whatever way you choose, but do relate. Chat, ask for things, listen for guidance, give suggestions (you *do* know some things you could do better than God is currently doing them, don't you?), give love, receive joy, or just say "thanks."

Give it a try. You have nothing to lose but your doubt. As the atheist, who was going through some rough times, said, "I sure wish I believed in God."

Remember: your wishes can come true.

The following thoughts on God may stir a few of your own.

Serve God, that He may do the like for you. — *The Teaching for Merikare (2135-2040 B.C.)*

What is God? Everything. — *Pindar (518-438 B.C.)*

Beauty is the gift of God. — *Aristotle*

Even God lends a hand to honest boldness. — *Menander (342-292 B.C.)*

I speak Spanish to God, Italian to women, French to men, and German to my horse. — *Charles V*

When God wounds from on high he will follow with the remedy. —*Fernando de Rojas*

I treated him, God cured him. — *Ambroise Par (1517-1590)*

God is usually on the side of the big squadrons and against the small ones. — *Roger de Bussy-Rabutin (1618-1693)*

Belief is a wise wager. If you gain, you gain all; if you lose, you lose nothing. Wager, then, without hesitation, that He Exists. — *Blaise Pascal (1623-1662)*

If God were not a necessary Being of Himself, He might almost seem to be made for the use and benefit of men. — *John Tillotson (1630-1694)*

Has God forgotten all I have done for him? — *Louis XIV (1709) (Louis also said, when a coach arrived precisely on time, "I almost had to wait.")*

To believe in God is impossible—not to believe in Him is absurd. — Voltaire

Live innocently; God is here. — *Linnaeus (1707-1778)*

For I bless God in the libraries of the learned and for all the booksellers in the world. — *Christopher Smart*

The universe is the language of God. — *Lorenz Oken (1779-1851)*

Of course God will forgive me; that's his business. —*Heinrich Heine (Last words, 1856)*

In the faces of men and women I see God. — *Walt Whitman*

Visitor: "Henry, have you made your peace with God?"
Thoreau: "We have never quarreled."

God forbid that I should go to any heaven in which there are no horses. — *Robert Bontine (1853-1936)*

God hid the fossils in the rocks in order to tempt geologists into infidelity. — *Sir Edmund Gosse*

The Lord God is subtle, but malicious he is not. — *Albert Einstein*

next to of course god america i love you land of the pilgrims' and so forth — *e. e. cummings*

God is a verb. — *Buckminster Fuller*

I could not say I believe. I know! I have had the experience of being gripped by something that is stronger than myself, something that people call God. — *Jung*

Isn't God special? — *Church Lady*

If only God would give me some clear sign! Like making a large deposit in my name at a Swiss bank. —*Woody Allen*

It's good to be
just plain happy;
it's a little better to know
that you're happy;
but to understand
that you're happy
and to know why and how
and still be happy,
be happy in the being
and the knowing, well
that is beyond happiness,
that is bliss.

HENRY MILLER

Nothing Is Too Good to Be True

Ready for a pop quiz? OK. Consider this statement: "If something is too good to be true, it is."

Pop quiz question: "What does *it* refer to?"

(A) "too good" (If something is too good to be true, it is, therefore, not true.)

(B) "true" (If something is too good to be true, it is true.)

BZZZZZZZ. Time's up.

The correct answer is (B): if something is too good to be true, it probably is true. The answer most people spontaneously arrive at, however, is (A).

LESSON: Negative thoughts lead to negative assumptions!

SCORING: Give yourself 50 points if you chose answer (A). Give yourself 50 points if you chose answer (B). Give yourself 100 points for taking the test.

GRADING: If you got more than 20 points, congratulations! You get an A+. Give yourself a gold star. Excellent work. Superb. Bravo. Hurrah! Good for you.

That's the pop quiz. How did you do?

Too good to be true?

It is.

Mirth is like
a flash of lightning,
that breaks through
a gloom of clouds,
and glitters for a moment;
cheerfulness keeps up
a kind of daylight
in the mind,
and fills it with a steady
and perpetual serenity.

JOSEPH ADDISON
1672-1719

Uplifting Acronyms

If we have a life-threatening illness, sometimes the very sound of the name—or the condensed version of the name (CA for cancer, MS for Multiple Sclerosis, etc.)—can strike fear into our hearts.

So change the meaning of the abbreviations. They're just letters. Assign other words to them, uplifting words. Then, whenever you hear people say the letters, you can smile. To them it means one thing; to you it means something else.

CA can be *Creating Always* or *Carefree and Alive* or *Caring for All*.

MS could be *Mighty Spiritual* or *Making Success* or *Mirthful Snuggle*.

AIDS might become *And I'm Doing Swell* or *Always I'm Dancing and Singing* or *Another Interesting Day in Spirit*.

You can also invent acronyms for treatments you don't like; shots, for example. *Sure Helps Overcome The Symptoms* or *Sure Heals Over The Seasons*.

You can do it with any words or abbreviations you don't like. They're just letters. Letters can represent anything you want. Might as well let them represent something uplifting.

*Without this playing
with fantasy
no creative work has ever
yet come to birth.
The debt we owe to
the play of imagination
is incalculable.*

JUNG

Visualization

Creative visualization is holding an image of the direction we want to go, of what we want to achieve, of the things and people we want to be with, and of what we want to become. It uses as many senses as possible.

Visualization is something we all do all the time anyway, either positively or negatively. It's the plan—the blueprint—we create. Then we construct our lives from that.

If we were to ask you to draw a square, a triangle, and a circle, you would probably be able to do that without "thinking" too much about it. You'd have an almost immediate image of each of those shapes. That image would come from visualization.

The use of the term *visual* in *visualization* is, perhaps, misleading. Yes, some people see clear, Technicolor images, but others have more a sense of what they're "visualizing," while for still others, "visualization" is more a process of hearing. Visualization can take place through any one or any combination of the five senses.

Perhaps a better word might be *imagine*—to put an *image* of something *in* to your awareness. Either word works fine. We'll use *visualization* because that's the term that has generally come to describe the process of using the mind and emotions as tools for consciously creating physical reality.

We say "consciously" because we *un*consciously use visualization to create our lives. Almost everything we've done, we probably "thought about it" before we did it, and that "thinking about it" includes visualization. We project ahead in our imagination. We try to imagine what the situation will be like.

*His imagination
resembled the wings
of an ostrich.
It enabled him to run,
though not to soar.*

LORD MACAULAY
On John Dryden
1828

We imagine what we would like it to be. We imagine all the things that might go wrong.

Therein lies the rub. Many people create their own *negative* reality by doing *negative visualization.* We've quoted a couple of times the saying, "What you fear may come upon you." Negative visualization is the process by which it comes about. We worry so much about something that we create an image of failure, terror and terribleness. Then we go about fulfilling our vision.

This process is not a total failure: we do, after all, get to be "right." "I knew it!" we think. "That wasn't worry; that was *accurate perception.*"

As Henry Ford said, "If you think you can do a thing or think you can't do a thing, you're right." The good news about this is that it seldom turns out as bad as we imagined. We're relieved when the other shoe finally drops, and we discover catastrophe is merely disaster.

We, naturally, are suggesting you use this powerful tool of the imagination for your upliftment, healing and joy, that you use it as yet another method of getting what you really want and, of course, not hurting anyone else in the process.

Positive visualization accomplishes the positive in the same way that negative thinking accomplishes the negative. It helps us "preview" goals, makes us comfortable with the reality we're creating, and lets us know when to say yes and when to say no as opportunities arise. (The ones that fulfill our vision, we follow; the ones that run counter to our vision, we let pass.) And, somehow, our thoughts seem to attract to us the realities our imagination creates.

For the balance of the book, when we use the word *visualization,* we'll be referring to *positive*

*The imagination
may be compared
to Adam's dream—
he awoke
and found it truth.*

KEATS

visualization. We just wanted you to know that *all* thinking incorporates visualization and that all visualization tends to manifest itself in physical reality.

How do *you* visualize? What senses do you personally use? What's it like? It's easy to find out. Think of the Eiffel Tower. Now think of the Statue of Liberty. Now think of a lemon. Now think of a rose. What color is the rose? If it's red, make it yellow; if it's yellow, make it red. Think of a lake. Think of a glass of water. What does your bathroom look like? What color is your car?

However you got those images, that's how *you* visualize.

One important point about visualization: *Never lose in your imagination.* In your imagination, you can have it precisely the way you want. Have it that way. When visualizing, you're not limited to any physical reality. You can fly. You can be always joyful. You can be perfectly healthy. You can be perfectly loved. You can be perfectly loving. So be it.

In the next several chapters, we'll discuss the many uses of visualization.

*We would often be sorry if
our wishes were gratified.*

AESOP

For the Highest Good
of All Concerned

Whenever asking for something (and visualization is a form of asking), you might find it a good idea to underwrite your request with an insurance policy.

The insurance policy we suggest: preface and/or follow all your requests with "for the highest good of all concerned."

We are powerful creators. We might ask for something—a solution to a problem, say—and, by the time it comes to pass, it has more problems attached to it than the problem it was intended to solve: it isn't "the right color" (or some such omitted detail), we no longer need it, we already have two others, or we simply no longer want it.

Sometimes putting requests in motion is like ordering room service in a bad hotel. We place the order at ten. By midnight nothing's come, so we give up and go to sleep. At 3:00 a.m., there's a pounding at the door, "Room service!"

"I don't want it anymore."

"But you ordered it."

"That was at ten o'clock."

"We were very busy tonight."

"Well, I don't want it now."

"Did you cancel your order?"

"No. The phone lines were busy."

"How many times did you try?"

"Three."

If we really want to live,
we'd better start
at once to try;
If we don't
it doesn't matter,
we'd better start to die.

W. H. AUDEN

"That wasn't enough."

"Well, I still don't want it."

"You ordered it. You've got to eat it."

"No, I don't."

"It'll be outside your door. You'll have to step over it in the morning."

"Fine. Now, leave me alone."

"And you have to pay for it."

"I'll do nothing of the kind."

"Then we won't bring you breakfast."

"Fine. Now, go away."

"What about my tip?"

"What tip?"

"It's customary to offer a gratuity when someone brings you room service. Especially at three o'clock in the morning."

"But I didn't *want* room service at three o'clock in the morning."

"Did you tell them that when you placed the order?"

"No."

"Then it's not *our* fault. It's certainly not *my* fault. I did my job. I think I deserve a tip."

"You're not getting a tip. Now, leave me alone."

"The maid's a friend of mine. I'll tell her not to clean your room tomorrow."

"I'm checking out tomorrow."

"The bellboy's a friend of mine, too. You'll have to carry your own baggage."

There are
two tragedies in life.
One is to lose
your heart's desire.
The other is to gain it.

GEORGE BERNARD SHAW

"Write yourself a tip on the bill. Now, let me get some sleep."

"Could you sign the bill, please?"

"What?"

"If you give a tip, you have to sign the bill."

"Why?"

"Hotel policy."

Sound familiar?

To get what we want—and only what we want, and all of what we want—it's good to be as specific as possible. But it seems that, no matter how many details we include, the fickle finger of fate can add a few we never considered.

That's where "the highest good" comes in. Do all that you can; then ask for it in the name of the highest good of all concerned. That way, no matter what happens, what comes to you will be right, and the timing will be perfect.

This is especially true when making requests for others. We don't know what would always be the best for *ourselves,* so how can we hope to know what would be best for someone else?

An elderly woman we heard about was in a coma. Her friends and family prayed, affirmed and visualized unceasingly that she live. The coma continued for weeks. The woman finally awoke from the coma and said in perfectly lucid tones to those gathered around her bed, "Let me go. I've seen what it's like on the other side. I want to go there. You're all holding me here. I love you. If you love me, let me go." She closed her eyes, returned to the "coma," and a few hours later—after the message of "let go" was spread among her family and friends—she died.

The highest good.

CICERO
106-43 B.C.

If her friends had sent their prayers, affirmations and visualizations to her *for her highest good and the highest good of all concerned,* she may have been able to make her transition with less struggle.

This, of course, is an extreme example. But how often have we wished for our friends, "I hope he gets that job" or "I hope they stay together" or "I hope she sells her house"? Maybe the new job, staying together and selling the house aren't for their highest good. Maybe later they'll say, "I sure hate this job" or "We should have broken up long ago" or "I wish I had my house back," at which point we can only tell ourselves, "But that's what they *said* they wanted."

What people say they want and what they really want when it actually comes to pass are often two different animals.

What we don't know, fully and absolutely, is the future. We don't know what will happen or how things will be different or how we will have changed. What we ask for today, we may not want tomorrow. This is why it's a good idea to make a list of all the things you're asking for—your list of goals. When you no longer want something (maybe because you got something better), cross it off. Tell yourself, "Thank you, but I no longer want this."

When asking for things, some people also like to add "this, or something better." If we want ten million dollars, but we get twenty million, that would be OK, wouldn't it? Some people put an upper limit on their receiving by the way they ask. "This, or something better, for my highest good and the highest good of all concerned" encompasses all variables, changes, extremes and conditions.

*The tendency of
man's nature to good
is like the tendency of
water to flow downwards.*

MENCIUS
372-289 B.C.

You can relax after asking. (Relax from worrying, that is. You'll probably have to take certain actions in order for things to take place.)

"For my highest good and the highest good of all concerned" is a statement of faithing. It trusts that there is some Higher Power—Mother Nature, Father God or whatever else you care to call It—who is taking care of us, who is there to nurture and support us, who knows what we want before we know we want it, and who is happy to give it to us.

In the beginning
God created the heaven
and the earth.

And the earth was
without form, and void;
and darkness was upon
the face of the deep.
And the Spirit of God
moved upon the face
of the waters.

And God said,
Let there be light:
and there was light.

THE FIRST BOOK OF MOSES,
Called GENESIS 1:1-3

Light

The concept of *light* as a gift from "someplace greater" to humankind seems to be ageless and universal. It spans time, geography and belief. It's central to almost every religion and spiritual practice.

In approximate historical order, let's look at how *light* is viewed by the major religions of the world today.

Hinduism, one of the oldest religions in the world (500 million adherents), was founded around 1500 B.C. One of the sacred texts is the *Brihadaranyaka Upanishad,* which states (1.3.28):

Lead me from the unreal to the real!
Lead me from darkness to light!
Lead me from death to immortality!

Light is equated both with reality and immortality. "En*light*enment" is a Hindu's highest goal.

Judaism was formally founded around 1300 B.C.E. ("Before the Common Era.") There are approximately 17 million Jews in the world today, almost half of them in North America. Jewish scripture is abundant with references to light, beginning with "In the beginning," quoted on the facing page.

The Old Testament of the Bible—the sacred texts as well as the story of the Chosen People—includes some of the most beautiful references to light ever written.

"And the Lord went before them by day in a pillar of a cloud, to lead them the way; and by night in a pillar of fire, to give them light." (Exodus 13:21)

Ye are the light
of the world.
A city that is set on a hill
cannot be hid.

Neither do men
light a candle,
and put it under a bushel,
but on a candlestick;
and giveth light unto
all that are in the house.

Let your light
so shine before men,
that they may see
your good works,
and glorify your Father
which is in heaven.

MATTHEW
5:14-16

"Lord, lift thou up the light of thy countenance upon us." (Psalm 4:6)

"The Lord is my light and my salvation; whom shall I fear? the Lord is the strength of my life; of whom shall I be afraid?" (Psalm 27:1)

"Arise, shine; for thy light is come, and the glory of the Lord is risen upon thee." (Isaiah 60:1)

"I shall light a candle of understanding in thine heart, which shall not be put out." (II Esdras 14:25)

"The light that cometh from her [wisdom] never goeth out." (Wisdom of Solomon 7:10)

Buddhism, founded by Gautama Buddha around 525 B.C., has about 250 million followers worldwide. Buddha is often referred to as "The Light of Asia." "En*light*enment," in fact, is what transformed endarkened Siddhartha Gautama into "Buddha" ("the Enlightened One").

Christianity, was formed in the year 0 by Jesus the Christ. (Actually, it was formed by his followers after his death.) The many variations of Christianity have about a billion followers in the world. Jesus said of himself, "I am the light of the world: he that followeth me shall not walk in darkness, but shall have the light of life." (John 8:12)

He told his followers, "Yet a little while is the light with you. Walk while ye have the light, lest darkness come upon you." (John 12:35) (Sounds a little like one of our repeated spurs to action.)

After he left the earth physically, Jesus sent "an advocate" in the form of the Light of the Holy Spirit, which first appeared to the disciples as tongues of fire (light).

Beyond plants
are animals,
Beyond animals is man,
Beyond man
is the universe.
The Big Light,
Let the Big Light in!

JEAN TOOMER

Islam was founded by the Prophet Mohammed in 622 A.D. and has about 500 million followers worldwide. The sacred text of Islam is the Koran. This passage from the Koran (24:35) leaves little doubt as to Islamic beliefs about light:

> God is the light of the heavens and of the earth. His light is like a niche in which is a lamp—the lamp encased in glass—the glass, as it were, a glistening star. From a blessed tree it is lighted, the olive neither from the East nor of the West, whose oil would well nigh shine out, even though fire touched it not. It is light upon light. God guideth whom He will to His light, and God setteth forth parables to men.

The Native Americans of both North and South America had many religions, but most have a common thread of The Great Spirit, Mother Earth and the various colors of Light. This North American Indian song illustrates the latter:

> May the warp be the white light of morning,
> May the weft be the red light of evening,
> May the fringes be the falling rain,
> May the border be the standing rainbow.
> Thus weave for us a garment of brightness.

Or from the poem "The Flight of [the Aztec] Quetzalcoatl":

> It ended . . .
> With his body changed to light,
> A star that burns forever in that sky.

*There are two ways
of spreading light:
to be the candle
or the mirror
that reflects it.*

EDITH WHARTON

Now, if all this talk about God and light isn't quite up your avenue, how about Ancient Philosophers?

The Greeks liked light. Pindar (518-438 B.C.) wrote, "Creatures of a day, what is a man? What is he not? Mankind is a dream of a shadow. But when a god-given brightness comes, a radiant light rests on men, and a gentle life."

The Romans were fond of light, too. "On a dark theme I trace verses full of light," wrote Lucretius (99-55 B.C.), "touching all the muses' charm."

The pagan gods used light. "The evening is come; rise up, ye youths," spoke Catullus (87-54 B.C.). "Vesper from Olympus now at last is just raising his long-looked-for light."

Not happy with Greeks, Romans and pagans? How about *poets*?

Dante, in the early 1300s, declared that Beatrice ". . . shall be a light between truth and intellect." Three hundred and fifty years later, Henry Vaughan calmly informed us,

I saw Eternity the other night
Like a great ring of pure and endless light.
All calm, as it was bright;
And round beneath it, Time in hours, days,
    years,
Driv'n by the spheres
Like a vast shadow moved; in which the world
And all her train were hurled.

A hundred-or-so years later, Wordsworth advised us, "Come forth into the light of things, / Let Nature be your teacher." And Lord Byron either heard a song from without or (as we like to think) a sound from within when he wrote:

It is eternity now.
I am in the midst of it.
It is about me
in the sunshine;
I am in it,
as the butterfly
in the light-laden air.
Nothing has to come;
it is now.
Now is eternity;
now is the immortal life.

RICHARD JEFFERIES
The Story of My Heart (1883)

A light broke in upon my brain—
It was the carol of a bird;
It ceased, and then it came again,
The sweetest song ear ever heard.

Emily Dickinson enjoyed one of the qualities of light: *"Phosphorescence.* Now, there's a word to lift your hat to," she wrote. "To find that phosphorescence, that light within, that's the genius behind poetry."

Closer to our time, Theodore Roethke pointed out, "The word outleaps the world, and light is all." More down to earth, he wrote, "Light listened when she sang."

Which brings us to one of the favorite poetical uses of light—to describe one's beloved. The most famous, perhaps, is Shakespeare's "But, soft! what light through yonder window breaks? / It is the east, and Juliet is the sun!"

Robert Burns was a bit more, well, Scottish with the light of love:

The golden hours on angel wings
Flew o'er me and my dearie;
For dear to me as light and life
Was my sweet Highland Mary.

Tennyson, at the tender age of thirty-three, remarked upon seeing the gardener's daughter,

Half light, half shade,
She stood, a sight to make an old man young.

All right. Enough poets. How about *artists?* Michelangelo wrote, "I live and love in God's peculiar light," and, during an interview, Marc Chagall once

There was a young lady
named Bright,
Whose speed was far
faster than light;
She set out one day
In a relative way,
And returned home
the previous night.

ARTHUR HENRY REGINALD BULLER

made this, well, peculiar comment, "Do not leave my hand without light."

And of light and death? Goethe's last words were "More light!" while Teddy Roosevelt requested, "Put out the light." Herder's self-written epitaph was "Light, love, life." Longfellow seemed to accept the notion that light is to be found on either side of death: "The grave itself is but a covered bridge / Leading from light to light, through a brief darkness."

All this too airy-fairy for you? What about good old psychology? What Jung said in *The Practice of Psychotherapy* may enlighten you:

> The unconscious is not just evil by nature, it is also the source of the highest good: not only dark but also light, not only bestial, semihuman, and demonic but superhuman, spiritual, and, in the classical sense of the word, "divine."

If you're not interested in religion, poetry, philosophy, art, parting words or psychology, we'll just have to appeal to your *patriotism!*

> Oh, say, can you see
> by the dawn's early light,
> What so proudly we hailed
> at the twilight's last gleaming?

(As George M. Cohan—who should know— pointed out, "Many a bum show has been saved by the flag.")

Why have we gone through all this? Isn't this book long enough already? Well, this was just our meandering way of illustrating that there are many

*Light seeking light doth
light of light beguile.*

SHAKESPEARE

kinds of light. Our suggestion? Whichever kind you believe in, use it.

Imagine, if you will, a pure, white light surrounding, filling and protecting you, all of your activities, everyone and everything around you. Ask for this light for your highest good and the highest good of all concerned.

Just as darkness is merely the absence of light, not a real thing in itself, perhaps negativity, another form of darkness, is simply the absence of another kind of light.

Where does the darkness go when you turn on the light? What happens to your fist when you open your hand? Where does your lap go when you stand up? If you work with the light (and ask the light to work with you), you may find yourself asking the question, "What happens to negativity when I call in the light?"

You can think of light as an acronym: *Luxuriating In Good Happy Times,* perhaps, or *Loving Intensely Gives Higher Thinking,* or *Laughing Internally Gets Hilarious Teachings,* or *Living In God's Holy Thoughts.* Invent any others you choose.

The idea is that *if there is* a power in light you can call on, you might as well use it. If there's not, you're not losing much except the few seconds it takes to think, "I ask the light to surround, fill, and protect me and everyone and everything around me for my highest good and the highest good of all concerned." (In a pinch, you can shorten it to: "Light! Highest Good!")

It's one of those you-have-little-to-lose-and-everything-to-gain suggestions. Try it. Play with it. See what happens. We're not asking you to *believe* anything, just experiment. Based upon your results, you'll know if there's something to it or not.

Joy is the sweet voice,
joy the luminous cloud—
We in ourselves rejoice!
And thence flows all that
charms or ear or sight,
All melodies the echoes
of that voice,
All colors a suffusion
from that light.

COLERIDGE

The Colors of Light

As long as we've suggested you experiment with light, let us tell you about the colors of light, too. People who are sensitive to such things have noticed that certain colors have certain effects.

This is probably not surprising. You may have felt a difference between walking into, say, an all-yellow room and walking into an all-blue room. The investigation of color and its effects on people is now considered by many a legitimate scientific study.

The white light contains all colors. When you mix paints, all the colors mixed together form a sort of murky green-brown. When you combine all colors of direct light, however, it makes white. On a color TV, for example, when the screen is white, all the primary colors are on full. The absence of all colors is black.

You've probably seen light go through a prism and become the colors of the rainbow. Rainbows are formed, in fact, by water molecules in the air acting as billions of tiny prisms.

When you want the benefit of all colors, use white. When you want specific results, you can use specific colors. Here's a summary of the colors of the visible spectrum and some of their potential uses.

Red is the color of intense, physical energy. When you need a powerful burst of energy, imagine red or look at something red. Coke does not put caffeine in its cola and paint the cans bright red for nothing. They're selling *energy*—raw, physical energy. The Real Thing! The Pause That Refreshes! Coke Is It!

This powerful physical energy, if overdone, sometimes leads to delusions of grandeur. As

For memory has painted
this perfect day
With colors
that never fade,
And we find at the end
of a perfect day
The soul of a friend
we've made.

CARRIE JACOBS BOND

Edmond Rostand noted, "I fall back dazzled at beholding myself all rosy red, / At having, I myself, caused the sun to rise."

When the red gets rowdy, it's often associated with mischief: "Three jolly gentlemen, / In coats of red, / Rode their horses / Up to bed." (Walter de la Mare) If the physical actions go too far, red becomes associated with crime: "caught red-handed" or "My case is bad. Lord, be my advocate. / My sin is red: I'm under God's arrest." (Edward Taylor)

The intense physical energy is also why red is the color most often associated with sexuality: red-light districts and scarlet letters. As John Boyle O'Reilly wrote, "The red rose whispers of passion / And the white rose breathes of love; / O, the red rose is a falcon, / And the white rose is a dove."

Orange is the next color in the spectrum. Orange is a color of energy, too, but a quieter, more sustaining energy. You'd use red if you needed a burst of energy; orange, for a more enduring strength.

"The red earth" of the South is really more orange in color. ("The orange earth of Tara" doesn't sound too romantic.) Edwin Markham's description of Abraham Lincoln incorporates the orange quality of abiding strength: "The color of the ground was in him, the red earth, / The smack and tang of elemental things."

Yellow is the color of the mind—joyful, purifying, mental energy. It's the color of lemons (a happy fruit), smile buttons, and Joy dishwashing detergent. (Lily Tomlin: "A friend of mine asked her four-year-old daughter, 'Do you know what joy is?' and the daughter answered, 'Yes. It's what gets your dishes so spotlessly clean you can see yourself.' ") Yes, yellow light *does* bring clarity.

Dear friend,
all theory is gray,
And green
the golden tree of life.

GOETHE

The thing we most often associate with yellow is the sun. The sun has been described as "glorious" (Shakespeare or Coleridge, take your choice) and "colossal" (Wallace Stevens)—qualities we could certainly apply to the mind (on a good day).

As Daniel Webster observed, "Knowledge, in truth, is the great sun in the firmament. Life and power are scattered with all its beams." Or, as Theodore Roethke said in the more fervid tones one can succumb to when wrought with mental enthusiasm: "The sun! The sun! And all we can become!"

Green is the color of healing and the color of learning; brilliant, emerald green. "The Lord is my shepherd; I shall not want. He maketh me to lie down in green pastures: he leadeth me beside the still waters." (Psalm 23: 1-2) "That happy place, the green groves of the dwelling of the blest." (Virgil)

Andrew Marvell marveled in 1651, "Annihilating all that's made / To a green thought in a green shade." The "annihilation" is that of illness when the ease of green confronts dis-ease, or when the green of learning confronts ignorance. "Keep a green tree in your heart and perhaps the singing bird will come." (Chinese proverb)

Of course, healing and learning are active processes. When you think of green, think of actively healing yourself, through physical action and through active visualizations. Think of vigorously learning all you can about yourself and your life. "April prepares her green traffic light and the world thinks Go." (Christopher Morley)

"*Blue* color is everlastingly appointed by the Deity to be a source of delight." John Ruskin said it in 1853 better than we could have today. Blue is a color of spirit, of calm, of peace. "Blue, darkly, deeply, beautifully blue." (Robert Southey)

And God smiled again,
And the rainbow appeared,
And curled itself
around his shoulder.

JAMES WELDON JOHNSON

As the sun is yellow and usually associated with sunny thoughts, so the sky is high and blue, and the sea is deep and blue. High and deep: two good descriptions of spirit. "The spacious firmament on high, / With all the blue ethereal sky." (Joseph Addison) "The sea! the sea! the open sea! / The blue, the fresh, the ever free." (Barry Cornwall)

The Apache have a chant: "Big Blue Mountain Spirit, / The home made of blue clouds / I am grateful for that mode of goodness there." And the final word on blue will go to Coleridge (dear Coleridge), who reminds us that "Saints will aid if men will call: / For the blue sky bends over all!" (You'd think he wrote these to order for us, wouldn't you?)

Purple is the color of royalty—the inner royalty that is the true you and the outer royalty of the Divine. We seem to associate purple with kings, queens and the primary color in stained-glass windows.

Use purple when you want to feel cloaked in the grand, magnificent, noble, majestic, stately One of the universe, or the grand, magnificent, noble, majestic, stately presence within you.

It's also fun mixing colors. If you have, say, "the blues," you might add the physical energy of red, which would make a more active purple. Or you could add to blue some mental energy (yellow), which would give you the green of healing; red would give you the more stable physical energy of orange.

If you were being a little too yellow—thinking too much at the expense of action (cowards, who sacrifice action for fearful thoughts, are often called "yellow")—you could add some highly physical red, which would give you a steady, reliable orange to carry out your physical tasks. Or you could add blue

My heart leaps up
when I behold
A rainbow in the sky:
So was it
when my life began;
So is it now I am a man;
So be it
when I shall grow old,
Or let me die!
The child is
father of the man;
And I could wish
my days to be
Bound each to each
by natural piety.

WORDSWORTH

to the yellow to make green and be ready for some active healing or learning.

If you add too many colors, don't worry: unlike mixing paints, when you overmix light, the worst you can end up with is white.

Use the colors you feel drawn to. Think about them surrounding and filling you with their energy. You can also look at sheets of colored paper, or wear clothes of the colors you want to imbue yourself with. As always, ask for them to impart their energy for your highest good and the highest good of all concerned.

PETER: A lovely meditation tape, which encompasses the colors of light, is John-Roger's "Meditation for Loving Yourself." It's $10.00, postpaid, from Prelude Press, 8165 Mannix Drive, L.A., CA, 90046; 800-LIFE-101.

My special place.
It's a place no amount
of hurt and anger
Can deface.
I put things
back together there
It all falls right in place—
In my special space
My special place.

JONI MITCHELL

Make a Sanctuary

If you wanted to learn woodcrafting, you'd probably want not just tools, but a workroom. If you wanted to become an artist, you'd probably want not just paints, but a studio. If you wanted to become a gourmet cook, you would probably want not just pots and pans, but a kitchen.

If you want to become a "gourmet visualizer," you might want not just the techniques of visualization but also a place for you to use them. We call this place a sanctuary.

A sanctuary is a place you build in your imagination. It's an inner place for you to go to visualize, contemplate, meditate, affirm, do spiritual exercises, solve problems, get advice, heal yourself, relax, have fun, hang out, and communicate with yourself and others.

We call it a *sanctuary* because the word seems to incorporate the qualities of preciousness *(sanctity)*, retreat, getting away from it all, safety and refuge. You can call your inner place whatever you choose. Some call it a workshop; others, a shrine or an inner sanctum. The name is not important. Building and using it is.

You build a sanctuary in your imagination. The nice thing about building in your imagination is that the time between design and construction is almost nonexistent. You can try something out, see how you like it, change it, see how you like that, and change your changes, all in a very short time.

To show you how quickly this can happen: imagine the Statue of Liberty. See the right arm holding up the torch and the left arm holding the tablets. (In the United States, by the way, the Statue of

A harbor,
even if it is a little harbor,
is a good thing,
since adventures come into
it as well as go out,
and the life in it
grows strong,
because it takes
something from the world
and has something
to give in return.

SARAH ORNE JEWETT

Liberty's tablets have July 4, 1776 engraved on them, the date of the signing of the Declaration of Independence. In France, the tablets of a much smaller Statue of Liberty have July 14, 1789 engraved on them, the date of the Storming of the Bastille. Now that you know that, don't you wish Trivial Pursuit were popular again?)

Imagine that Lady Liberty has gotten tired of holding up her right arm all these years. (She's a she: the artist's mother posed for the statue.) Imagine her switching the tablets to her right arm and the torch to her left. Then see her holding aloft the torch in her left hand while holding the tablets in her right.

That didn't take long. Can you imagine how long that would have taken to do in real life? Heck, it took them two years and Lee Iacocca just to *clean* it.

As we mentioned earlier, some people see clear pictures, others have a vague sense of it, while others don't see much but they listen carefully and "know" something happened.

If we asked you to draw a very rough sketch of the Statue of Liberty with the torch in her left hand, you could probably do it, even though you had never seen a left-handed Liberty before. You would be drawing your visualization of it, from your creative imagination.

Before constructing your sanctuary, you might want to read through this whole chapter first. That way you'll have an idea of what size to make the sanctuary, what shape, what location, etc.

When you finally decide to construct it, you might want to do it with your eyes closed but while standing and moving. This physical movement helps the body feel that the sanctuary you're constructing is real.

*Can success change
the human mechanism so
completely between one
dawn and another?
Can it make one feel
taller, more alive,
handsomer,
uncommonly gifted
and indomitably secure
with the certainty
that this is the way life
will always be?
It can and it does!*

MOSS HART

You can have as many workers as you want, or you can snap your fingers and things will just appear. Want to change the color of the whole place? Snap your fingers, it's done. Want to make it twice as large? Snap, it's larger.

In constructing your sanctuary, keep in mind the following story. Moss Hart, the playwright and director, bought an estate outside New York and began landscaping it. He moved a large hill from one location to another, redirected the course of a stream, and rearranged trees so the effect would be more aesthetically pleasing. When George S. Kaufman came to visit and saw the changes Hart had made, he commented, "This is what God would do if He only had money."

When building your sanctuary, be a god with lots of money—because in your imagination, *you are*.

We'll suggest uses for the sanctuary later, but for now we'll just describe their basic function. Their size, shape, design, etc., etc., is entirely up to you. Ready? Here we go . . .

Location. Your first choice is location. Where would you like your sanctuary to be? It can be anyplace, either real or imagined: on a mountain top, floating over the ocean, on the moon, in a valley. Landscape it as you please: add rivers, rock formations, galaxies, and shrubbery at will.

Outside. What do you want the outside of the sanctuary to look like? Choose a size (from enormous to moderate to cozy), shape (cathedral to cottage to geodesic dome), color (the full color spectrum, plus colors we can't physically see), and so on.

Entry Way. The entry way to your sanctuary is special. It permits only you to enter. How does it know it's you? Do you have a special key? Does it read your handprint? Do you have secret words,

Three things are to be
looked to in a building:
that it stand
on the right spot;
that it be securely founded;
that it be
successfully executed.

GOETHE

such as "Open sez me"? Or does it just automatically recognize you?

White Light. Just inside the doorway, create a perpetual white light. Whenever you enter or exit your sanctuary, you automatically pass through a column of pure, white light. You know that as you do, you are surrounded, filled, protected and healed by this light and that only that which is for your highest good and the highest good of all concerned takes place while you're in your sanctuary.

Main Room. What would you like the main room of your sanctuary to be like? Large? Small? Carpeted? Wood floors? Grass? What about the walls, ceiling, windows? How is it decorated? Snap into place whatever you want and, if you're not entirely satisfied, snap your fingers and create something else.

Information Retrieval System. This can be in the main room or in a special room by itself. It's a way of getting information about whatever you want to know. It could be a computer terminal, a staff of researchers, a telephone or anything else. All you need is a method of asking questions and receiving the answers.

Video Screen. Again, this can be in the main room or in its own room. It can be any size, from hand-held to wall-size. Have some comfortable chairs in front of it so you can relax and watch TV. What will you watch? Mostly the story of your life. You're the star; everyone else is just extras. You can also use it to play videos given to you from the information retrieval system. Surrounding the screen should be a white light that can go off and on.

Ability Suit Closet. This is a closet of suits. For every ability you have or would like to have—painting, flying, being rich, playing piano—there's a

*We must reserve
a back shop all our own,
entirely free,
in which to establish
our real liberty
and our principal retreat
and solitude.*

MICHEL EYQUEM DE MONTAIGNE
1580

suit that, when you put it on, instantly gives you that ability. When you're done with the suit, throw it on the floor. It automatically hangs itself back in the closet. That's just one of the abilities of the ability suits.

Ability Practice Area. This is a place where you can try different abilities on for size. You put on the ability suit for, say, gourmet cook, and the ability practice area becomes a master chef's kitchen. You can also use this area to practice abilities as you develop them.

People Mover. This is the way you can invite others into your sanctuary. (Remember, only you can come and go by way of the main entrance.) It can be an escalator or an elevator or one of those "beam me up, Scotty" devices from *Star Trek* or whatever else you imagine.

White Light by People Mover. Place a perpetual white light by the entrance of the people mover. In that way, anyone who comes into your sanctuary is automatically surrounded, filled and protected by the white light, and only that which is for his or her highest good and the highest good of all concerned can take place. Make sure the column of light is located in such a way that anyone visiting your sanctuary passes through it both on entering and on leaving.

Healing Center. This can be a multiroom wing of your sanctuary. Here, all the inner healing arts are practiced. You are attended by all known and imagined healers—past, present and future. The latest to the most ancient technology is available, as are all future discoveries.

Sacred Room. This is a special room within your sanctuary. It's for you to commune with yourself—to meditate, contemplate, do spiritual exercises,

If you call him
your Master will hear you.
Seven bars on the door
will not hold him
Seven fires burning bright
only bring him delight.
You can live
the life you dream.

JUDY COLLINS

visualize, and just be. You can also invite special friends into this room of communion.

Master Teacher. A special feature of your sanctuary is the presence of a special teacher, a friend, someone who knows everything about you, who cares for you totally and who loves you unconditionally. How do you discover your Master Teacher? Easy. Just stand in front of the people mover and say, "Would my Master Teacher please come forward?" From the column of white light in front of the people mover will emerge your Master Teacher. Take some time. Get acquainted. Show off your sanctuary. Spend some time together in the sacred room.

This is the basic outline for a sanctuary. Keep in mind that it's *your* sanctuary. You can add anything else you like. There are no limitations other than the ones *you* place there. We, naturally, recommend limitlessness.

In the following sections we'll put your sanctuary to good use.

By means of an image
we are often able to hold on
to our lost belongings.
But it is
the desperateness of losing
which picks
the flowers of memory,
binds the bouquet.

COLETTE

MRS. MALAPROP:
Illiterate him, I say,
quite from your memory.

RICHARD SHERIDAN
1775

The Healing of Memories

Most of us have memories of past hurts, disappointments and fears that keep returning, causing pain, resentment, guilt or fear. These situations may be from hours ago or years ago. When this happens, we're letting a memory of something *then* negatively affect us *now*. Fortunately, memories—like any other part of our being—can be healed.

Here's a simple technique for the healing of memories. Go into your sanctuary, making sure you pass through the white light at the entry way. Have a seat in front of your video screen. You may want to ask your Master Teacher to join you. If so, stop by the people mover and pick up your MT on the way.

Let the white light surrounding the screen be off. On the screen, see the situation you feel upset about. Let it play itself out, and watch it as you would a movie. After it's over, go back and freeze-frame a moment you found particularly upsetting.

Imagine you have a large paintbrush full of black paint in your hand. Take the paintbrush and make a large, black *X* across the upsetting image on the screen. Let the image and the paint fade.

Now, illuminate the white light around the edges of the video screen. See the situation again, but this time, let it happen *exactly the way you would have liked it to have happened*. (Remember, never lose in your imagination.)

This process actually *replaces* the painful or fearful memory with a joyful, contented one. For some situations, you may need to repeat it a few times; in other cases, once will do.

Neither a lofty degree
of intelligence
nor imagination nor both
together go to the
making of genius.
Love, love, love,
that is the soul of genius.

MOZART

Healing Your Body

The healing center of your sanctuary is a powerful place. There, healing can take place instantly. Some people like to have their Master Teacher come along when they go for healing. (Some people have their Master Teacher with them all the time. In your sanctuary, your Master Teacher has infinite time to spend with you.)

The healing of the body in your healing room is limited only by your imagination. You can be given the Miracle Shot (painlessly, of course) or take the Miracle Pill. You can have healers place their hands on you and heal you by touch. You can stand under different colors of light and be healed in that way.

In your healing room is an infinite supply of replacement body parts, especially stocked for your body. You can snap out any part that's not quite up to par and snap in a perfect part. It only takes a second. You can do it yourself or have a whole team —like the pit crew at the Indianapolis 500—do it for you.

If you know you're having trouble with, say, your liver, snap out the old liver and snap in a new one. Heart? Snap out, snap in. (You can also replace your whole circulatory system—blood and all— while you're at it.) Immune system? Easy. Snap, snap.

Before you do this, you might want to look at some color drawings of what various organs look like and where they're located. The more vivid the image and your knowledge of the replacement body part, the better. You may have to replace a particularly recalcitrant part a hundred times, but that's OK. Whatever it takes, right?

*It is not enough
to have a good mind.
The main thing
is to use it well.*

RENE DESCARTES
1637

You can invite, through your people mover, the greatest medical experts in the world (any world) for consultation. They're always available, always have enough time, and never charge a cent. You can invite healers from past, present and future—real and imagined—to do work and to give advice.

Some people like to have a Master Healer to organize the comings and goings of all the other healers. Some people like to imagine their Master Teacher in a white coat and stethoscope. Others like the variety of new and different experts.

Anytime you hear of a new healing method or technique that interests you, go to your healing room and try it out. Let it work perfectly for you. Create new techniques for treating whatever ails you. And feel free to visit the healing room even when you're not sick. That way, you won't have to be sick in order to enjoy getting better.

As we've stated before, none of the inner work you do should replace the outer work of proper medical treatment. If your outer treatment reaches an impasse, however, the inner work might help the outer along.

Some people ask their inner doctors for help in diagnosing certain "mysterious" ailments. When they go to their regular (outer) doctors next, they say, "Just for the heck of it, why don't you check out _____." It's amazing how often _____ has something to do with it.

If you have any spiritual or religious beliefs, be sure to invite the healers of your tradition — via the people mover—into your sanctuary. And don't accept some assistant—go for the Top, the Head Honcho, the Big Enchilada.

You're worth it.

When bad men combine,
the good must associate;
else they will fall
one by one,
an unpitied sacrifice
in a contemptible struggle.

EDMUND BURKE
1770

Visualize Health

In addition to the work done in the healing center on your body from the "outside" (we realize it's all going on in your imagination), you can also do work on your body from the inside.

The technique is one made popular by Dr. Carl Simonton.* For years, Dr. Simonton has been using nontraditional methods for treating cancer patients who were diagnosed as "terminal." (When new patients enter his clinic for an initial consultation, Dr. Simonton looks them straight in the eye and asks, "When did you decide to die?")

The technique of visualization we're about to describe can be done in your sacred room, if you like, or in a special room of the healing center. You can, as always, have your Master Teacher come along. (The MT, naturally, has the ability to join you in any inner journeys you take; makes a great guide, in fact.)

The idea is to imagine whatever is *not* healthy about you as the Bad Guys and your own healthy body parts as the Good Guys. Then imagine them slugging it out. The Good Guys *always* win.

If, for example, you have cancer cells in your body, you can see those as, say, cowboy villains in black hats and your white blood cells as heroes in white hats. They meet at the OK Corral for a showdown. Much punching and gunplay later, the "black hats" are all in jail or boot hill, and the "white hats" are riding off into the sunset or going upstairs with Miss Kitty or doing whatever your white hats enjoy.

You can imagine the nasty cells being dog biscuits and the good cells being dogs; whenever a dog

*A catalog of Dr. Simonton's books and tapes can be yours by calling 1-800-338-2360. Outside the U.S.: 1-817-444-4073.

Imagination is very rapid;
it jumps from admiration
to love,
from love to matrimony
in a moment.

JANE AUSTEN

sees a biscuit, it eats it. Or imagine the good cells as Pac-Man (or Ms. Pac-Man) and the bad cells as the little white dots Pac-People devour.

The negative emotions often connected with life-threatening illness (fear, anger, guilt, blame, etc.) can be visualized away.

You can see anger, for example, as a fire (or burning embers or a fire-breathing dragon) and rivers (or fire hoses or waterfalls) flowing into the fire, extinguishing it at its source. Then you can let the water form a beautiful inner lake (or pond or reflecting pool) surrounded by peaceful trees (or mountains or rolling hills or—see how imaginative your imagination can be?).

Fear can be seen as an ice cube (or iceberg or icicle) being melted by the heat of the sun (or blowtorch or sauna).

If a visualization seems to "go bad" (the polar bear you've been chasing turns and starts chasing you), change it *at once*. (You run into the annual gathering of the National Polar Bear Hunter's Club: thousands of bear-hungry hunters who have spent the past week just *looking* for a bear.)

Remember: *Never lose in your own imagination.*

Another option is to imagine the harmful cells in your body *mutating* into non-life-threatening ones. The mutated cells might then cause a lesser illness and be gone, or they might mutate to a point where they no longer want to be in a human body and just leave. (There are all sorts of viruses and bacteria that want nothing whatever to do with the human body.)

We have several new strains of flu virus every year. That's because some of the viruses have mutated. They've discovered a non-life-threatening

You see things;
and you say, "Why?"
But I dream things
that never were;
and I say, "Why not?"

GEORGE BERNARD SHAW

variant of the AIDS virus, currently called HIV-2. The HIV-1 virus might just mutate itself into a harmless virus before an official "cure" is found. And before that happens universally, it can begin happening to the HIV cells in any individual's body.

If you have an organ that's not functioning properly—a heart, say—visualize it operating perfectly. See it doing its job flawlessly. In your imagination, hear and feel it beating with strength, regularity and vigor. If you have, for example, clogged arteries, see them open, clear and healthy.

These visualizations can be done anywhere, anytime. Let boredom and impatience be the reminders to do some inner work. The checkout line at the supermarket or a dull passage on the radio can be the perfect time to heal yourself.

The options, as you may have noticed, are endless. Be creative. Have fun. If you learn to enjoy the process of healing, you'll find that your health is more enjoyable, too.

*It would be a great thing
to understand pain
in all its meanings.*

PETER MERE LATHAM

Listen to Your Pain

What if pain were really your friend? What if it were giving you important information about your life, and, once you listened to and followed that information, it would go away?

We learned that guilt and resentment could be "angels at the gate," keeping us from traveling down pointless and destructive pathways of negative thinking. The same is true of pain.

We define pain as anything in your mind, body or emotions you wish wasn't there. It might be a physical pain (headache, sore muscles, upset stomach), an emotional pain (hurt, anger, fear) or a mental pain (confusion, doubt, rigidity).

All you have to do is talk to your pain. Ask it some questions. Listen to the answers. If the answers seem to make sense, follow the pain's advice.

Go into your sanctuary—gathering your Master Teacher along the way, if you like—and go to the sacred room. Imagine the pain leaving your body and sitting in a chair opposite you. Give the pain some human characteristics. How would Walt Disney animate it? What kind of Muppet would Jim Hensen make of it?

Then ask the pain some questions. You can make them up as you go along. Here are some possible starters: Do I embarrass you by talking to you? What payoff am I getting from having you? How am I using you? Is there anything I get to avoid by having you around? Is there some excuse you give me? What other information do you have for me? What would I have to take care of in order to let you go? Do you have any other advice for me?

One word
Frees us of all the weight
and pain of life:
That word is love.

SOPHOCLES
406 B.C.

Questions along those lines. You may be amazed how many knowledgeable answers the pain has. After you've gathered the information, say good-by to the pain and imagine it surrounded by a white light. See it fade away and disappear into this light, smiling and waving good-by, happy to be going on to other projects.

Then put the advice in motion. If you do the things you've been avoiding, you'll probably find that the pain doesn't need to be there reminding you anymore.

When you've learned the lesson the pain was sent to teach, it generally goes. How do you know when you've learned the lesson? When the pain is gone. If it remains, there's probably a seminar or two left to take.

If the pain is chronic, you've probably ignored lesser pains that could have given you the same information. When we need to change something, the messages telling us to get moving are like an alarm clock that keeps getting louder and louder until we finally wake up.

When you learn to listen to your pain and to take corrective action at an earlier point—when it's just discomfort or annoyance or mild sensations—you can usually avoid the alarm clock's loudest rings.

This can be a powerful process—to learn that guilt, resentment and pain are our friends. Could that mean that *everything* in our life is put here for our good?

Good question.

*Sometimes
I sits and thinks,
and sometimes I just sits.*

Meditate, Contemplate or "Just Sits"

In addition to visualization, you might like to try any number of meditative and contemplative techniques available—or you might just want to sit quietly and relax.

Whenever you meditate, contemplate or "just sits," it's good to ask the white light to surround, fill and protect you, knowing only that which is for your highest good and the highest good of all concerned will take place during your meditation.

Before starting, prepare your physical environment. Arrange not to be disturbed. Unplug the phone. Put a note on the door. Wear ear plugs if noises might distract you. (We like the soft foam-rubber kind sold under such trade names as E.A.R., HUSHER and DECIDAMP.) Take care of your bodily needs. Have some water nearby if you get thirsty, and maybe some tissues, too.

Contemplation is thinking about something, often something of an uplifting nature. Sometimes it's pondering a seemingly simple question with profound implications—the one we ended the last chapter with, for example. You could contemplate any of the hundreds of quotes or ideas in this book. Often, when we hear a new and potentially useful idea, we say, "I'll have to think about that." Contemplation is a good time to "think about that," to consider the truth of it, to imagine the changes and improvements it might make in your life.

Or you could contemplate a nonverbal object, such as a flower, or a concept, such as God. The idea of contemplation is to set aside a certain amount of

*Most of the evils in life
arise from man's being
unable to sit still
in a room.*

BLAISE PASCAL
1623-1662

quiet time to think about just *that*, whatever you decide "that" will be.

Meditation. There are so many techniques of *meditation*, taught by so many organizations, that it's hard to define the word properly. We'll give a capsule summary of some techniques from John-Roger's book, *Inner Worlds of Meditation*. (For more complete descriptions, you can get the book for $7 postpaid, from Mandeville Press, Box 3935, Los Angeles, CA 90051.)

You might want to try various meditations to see what they're like. With meditation, please keep in mind that *you'll never know until you do it*. We may somehow like to think we know what the effects of a given meditation will be by just reading the description, and that, in fact, is exactly what happens. We *think* we know; we don't *really* know. We suggest you try it, gain the experience, and decide from that more stable base of knowledge what is best for you at this time. And please remember to "call in the light" before beginning. We suggest you do not do these meditations while driving a car, operating dangerous machinery, or where you need to be alert.

Breathing Meditation. Sit comfortably, close your eyes, and simply be aware of your breath. Follow it in and out. Don't "try" to breathe; don't consciously alter your rhythm of breathing; just follow the breath as it naturally flows in and out. If you get lost in thoughts, return to your breath. This can be a very refreshing meditation—twenty minutes can feel like a night's sleep. It's also especially effective when you're feeling emotionally upset.

Tones. Some people like to add a word or sound to help the mind focus as the breath goes in and out. Some people use "one" or *God* or *AUM (OHM)* or *love*. These—or any others—are fine. As you breathe in, say to yourself, mentally, "love." As you

A powerful agent
is the right word.
Whenever we come upon
one of those intensely
right words
the resulting effect
is physical
as well as spiritual,
and electrically prompt.

MARK TWAIN

breathe out, "love." A few other tones you might want to try:

HU. HU is an ancient sound for the higher power. One of the first names humans ever gave to a supreme being was HU. Some good words begin with HU: *humor, human, hub* (the center), *hug, huge, hue, humus* ("The Good Earth"), *humble,* and, of course, *hula.* HU is pronounced "Hugh." You can say it silently as you breathe in, and again as you breathe out. Or, you can pronounce the letter *H* on the inhale and the letter *U* on the exhale. You might also try saying HU out loud as you exhale, but don't do it out loud more than fifteen times in one sitting; the energies it produces can be powerful.

ANI-HU. This tone brings with it compassion, empathy and unity. You can chant it silently (ANI on the inhale, HU on the exhale) or out loud (ANI-HU on the exhale). It makes a lovely group chant and tends to harmonize the group—in more ways than one.

HOO. This can be used like the HU. Some people prefer it. It's one syllable, pronounced like the word *who.*

RA. RA is a tone for bringing great amounts of physical energy into the body. You can do it standing or sitting. Standing tends to bring in more energy. Take a deep breath and, as you exhale, chant, out loud, "ERRRRRRRRAAAAAAAAA" until your air runs out. Take another deep breath and repeat it; then again. After three RAs, breathe normally for a few seconds. Then do another set of three, pause, then another set of three. We suggest you don't do more than three sets of three at any one time.

SO-HAWNG. The SO-HAWNG meditation is a good one to use when your mind wants to do one thing and your emotions another. SO-HAWNG tends to unify the two, getting them on the same track.

I do not know
whether I was
then a man dreaming
I was a butterfly,
or whether I am now
a butterfly dreaming
I am a man.

CHUANG-TZU
396-289 B.C.

This tone is done silently. You breathe in on SO and out on HAWNG. Try it with your eyes closed for about five minutes and see how you feel. You may feel ready to accomplish some task you've been putting off for a long time.

THO. THO is a tone of healing. The correct pronunciation of it is important. Take a deep breath, and as you breathe out say, "THooooo." The TH is accented; it's a sharp, percussive sound (and it may tickle your upper lip). It's followed by "ooooooo" as an extended version of the word *oh*. To do the THO meditation, sit comfortably, close your eyes, inhale and exhale twice, take a third deep breath, and on the third exhale, say, "THoooooo." Repeat three times this series of three breaths with THO aloud on the third breath. That's enough. It's powerful. Feel the healing energies move through your body. You can also chant THO inwardly as a formal meditation or any time during the day, even while doing something else. (But, again, as with all meditations, not while driving a car or operating potentially dangerous equipment.)

FLAME MEDITATION. This uses the power of fire to dissolve negativity. Put a candle on a table and sit so you can look directly into the flame, not down on it. Allow your energy to flow *up* and *out* into the candle. You may feel negativity or have negative thoughts. Don't pay any attention to their content; just release them into the flame. If you feel your energy dropping back down inside of you as though you were going into a trance, blow out the candle and stop the meditation. The idea is to keep the energy flowing up and out and into the flame. Do it for no more than five minutes to start. See how you feel for a day or so afterward. You may have more vivid dreams. If you feel fine otherwise,

Men grind and grind
in the mill of a truism,
and nothing comes out
but what was put in.
But the moment
they desert the tradition
for a spontaneous thought,
then poetry, wit, hope,
virtue, learning, anecdote,
all flock to their aid.

EMERSON

you might try it for longer periods. Twenty minutes a day would be a lot.

WATER MEDITATION. Take some water in a clear glass, hold it between your hands (without your two hands touching each other), and simply look down into the glass. Observe whatever you observe. You may see colors. You may see energy emanating from your hands. You may just see yourself holding a glass of water. Observe the water for five minutes, gradually working up to fifteen. Drink the water at the end of the meditation. Your energies have made it a "tonic," giving you whatever you may need at that time. As an experiment, you can take two glasses, each half-filled with tap water. Set one aside, and do the water meditation with the other. Then taste each. Don't be surprised if the one you "charged" tastes different.

E. The E sound is chanted out loud after meditation to "ground" you and bring your focus back to the physical. It's a steady "Eeeeeeeeeeeee" as though you were pronouncing the letter *E*. It begins at the lower register of your voice, travels to the upper range, then back down again in one breath. You begin as a bass, go through tenor, alto, onto soprano, and back to bass again. As you do this, imagine the sound is in your feet when you're in the lower register, gradually going higher in your body as your voice goes higher, finally reaching the top of your head at the highest note of the eeee, and then back down your body as the voice lowers. If you try it, you'll see that it's far easier to do than it is to explain. Do two or three E sounds after each meditation session.

These tones and meditations have worked for many people. We don't ask you to *believe* they will work. We simply ask you, if you like, to try them and see what happens. If they do work, you don't need belief; you've got knowledge. Your results will

The poet,
described in ideal
perfection,
brings the whole soul
of man into activity,
with the subordination of
its faculties to each other,
according to their relative
worth and dignity.
He diffuses a tone
and spirit of unity,
that blends,
and (as it were) fuses,
each into each,
by that synthetic and
magical power,
imagination.

COLERIDGE

dictate whether you'll use them often, sometimes, seldom or never. Some may work better for you than others; that's only natural. Use the ones that work best for you now and, every so often, return to the others to see if they will offer more.

These tones are also good to keep in mind when you find yourself "trapped" in negative thinking and can't think of a positive thought to think. Try one of these tones. The positive energy will help break the downward spiral of negative thought.

Some people think meditation takes time *away* from physical accomplishment. Taken to extremes, of course, that's true. Most people, however, find that meditation *creates* more time than it *takes*. One of the primary complaints people have about meditating is, "My thoughts won't leave me alone." Perhaps the mind is trying to communicate something valuable. If the thought is something to do, write it down (or record it on a tape recorder). Then return to the meditation. This allows the mind to move onto something else—such as meditation, for example.

As the "to do" list fills, the mind empties. If the thought, "Call the bank," reappears, you need only tell themind, "It's on the list. You can let that one go." And it will. (It is important, however, to *do* the things on the list—or at least to consider them from a non-meditative state. If you don't, the mind will not pay any more attention to your writing it down than you do, and it will continue to bring it up, over and over.)

When finished meditating, not only will you have had a better meditation, you will also have a "to do" list that is very useful. One insight gleaned during meditation might save *hours*, perhaps *days* of unnecessary work. That's what we mean when we say—from a purely practical point of view—meditation can make more time than it takes.

*The currents
of the Universal Being
circulate through me;
I am part and parcel
of God.*

EMERSON

Affirmations

An affirmation is a statement of positive fact. It's always worded in the present and usually begins with "I am." Affirmations are designed "to make firm" positive things about yourself.

Affirmations may be truer in the future, but the fullness of the affirmation is always claimed *here and now*. Affirmations can be said anywhere, silently or out loud. The more often they're used, the more real, true, solid and "firm" they become.

Setting aside periods of time especially for affirmations is valuable. Go to your sanctuary, sit in the sacred room and say a selected affirmation over and over again. After a while, go to the video screen and watch yourself living that affirmation fully.

Then go to the ability closet and put on the ability suit for that affirmation. Go to the ability practice area and experience yourself living that affirmation.

Affirmations are very powerful when you repeat them in front of a mirror while looking into your eyes. All the negative thoughts and feelings that keep you from fulfilling your affirmation will probably surface. Let them surface, and let them float away. Beneath all that "stuff" is a part of you that knows the truth of the affirmation.

Create your own affirmations to suit your particular situations. Remember to keep them a positive statement of the *present*. "I am healthy, wealthy and happy," not "I want to be healthy, wealthy and happy," or "Pretty soon, with enough luck, I'll be healthy, wealthy and happy."

Here are some affirmations to get you started. Pilfer these, and then go on to create your own.

Affirmations others have used . . .

"I am one pure of mouth, pure of hands." *(The Address to the Gods, 1700-1000 B.C.)*

"I am nearest to the gods." *(Socrates)*

"I am ready for Fortune as she wills." *(Dante)*

"I am not only witty in myself, but the cause that wit is in other men." *(Shakespeare)*

"I am coming to that holy room." *(John Donne)*

"I am in love with the world." *(Swift)*

"I am content." *(John Quincy Adams)*

"I am the maker of my own fortune. I think of the Great Spirit that rules this universe." *(Tecumseh)*

"I am on the side of the angels." *(Benjamin Disraeli)*

"I am the master of my fate; / I am the captain of my soul." *(William Ernest Henley, 1888)*

"I am as strong as a bull moose." *(Theodore Roosevelt)*

"Every day, in every way, I'm getting better and better." *(Emile Coue, 1857-1926)*

"I am absorbed in the wonder of earth and the life upon it." *(Pearl S. Buck)*

"I am the greatest." *(Muhammad Ali)*

"I am strong, I am invincible, I am woman." *(Helen Reddy)*

And here are some others you might try . . .

"I feel warm and loving toward myself."

"I am worthy of all the good in my life."

"I am one with the universe, and I have more than I need."

"I always do the best I can with what I know and always use everything for my advancement."

"I forgive myself unconditionally."

"I am grateful for my life."

"I love and accept myself and others."

"I treat all problems as opportunities to grow in wisdom and love."

"I am relaxed, trusting in a higher plan that's unfolding for me."

"I automatically and joyfully focus on the positive."

"I give myself permission to live, love and laugh."

"I am creating and using affirmations to create a joyful, abundant, fulfilling life."

". . .this, or something greater for my highest good, and the highest good of all concerned." (A good ending to all affirmation sessions, by the way.)

*Just trust yourself,
then you will know
how to live.*

GOETHE

Words of Encouragement

Go to your sanctuary and invite your Master Teacher in. Together, go to the sacred room. You sit down, close your eyes, and relax. Imagine your Master Teacher kneeling behind your chair and whispering gently into your ear a few words of encouragement, words you will use often on your path from illness to health, from negative thinking to positive focus, from desiring death to affirming life.

They're just a few words: three, four, five. Listen carefully. Your Master Teacher is repeating them, over and over. Listen. What are they? As your Master Teacher repeats them, relax; let them go deep. Hear them repeated, over and over. After a while it's hard to tell if the words are coming from your Master's mouth or from inside your own head.

Thank your Master Teacher for giving you those words. You escort your Master Teacher back to the people mover, and, as you turn, you see your words of encouragement emblazoned on the wall of your main room in golden letters. You realize that these aren't just words of encouragement; they are an accurate statement about you, here and now.

On a pedestal in front of the glistening words of encouragement is a gift from your master teacher. What is it? It represents your words of encouragement in a symbolic yet physical way.

Whenever you enter your sanctuary, while standing under the white light of your entry way, pause for a moment and read your words of encouragement. Let the words touch your heart. Whenever you feel challenged on your path, remember that those are not just words, but a fundamental truth about you.

*Always
forgive your enemies—
nothing annoys
them so much.*

OSCAR WILDE

Forgiveness

Yes, we are saving the best for last. The information in any one of these final three chapters, if applied with a genuine desire to be well, is more than enough to heal.

The first of these is forgiveness. Forgiveness may be the greatest healer.

We hold so much against ourselves, and against others; then we hold it against ourselves that we hold things against ourselves and others. The process of judging ourselves and others for not measuring up to some constructed image we have is a painful one. (PAINFUL = PAY-IN-FULL.)

The way out? Forgiveness. The process of forgiveness is such a simple one. It's so easy, most people don't realize how effective it can be, so they don't try it, and they don't find out how well it works.

To forgive yourself, all you have to do is say, "I forgive myself for _____," or "I forgive _____ (another) for _____," and fill in the blanks.

Notice that the forgiveness is unconditional. To forgive is to be willing to let go of any hurt, guilt, resentment or attachment to yourself or the person you're forgiving.

That's part one.

Part two is, "I forgive myself for judging myself for _____," and "I forgive myself for judging _____ (another) for _____."

The fact that we did something, or someone else did something, is of little concern. The real problem *for us* began when *we judged what happened as wrong, bad, improper, hurtful, mean, nasty, etc.* It's our *judgment* we really need to forgive. The action

*Forgiveness is the key
to action and freedom.*

HANNAH ARENDT

was just the action. Our *judgment* that the action was bad, etc., is what caused our difficulty.

If you're going to judge something, wait until all the evidence is in. Yes, so-and-so walked out on you, but two years later you met such-and-such, and thanks to so-and-so's departure you were free to take up with such-and-such, who is much more fun than so-and-so ever was; therefore, so-and-so's "desertion" was really a blessing in disguise and, had you known then what you know now, you would certainly have thrown so-and-so a *bon voyage* party.

How long does it take for all the evidence to come in? Give it at least five years: wait five years before judging anything.

"But in five years I won't remember that this even took place." Fine. Then forget it now. If it's not worth remembering for five years, it's not worth getting upset about now. How will you know if it's worth remembering for five years? Wait five years and see. Until then, "the jury's out."

What happens if we forget about the five-year moratorium on judgments (and, being humans, we probably will)? If you forget, then as soon as you remember, forgive yourself on the spot. Forgive yourself for judging, knowing it was the judgment— not the action—that caused the hurt, pain and separation.

Just say those forgiveness sentences to yourself. Try it. See what happens. It's one of those techniques that works by rote: you do it, it works. When should you do it? Whenever you're upset. All upset is caused by our judgment of a situation. Forgive the judgment, and the upset tends to fade.

You may have to repeat the forgiveness sentences several times, because you may have judged something several times. How many times does it

*To be wronged is nothing
unless you continue
to remember it.*

CONFUCIUS

take? You know the answer to that one by now: when the upset goes away, that was enough.

There's another element to forgiveness, and that's "forgetness." When it's forgiven, it's forgotten. Let it go. It's not worth holding on to. Some people would rather have the righteousness of their vindictiveness than be healthy. That's their choice.

Use the white light, your sacred room and your Master Teacher in your forgiveness process. Learn to forgive fully and completely. If you want health, wealth and happiness, you can't afford the luxury of lugging around all those unforgiven, unforgotten past events. Let them go.

Declare regular periods of General Amnesty during the day. Forgive yourself and everyone else for everything that happened (or failed to happen) since the last General Amnesty. Schedule them every few hours. Nothing from the past is worth polluting your present for any longer than that.

Forgiveness is simply a matter of declaring yourself forgiven. That can surface worthiness issues faster than almost anything we know. Tell yourself you are worthy of being forgiven. You are. And even if you don't *feel* worthy of forgiveness, forgive yourself anyway. Prove your unworthiness wrong again.

And then forgive it

(Forgiveness—and a great deal more—is used in Louise Hay's classic book, *You Can Heal Your Life*. Available for $12 postpaid from Hay House, 501 Santa Monica Boulevard, Santa Monica, CA, 90401. Also ask for their catalog of other Louise Hay books, tapes, etc.)

Thank God for tea!
What would the world do
without tea?—
how did it exist?
I am glad I was not
born before tea.

SYDNEY SMITH
1771-1845

The Attitude of Gratitude

As you learn to focus on the positive things in your here-and-now environment, take it one step further: be *grateful* for everything in your life.

Start with the outstanding things, then the good things, then the mundane things, then the not-so-good things, then the very not-so-good things, then the terrible things.

Why should you be grateful for the terrible things? First, you'll be meeting terrible things with feelings of gratitude, and gratitude feels so good. Second, the terrible things are part of your life, so there must be some reason why they're there. You might not know the reason yet, but, sooner or later, it will probably appear. So, be grateful until it does, and when it does, you'll be in the habit of gratitude.

Negative thinking simply cannot exist in a consciousness of gratitude. A nasty thought tries to take hold, and the attitude of gratitude says, "Thank you for that thought!" Such appreciation diffuses negative thinking almost at once.

Remember to be grateful for the things we often take for granted—our awareness, our senses, our bodies, our lives. Sure, we probably have things we could complain about, but we also have so much to be grateful for.

Who or what should you be grateful to? It doesn't matter. Take your choice. You can be grateful to the power company for the electricity, or Edison for inventing the light bulb, or the designer of the lamp, or the money to pay for the power, or God for the energy behind it all, or any combination. And that's for just a lamp.

But if a man
happens to find himself
he has a mansion
which he can inhabit
with dignity
all the days of his life.

JAMES MICHENER

Who gets the gratitude is not as important as *you feeling* the gratitude. The attitude of gratitude is just that: an attitude. It's such a free, abundant, happy attitude. That's why we're suggesting you find things to be grateful about—not so that the electric company gets thank-you notes, but so that you'll feel the joy of being grateful.

In his cassette tape *Meditation of Gratitude: A Key to Receptivity* ($12 postpaid from The Cosmos Tree, 301 E. 78th, NY, NY 10021), Roger Lane asks you to imagine yourself as a sweater, a simple wool sweater. He then goes through everything even a sweater has to be grateful for: the sheep, the spinners, the knitters, the people who grow the food to feed the knitters, etc.

And how much more we have to be grateful for than a sweater! If we were truly grateful for everything in our lives, we wouldn't have *time* for so much as a single negative thought.

Throw an inner gratitude party. Invite the people from your past and present into your sanctuary and thank them for all they've contributed to your life: teachers, lovers, friends, brothers, sisters, spouse(s), children and, of course, parents. See them come in, one by one, through the white light of the people mover. Express your gratitude. Then point them to the bar and buffet and welcome your next guest. (Your Master Teacher will know a great Master Caterer.)

Gratitude opens the place in you to receive. Whom do you prefer giving to: people who truly appreciate your gifts, or those who find fault with every little detail? The universe probably thinks as you do: let's give to the grateful.

And it does.

*And now I will show you
the most excellent way.*

*If I have the gift of prophecy
and can fathom all mysteries
and all knowledge,
and if I have a faith
that can move mountains,
but have not love, I am nothing.*

*If I give all I possess to the poor
and surrender my body to the flames,
but have not love, I gain nothing.*

*Love is patient, love is kind.
It does not envy, it does not boast,
it is not proud. It is not rude,
it is not self-seeking,
it is not easily angered,
it keeps no record of wrongs.*

*Love does not delight in evil
but rejoices with the truth.
It always protects, always trusts,
always hopes, always perseveres.
Love never fails.*

*And now these three remain:
faith, hope and love.*

But the greatest of these is love.

I CORINTHIANS 13

Loving

There are three magic words in healing—*I Love You.* When we say them, to others or to ourselves, all are healed.

As with *faithing,* we prefer the word *loving* to *love.* Loving includes the action necessary to bring about the qualities of love. Love is nice, of course, but love-in-action gets a lot more done.

Loving feels wonderful, but it's more than just a *feeling;* loving is a *decision.* We *choose* to be loving toward ourselves and others. This moment we choose. The next moment, we choose again. We always have a choice.

We can be lost in the gravity of our bad habits and negative thinking, but with each moment comes a new opportunity to choose loving. Now and now and now again.

It's usually not a grand choice preceded by golden trumpets and a chamberlain heralding, "Do you choose the joy of loving, or do you choose the quagmire of negative thinking?" Usually it's small choices: How do I respond to this information? Should I focus on the positive or the negative? Would eating this be taking care of myself? Would doing my exercises be loving me?

There may not be a "loving feeling" behind the decision to take a loving action, but we take the action anyway; that's part of the *decision* to be loving. That loving action often produces the loving feeling. When we act in a loving way—either toward ourselves or toward others—we usually start feeling loving. If we wait for the feeling of loving before we take a loving action, we might take only two or three loving actions a week.

*Because I am the only person
I will have a relationship
with all of my life, I choose:*

+ *To love myself
  the way I am now*
+ *To always acknowledge
  that I am enough
  just the way I am*
+ *To love, honor
  and cherish myself*
+ *To be my own best friend*
+ *To be the person I would
  like to spend the rest of
  my life with*
+ *To always take care of
  myself so that I can take
  care of others*
+ *To always grow,
  develop and share
  my love and life.*

RON AND MARY HULNICK
University of Santa Monica

Who is there to love in your life? Ultimately, you. As the song states, "Learning to love yourself is the greatest love of all." You're the only person you'll be with all the time for the rest of your life. Why not make it a loving time?

Choose to love yourself. *Do* loving things for yourself. *Act* toward yourself in a loving way. *Forgive* yourself for *everything*. *Be easy* on yourself. *Love* yourself *unconditionally*. When you learn to love yourself—warts, bumps, bald spots, love handles, habits, negative thinking, illness and all—you can love anyone or anything. Then you'll always be "in loving."

Did we say love the illness? Yep. Love it so much that it wouldn't even *dream* of harming you. Love it so much that if you told it, "I love you, but I could love you better if you were over there," it would go over there. Love it so much that you won't have any hate left in you about anything.

As Dale Evans (of Roy Rogers and Dale Evans) pointed out, "I'm so busy loving everything, I just don't have time to hate anything."

What's the answer? Loving. What's the question? It doesn't matter; the answer will still be loving.

It's the last word we want to leave you with, the first word in healing, the antidote to stress, the ease that dissolves dis-ease, the Magic Bullet of Joy, the vaccine against hatred, the positive action we can take when negative thinking flares, what we can always be grateful for, proof positive that the blessings already are, the heart of forgiveness—

Loving.

*Stay at home
in your mind.
Don't recite
other people's opinions.
I hate quotations.
Tell me what you know.*

EMERSON

For Further Study: Organizations Founded by John-Roger

This is Peter, stepping out of my co-author character to tell you about some of the organizations founded by John-Roger.

J-R must like founding organizations. I certainly *hope* he likes founding organizations—he's founded enough of them. It's probably more accurate to say that organizations formed around John-Roger; he stands still for a while and teaches, and the people listening to him form organizations by which these teachings can be shared with others.

Now that you've had a taste of J-R's teachings (through this book), you might like to explore some more. (In this book we have barely scratched the surface—he's been at it nonstop for the past 27 years.)

I'll be brief. You might want to ask your Master Teacher which, if any, of these you might like to pursue.

Insight Seminars provides workshops on personal development. The flagship seminar—and a great place to start—is Insight I, The Awakening Heart Seminar. Insight Seminars are offered in dozens of cities all over the world. I can't recommend them too highly. Insight Seminars, 2101 Wilshire Blvd., Santa Monica, CA 90403; 213-829-9816 or 800-777-7750.

The Center Store carries a broad range of books, tapes, and other educational materials on personal growth. You might ask about the book *One Minute Self-Esteem,* or the book/tape package *250 Ways to Enhance Your Self-Esteem*, both by Candy Semigran. The Center Store also carries a series of audio tapes by John-Roger. Please contact the store for more information about their full line of products. Center Store, 2101 Wilshire Blvd., Santa Monica, CA 90403; 213-453-0071 or 800-344-4976.

The Heartfelt Foundation is dedicated to service. They do various community projects, large and small, all over the world. If you'd like to take part— or organize a service project in your community— give them a call. 2101 Wilshire Blvd., Santa Monica, CA 90403; 213-828-0535.

Institute for Individual and World Peace. Just as it says. If you want to learn more about peace and how you can effect it—or if you have any ideas to contribute—drop them a line. 2101 Wilshire Blvd., Santa Monica, CA 90403; 213-828-0535.

University of Santa Monica. Offers an M.A. in Applied Psychology, including the Awakening the Inner Counselor program. Approved by the State of California. Write or call for a brochure. 2107 Wilshire Blvd., Santa Monica, CA 90403; 213-829-7402.

University of Santa Monica Center for Health. A gathering of health professionals dedicated to treating the patient, not just the symptoms. They work toward both the elimination of illness and the enhancement of wellness. They also have a division, the Santa Monica Institute for Stress Related Disorders. Call or write for a brochure. 2105 Wilshire Blvd., Santa Monica, CA 90403; 213-829-0453.

Movement of Spiritual Inner Awareness (MSIA) is for those who want to live in a way that makes spirit and God a part of their lives. MSIA has no formal membership, dues, rules or dogma. It encourages people in their own experience of the divine, without restricting personal choices. The booklet "About MSIA" describes MSIA and its goals. You can also find out if J-R's TV show "That Which Is" is available in your area. Write or call MSIA, Box 3935, Los Angeles, CA 90051; 213-737-4055.

Discourses. John-Roger's Soul Awareness Discourses are the most complete, effective and delightful course in Spirit I know. You simply read one a month at your own pace. Each Discourse contains about 30 pages of text and more than 60 blank pages for your own daily notes, reminders, dreams, discoveries, affirmations or anything else you'd like. They're $100 per year (12 Discourses), and I can't recommend them too highly. For more information, please contact MSIA.

Mandeville Press. Publishes J-R's earlier books, including *Relationships—The Art of Making Life Work, The Power Within You,* and *Wealth and Higher Consciousness.* On a more spiritual note, there's *Loving...Each Day, The Spiritual Promise, The Spiritual Family* and *The Way Out Book.* Other books are available. They also publish *The New Day Herald,* a bi-monthly newspaper of articles on, mostly, loving. A vast collection of John-Roger on audio and video tapes is available, looking at life from a spiritual yet practical point of view. A free catalog is available from MSIA.

Other Books (and Stuff) Published by Prelude Press

This is still Peter. I thought I'd tell you about some of the books published by Prelude Press. This may seem like a shameless commercial. It is not. As author (or co-author) and publisher of these books, I say it's not a commercial—it is an exercise in blatant egoism.

You Can't Afford the Luxury of a Negative Thought Cases

This book is available at case discounts: 10 copies, $100.00.

Focus on the Positive: The You Can't Afford the Luxury of a Negative Thought Workbook

By John-Roger and Peter McWilliams. Specific excercises to help you eliminate the negative and latch onto the affirmative. Trade Paperback, $12.

You Can't Afford the Luxury of a Negative Thought Audio Tapes

Every word of the book on eight cassettes. A new recording, read by David Warrilow (who, if you ask me, has the greatest voice since Orson Welles), with a special meditation by John-Roger (the *Meditation for Loving Yourself*). Only $22.99.

You Can't Afford the Luxury of a Negative Thought Watch

A quiet, tasteful wristwatch—with a message: you can't afford the luxury of a negative thought. Let this watch remind you of that important (but often forgotten) fact each time you check the time. One size fits most. $35.

LIFE 101: Everything We Wish We Had Learned About Life in School—But Didn't

The overview book of the *LIFE 101 Series*. The idea behind *LIFE 101* is that everything in life is for our upliftment, learning and growth—including (and, perhaps, especially) the "bad" stuff. "The title jolly well says it all," said *The Los Angeles Times*—jolly well saying it all. 400 pages. Paperback, $5.99. Hardcover, $18.95.

LIFE 101 Audio Tapes

The entire book, complete and unabridged on five 90-minute audiocassettes. A new recording read by Academy Award Nominee Sally Kirkland, Christopher McMullen and Yours Truly. Five tapes, $19.99

LIFE 101 Watch

A Paul LeBus designed wristwatch with all the color and fun of the cover of *LIFE 101*. The words on the watch face read "Time to enjoy...LIFE 101." $35. One size fits most. (If you want to see what the watch looks like, please see the cover of the book *DO IT!* at your local bookstore.)

DO IT! Let's Get Off Our Buts

DO IT! is a book for those who want to discover—clearly and precisely—their dream; who choose to pursue that dream even if it means learning (and—gasp!—practicing) new behavior; who wouldn't mind having some fun along the way; and who are willing to expand their comfort zone enough to include their heart's desire—and maybe even a dance floor. Hardcover. 500 pages. $20.

DO IT! Audio Tapes

Every word of the book, read by Sally Kirkland, Christopher McMullen and Yours Truly. Six tapes, $22.99.

John-Roger's Meditation for Loving Yourself

This is the most beautiful meditation tape I know. It lasts a little over half an hour. The meditation is repeated on side two. (That way, all you have to do is turn the tape over—no rewinding.) John-Roger is "backed" by a lovely musical score composed and performed by Scott Fitzgerald and Rob Whitesides-Woo. The tape is $10 and highly recommended. This meditation is also included in the audio cassette package of *You Can't Afford the Luxury of a Negative Thought*. (It's on side two of tape eight. That means rewinding!)

How to Survive the Loss of a Love

This is an entirely new edition, completely revised and updated. Hardcover, 212 pages, $10. Also available on unabridged audio tapes, read by the authors Melba Colgrove, Harold Bloomfield and Yours Truly. $9.99.

The Personal Computer Book

A compilation and updating of all my earlier introductory computer books. If you're looking for an enjoyable, nonintimidating introduction to what personal computers are and what they do, you'll enjoy this book. Trade paperback, $19.95.

To order any of these books, please check your local bookstore, or call

1-800-LIFE-101

or write to

Prelude Press
8165 Mannix Drive
Los Angeles, California 90046

Call or write for our free catalog!

Index

Burke, Edmund, quote, 556
Burns, Robert, quote, 523
Burton, Robert, quote, 86
Business Week (magazine),
  quote, 311
Bussy-Rabutin, Roger de,
  quote, 492
Butler, Samuel, quote, 372
Byron, Lord, quote, 521-523

C

California, 3, 19, 45
Cancer, 79, 81
  and smoking, 314
  description, 85
  now considered curable, 307
  remission of, 85-87
Career, 39, 81, 177
  SEE ALSO Work (job)
Carlyle, quote, 177-179
Catch-22, 149-151
Catullus, quote, 521
Centers for Disease Control,
  AIDS disease study, 317
Cerf, Christopher, 311
Chagall, Mark, quote, 525
Chanel, Coco Gabrielle, quote,
  348
Change, 164-167
Channing, William, quote, 26
Charities (organizations), and
  needy 253-255
Charity, 250-255
  definition, 251-253
  vs. pity, 251-253
  vs. service SEE Service
Charles V, quote, 492
Child, Lydia Maria, quote, 180
Childhood, as indicator for fu-
  ture, 66-69
Children, 286-287
  attention, need for, 69
  attention, when sick, 411-413
  deaths, 313
  respect for, 68

training, 67, 69, 437, 465
training, for unworthiness, 69
training, positivity, 91
training, praise and punishment, 69
Chinese proverb, quote, 533
Chocolate cake, 197, 437-445
Choose, 63, 150
  by default, 237
  life, 149-153
  people you want, 171, 291-293
  positive or negative focus, 129
  technique, not duty, obligation,
  169
  vs. right and wrong, 57
  what you want, 171, 206, 219-
  225, 285
Christianity, and light, 517
Chuang-tzu, quote, 250, 572
Church Lady, quote, 493
Churchill, Winston, quote, 2,
  230, 368, 378, 428
Cicero, quote, 510
Cinch by the inch..., 353
Cohan, George M., 525
Coke, The Real Thing, 529
Coleridge, quote, 528, 533
Colette, quote, 136, 550
Colgrove, Melba, 145
Collins, Judy, quote, 266, 548
Colors, technique, 529-537
Comet Kohoutek, 308
Commit to life, 154-155
Commitments, 185-191
  technique, seven suggestions
  185-189
  to yourself 187
  SEE ALSO Agreements
Common sense, 91, 92
Complaining, 272-275
  technique to handle, 273-275
Complaining consciousness, vs.
  attitude of gratitude, 129
Completion, technique, 187
Compulsive sex, 75, 401
Confucius, quote, 588

Conrad, Joseph, quote, 178, 326
Contemplation, 193, 489, 567-
569
Coolidge, Calvin, quote, 426
Corinthians, I, quote, 110, 594
Cornwall, Barry, quote, 535
Coue, Emile, quote, 580
Courage, 106, 166, 196
mastery of fear, 165
Cousins, Norman, quote, x,
134, 160, 280, 281
C.P.A. SEE Create, promote or
allow
Crabbe, George, quote, 40
Create, promote or allow, 417-
431
Creation, 288
Bible, 514
Creative power, 431-433
key is accountability, 433
Creative power of thoughts
SEE Thoughts, creative
power of
Creativeness, 208
Creativity, 289, 489
Creators, powerful, 505
Crises, value, 44
Cruising, 75
Curran, John Philpot, quote,
374

D

Dali, Salvador, quote, 204
Dangerfield, Rodney, respect,
421
Dante, quote, 521, 580
Darwin, Charles, quote, 70
Dating, 73
Day, Clarence, quote, 116, 488
De la Mare, Walter, quote, 531
Death, 59, 60, 82, 91, 110, 116,
118, 160
acceptance of, 100
acceptance of your own, 147
and eternity 111-112

and religious belief, fear based
on, 111-113
and the soul, 111-112
beliefs about, 111-115
crash course in, 99-101, 109-115
example, woman in coma, 509
fear of, 78, 82, 98
fear of, as affirmation, 99
fear of, handled, result, 115
fear of, technique to handle,
111-115
fear of, useless, 109
life after, 211
shadow of, 102
struggle against, 149
Death wish, 75
SEE ALSO Desire to die
Decision by default, 237
Declaration of freedom, 377
Degenerative illnesses, 85, 87
Denial, 139, 143
Depression, 33, 143-145, 161,
197, 461
causes, 193, 233
clinical, 461
technique, movement, 461
Descartes, Rene, quote, 554
Desire goal above all else, 209-
211
Desire to die, 59, 61, 71, 81, 99
reversed, 85-87
Desire to hide, 59
Desire to live, 85-87
live fully each moment, 163
reason, 162
technique to strengthen, 161-
163
Desires, 54, 55-61, 221, 239,
467-469
attachment to, 73
based on involvement, 233
can be changed, 61
technique to handle, 469
unconscious, 61
value, 208
Despair, 63, 197

Huxley, Thomas Henry, quote, 340, 376
Hypochondria, 79

I

Iacocca, Lee, 541
Idea whose time has come..., 47
Illness, 59, 63, 164, 197
  causes, 233
  cure, acronyms, 497
  cure, medical care, 299
  cure, payoffs, technique to handle, 415
  cure, technique, nurture yourself, 415
  cure *SEE ALSO* Goals, achieving; Laughter, and healing
  genetic predisposition to, 79
  healing, technique, 87, 553-555
  payoffs, 411-415, 563
  technique, gratitude daily, 141
  SEE ALSO Disease
Illusions, 65, 72, 101, 103
Imagination, 502, 503, 539
  SEE ALSO Visualization
Imaging *SEE* Visualization
Ineffectiveness, 197, 199
Ingersoll, Robert Green, quote, 302
Inner kingdom, 91
Inner vision, 53
Inner voice, 425, 427, 455
Inner Worlds of Meditation (book), 569
Insanity, temporary, 195
Insecurity *SEE* Unworthiness
Insight Consulting Group, 231
Insurance life-expectancy tables, 327-329
Insurance reports of victims, 421-423
Integrity, 601
Intention, 55, 57, 59, 155
Involvement, 201, 209
  indicates desire, 233

Isaiah, quote, 517
Isherwood, Christopher, 480
Islam, and light, 519

J

James (Bible), quote, 240
James, William, quote, 44, 384
Jeans, Sir James, quote, 246
Jefferies, Richard, quote, 522
Jefferson, Thomas, 49
  quote, 48
Jerome, Jerome Klapka, quote, 177
Jesus
  and disciples, 453-455, 517
  faith of a mustard seed, 239
  love your enemies..., 453
Jewett, Sarah Orne, quote, 540
John (Bible), quote, 454, 517
John-Roger, 569, 599
Johnson, James Weldon, quote, 534
Jones, Ernest, quote, 370
Joy, 91, 99, 130, 133, 155, 465, 467
  achieving, 237
  have it and have it abundantly, 65
  of service, 257, 261
  SEE ALSO Service
  technique to create more, 205
Judaism, and light, 515
Judgments, 133, 451, 585
  and disease, 269
  and forgiveness, 584, 587
  technique, wait five years, 587
Jung, quote, 493, 498, 525

K

Kaposi's sarcoma, 79, 317
Katzoff, Dr. S. L., quote, 314
Kaufman, George S., quote, 543
Keats, quote, 502

Lowell, James Russell, quote, 474
Lucretius, quote, 521
Lyme disease, 81, 307

M

Macaulay, Lord, quote, 500
Macbeth, quote, 84
Macdonald, Dr. Ian G., quote, 314
Madonna, 201
Malloch, Douglas, quote, 322
Man Who Was Tired of Life, The (quote), 334
Managing Accelerated Productivity, 231
Mann, Thomas, quote, 300
Manure, 77
Markham, Edwin, quote, 531
Martial, quote, 432
Martians build canals, 304
Marvell, Andrew, quote, 533
Marx, Groucho, quote, 186
Master Plan, in heart, 93-95
Master teacher, 548-549, 553, 563, 583
Mastery, 455
Match of thoughts, feelings, actions, 193-199
Matthew (Bible), quote, 453, 516
Mazarin, Jules Cardinal, quote, 116
McDonald's Big Mac Attack, 181
McLaughlin, Mignon, quote, 396
McWilliams, Peter, 145-147
Medical conditions, technique, record symptoms, 134
Medical theory, thoughts and health, 45
Medicine, 295-297
  miracles, 295-297
  traditional, and alternative therapies, 339-343

Meditation, 193, 489, 569
Meditation of Gratitude: A Key to Receptivity (cassette tape), 593
Meditation for Loving Yourself (cassette tape), 537
Meditations
  technique, 569-577
Memories, 550-551
  healing, technique, 551
  of past, 135, 137
Menander, quote, 492
Mencius, quote, 512
Mencken, H. L., quote, 60
Mental illness, 33
Mercer, Johnny, 123, 467
Michelangelo, quote, 472
Michelangelo's David, 472
Michener, James, quote, 592
Miller, Henry, quote, 494
Milton, John, quote, 22, 66
Mind, 52, 479
  addicted to being right, 41
  description, 23-27
  focus, technique, 569, 571-573
  looks for negativity, 25, 31-33
  quiet, as cure, 86
  worshiping, 125
Miracles, 139-141
Miseria Libere Companio, 273
Mistakes, 410
Mitchell, Joni, quote, 17, 538
Mohammed, 519
Moider, 16
Money, 51, 179
Montaigne, Michel Eyquem, quote, 218, 546
Montessori, Maria, quote, 356
Monty Python (movies), 37-39 283
Moonlighting (TV show), 109
Mother Nature, 513
Mourning, 142-147
  three phases, 143

Mouse experiment, 265
Mozart, quote, 552
Muir, John, quote, 118
Muppets, 563
Murray, W. H., quote, 154

N

NAACP (organization), 177
Napoleon, quote, 179
Native American religions, 519
Nature, 118, 472
Navasky, Victor, 311
Nazis, 243
Needs, 221
Negaholics Anonymous, 409
Negative behavior, 413
Negative feedback, 357
Negative information
  technique to use, 134
  value, 133
Negative thinking, 5, 51, 133,
    153, 181, 355-357, 427, 447
  addictive quality of, 41-43
  and life-threatening illness, 3,
    7, 71, 77
  and the body, 28-33, 81, 141
  and the emotions, 34-39
  and the mind, 22-27
  as a luxury, 3, 45
  as addiction, 41, 291, 359
  as an epidemic, 79
  as disease, cure for, 91
  causes, 233
  contributors, 397-403
  habit of, 41-43, 45, 183
  origin, 63-69
  promotes conditions for oppor-
    tunity, 77
  responsibility for what we keep,
    355
  result, 193
  technique, 93, 167, 291, 349-
    353, 361, 363, 577
  technique to handle, 361-409,
    573

technique to handle, goal, 367
technique to handle, partnership, 381
technique to handle, say "No,"
  385
technique to handle, tests, 369
technique to handle, tracking,
  379
technique to handle, write, 387
unnecessary, 175
vs. positive action, 355
yield negative results, 53
Negative thoughts SEE Negative thinking
Nehru, Jawaharlal, quote, 80
New England conscience, 438
New York Times (newspaper),
  quote, 304
New Yorker (magazine), 283
News media
  method of reporting, 305-309
  not always expert, 304-317
Newspapers SEE News media
Newsweek (magazine), quote,
  308
Newton, Howard W., quote, 420
Newton-John, Olivia, 201
Nichol, F. W., quote, 226
Niebuhr, Reinhold, 458
  quote, 196
Nietzsche, quote, 162
Nin, Anais, quote, 106, 382
North American Indian song,
  quote, 519
Nostradamus, 19, 21

O

Observation, 457, 478-481
  acceptance, tool of, 479
  technique, 479-481
O'Flaherty, Liam, quote, 74
O'Hara, Scarlett, quote, 108
Oken, Lorenz, quote, 493
O'Neill, Eugene, quote, 109
Openness, 51

result in activity, objects, 49
SEE ALSO Positive thinking;
Negative thinking
Three magic words, 595
Tillotson, John, quote, 492
Time (magazine), 113
quote, 306
Titanic, 325
To be or not to be..., 149
Tomlin, Lily, quote, 531
Tones, 569-573
Too good to be true, 495
Toomer, Jean, quote, 518
Treating Type A Behavior and
Your Heart (book), 267
Trump, Donald, 49, 199
Trust yourself, 582
Truth, 125, 190, 248, 338
vs. correct, 55
vs. profound truth, 55
Trying SEE Actions
T-shirt, quote, 105
TV reporting SEE News media
Twain, Mark, quote, 144, 152,
156, 165, 172, 175, 177,
184, 188, 192, 224, 352, 570
Twelve Steps, 405-409
20/20 vision of hindsight, 325

U

Ulmer, Diane, R.N., 267
Unamuno, Miguel de, quote, 42
Unconscious, 75, 499
Understanding, 119, 143-147
Unworthiness, 63-69, 161, 199
as an illusion, 65
examples of cover-up, 65

V

Van Dyke, Henry, quote, 20
Vanbrugh, Sir John, 456
Vaughan, Henry, quote, 521
Vega, Lope de, quote, 198

Velpeau, Dr. Alfred, quote, 312
Victim, 421, 425
as habit, 421
stories, 421-423
Viewing point, 7
Vinci, Leonardo da, quote, 49
Virgil, quote, 533
Visualization, 193, 209, 499-503
creative, 499
example, 539-549
negative SEE Worry
positive, 501
using, 551, 551
Voltaire, quote, 92, 138, 179,
190, 222, 264, 282, 316,
486, 492

W

Wants, 221
Warner, Charles Dudley, quote,
173
Watt, William W., quote, 324
Waugh, Evelyn, quote, 278
Wealth, consciousness of, 51
Webster, Daniel, quote, 338, 533
Weeping, 465
Weight control, 437-445
SEE ALSO Overeating, tech-
nique to handle
Weil, Simone, quote, 72
Weill, Alexandre, quote, 313
Welles, Orson, quote, 398
Well-being, 87
Wellness, 87
Wellness Community (organiza-
tion), 559
Wesley, John, quote, 256
West, Mae, quote, 30, 170, 202,
442
Wharton, Edith, quote, 164, 520
What do you want?, 219-225
White light, 163, 393-395, 526,
529, 545, 547, 565, 567, 589
Whitman, Walt, quote, 112, 492

Y

Z

You have delighted us
long enough.

JANE AUSTEN